# Mr. Dooley's America

FINLEY PETER DUNNE

*in a caricature by "Spy," considered by old friends to be the best likeness in existence.*

# Mr. Dooley's America

## A LIFE OF FINLEY PETER DUNNE

BY

ELMER ELLIS

ARCHON BOOKS
1969

66048

*Copyright 1941 by Alfred A. Knopf, Inc.*
*Reprinted 1969 with permission*
*in an unaltered and unabridged edition*

*SBN: 208 00734 2*
*Library of Congress Catalog Card Number: 69-18271*
*Printed in the United States of America*

FONTBONNE LIBRARY

PS
3507
U6755Z6

TO

*My Critic and Collaborator*

RUTH CLAPPER ELLIS

# PREFACE

One attempts a book on Finley Peter Dunne with considerable hesitation, for biography was frequently a subject of Mr. Dooley's devastating wit.

"Which wud ye rather be, famous or rich?" Mr. Hennessy once asked the great philosopher.

"I'd like to be famous," said Mr. Dooley, "an' have money enough to buy off all threatenin' biographers."

My interest in Peter Dunne grew out of a parallel study of the history of the times and the reading of Mr. Dooley's observations. I acquired the habit of adding sparkle to lectures on American history at the University of Missouri by frequent quotation from Mr. Dooley's vast store of humor and wisdom. Quotation led to the collection of suitable material, and eventually that led to an invitation to select and edit an anthology of Mr. Dooley's essays. The manuscript was prepared, and correspondence with Peter Dunne regarding it was ended by his death in 1936. Subsequently the anthology was published, and it was greeted with generous appreciation by virtually every newspaper and periodical in America which comments upon books.

With the encouragement which came from the reception of *Mr. Dooley At His Best*, I commenced to gather material relating to Dunne's influence as a political force. A fellowship from the John Simon Guggenheim Memorial Foundation enabled me to devote a full year toward a biographical study which would attempt to evaluate Dunne's influence upon his times. The answer is admittedly speculative and incomplete, but the resulting biography is a necessary preliminary to any scholarly judgment on the questions involved.

Acknowledgment is made to Peter Dunne's family for unstinted co-operation in carrying out the work. At the time of his death Dunne had written a substantial portion of a projected volume of recollections. While hardly autobiography in the strict sense, these reminiscences contain many useful biographical hints. I have had unrestricted use of the recollections, as well as of Dunne's file of correspondence, both of which are the property of Mrs. F. P. Dunne. Next in importance to these was a collection of Dunne's letters to his sisters, made available to the writer by Miss Charlotte Dunne.

In addition to these, other revealing documents have been supplied by friends of Peter Dunne. Mrs. Francis P. Garvan, Mrs. Charles Dana Gibson, Robert Hamill, Wayne Johnson, and Michael Straus each supplied a substantial number of useful letters from Dunne. Charles Scribner not only furnished Dunne's letters to the Scribner firm, but also the interesting group which Dunne wrote to Michael Monahan. Smaller groups of letters were loaned by Margaret Cobb Ailshie, Ray Stannard Baker, Herbert L. Jones, Addison W. Kelly, Mrs. William Kent, John T. McCutcheon, and Joseph T. Ryerson.

As important on the biographical side as the letters were the interviews which I was privileged to secure. While it is not possible to list all of these here, the most valuable, aside from those with members of Dunne's immediate family, were with the following: George Ade, Ray Stannard Baker, the late James O'Donnell Bennett, the late H. B. Chamberlain, Charles Collins, T. A. Daly, Charles H. Dennis, Theodore Dreiser, John C. Eckel, Charles Dana Gibson, Charles Hamill, Laurence Hamill, Mrs. Robert Hamill, Robert Hunter, Herbert L. Jones, Wayne Johnson, William K. McKay, the late John J. McKenna, Arthur E. Pattison, John S. Phillips, Leigh Reilly, the late Wallace Rice, Michael Straus, Mark Sullivan, Timothy G. Turner, James W. Wadsworth, J. S. Wheelright, H. J. Whigham, and Henry Ten Eyck White.

In addition to these, the following have written substantial reminiscences or have written answers to a series of prepared questions relating to Peter Dunne: John C. Eckel, W. J. Etten, Hugh Fullerton, Hutchins Hapgood, John Kelley, Walter E. Mellinger, Arthur W. O'Neill, Edgar E. Owen, and John R. Patterson.

Acknowledgment of a special nature should be made to several very helpful friends. Charles Collins, of the " Line o' Type or Two " of the *Chicago Tribune*, has been extraordinarily generous in suggestions for finding material in out-of-the-way places, and in assisting in solving problems concerning Chicago journalism and history. Wayne Johnson has been extremely helpful in retracing Dunne's steps about New York; Bessie L. Pierce of the University of Chicago permitted the use of the manuscript of Volume III of her *History of Chicago* for background material. Franklin P. Adams, John Beffel, W. J. Burke, Herbert A. Kellar, Franklin J. Meine, Allan Nevins, Will Payne, and William Allen White have all been generous with useful suggestions for discovering material.

The staffs of the libraries at the University of Missouri, the Chicago Historical Society, the Newberry Library, the Chicago University Library (especially its Department of Photographic Reproductions), the Chicago Public Library, the New York Public Library, the Columbia University Library, and the Library of Congress have all been most generous in their assistance. A special debt is acknowledged to the staff of the Henry E. Huntington Library, where the manuscript was prepared.

Most of the chapters have been read and criticized by one or more persons who are familiar with that part of Dunne's career dealt with in them. For this helpful service, especial thanks are due to the following: Charles H. Dennis of the *Chicago Daily News*, Father Gilbert J. Garraghan, S.J., of Loyola University, Charles Hamill, Laurence Hamill, Wayne Johnson, Willoughby Johnson, John S. Phillips, and Mark Sullivan.

Mrs. F. P. Dunne and Charles Scribner's Sons have been very generous in permitting quotations from Dunne's works. In order to keep the footnotes at a minimum, only those quotations from Dunne's writings which are not easily available in book form are annotated.

ELMER ELLIS

*July* 1, 1941

# CONTENTS

ILLUSTRATIONS

# Mr. Dooley's America

# A CHICAGO CHILDHOOD

PETER and John Dunne, twin sons of Peter and Ellen Dunne, were baptized in St. Patrick's Church on July 19, 1867.[1] The boys were but nine days old and had been carried the few steps across Adams Street that separated the Dunne home from the church. There was nothing unusual in this, as they were born into an environment that was Irish, Catholic, urban, and American. For the Dunnes were all of these, and St. Patrick's Church was the center of the middle-class Irish life on Chicago's near west side. In the blocks adjoining the church lived several brothers and sisters of the father of the twins. In fact, two of them, Patrick Dunne and Mary Riordan, acted as the twins' godparents. Another brother, Dennis, had been the pastor of St. Patrick's since 1854, and was now Vicar General of the Diocese. But he was too busy to baptize the twins, so the eldest of Mary Riordan's two boys who had entered the priesthood performed that office for his cousins, with

1 Baptismal Registrar of St. Patrick's Church.

the parents perhaps as unconscious as the babes that the young priest was destined to become a famous archbishop.[2]

The boys' father, Peter, had left his native Queens County, Ireland, with his parents when a child of six, and had gone to Chatham, New Brunswick, where other relatives were living. It was there that he and his brothers were trained in the craft of ship's carpenter. They followed this trade after they moved to Chicago, doing other types of carpentry as well, and some of them branched out into the retail lumber business in a small way. The Dunnes were a pious, churchly family. Among his brothers, nephews, and cousins, the elder Peter Dunne numbered nearly as many priests as there were ship's carpenters. He himself took life seriously, and carried out his duties, both religious and secular, with unfailing regularity. He had some education, aside from his trade, and was a regular reader of religious publications. In his later years his trips to the confessional were reduced to annual visits, preceded by a week of study and contemplation that dominated the household for that period. Although no teetotaler, his strong sense of duty made him allow a building which he owned to stand idle when the only available tenant was a saloon-keeper with his attendant gambling establishment. His piety did not degenerate into hypocrisy. All evidence would indicate that Peter Dunne was like his brother Michael, one of whose letters relating to the disposal of New Brunswick property belonging

[2] Reverend P. W. Riordan, Archbishop of San Francisco, 1883 to 1914.

to the two brothers happens to have been preserved. After detailing to their agent certain private charities, and "three pounds to the priest of Chatham parish for charitable purposes," he added: "In giving these . . . you will please not mention my name."[3]

In appearance the elder Peter Dunne was a moderately tall, heavily built man, with a full beard. He spoke with the deep rich brogue of one who had spent most of his life among Irish people of little formal education. His solidity of character was not purely religious, for he was also a Democrat in politics and an Irishman in national sentiment. Except perhaps in local contests he never broke a long record of consistent support of the Jacksonian political party. His usual conversation was on political subjects, he was an active party worker at election time, and he was a constant reader of the political newspapers of Chicago. Although his brother Dennis, the pastor of St. Patrick's, had been the outstanding Unionist among the Catholic clergy of Chicago during the Civil War,[4] Peter had remained a more typical Democrat, which is to say, more skeptical of the federal government's purpose during the war. He had few memories of Ireland that were his own; but like most of the people of his descent, the spirit of Irish nationality was strong within him, and he was a regular supporter of the various societies of Irish-Americans working for the independence of Ireland from English rule. Like

[3] Michael Dunne to George Herr, Esq., March 23, 1852. F. P. Dunne letters.

[4] Frederick Francis Cook: *Bygone Days in Chicago* (Chicago, 1910), pp. 97–98; Joseph J. Thompson: "The Irish in Chicago," *Illinois Catholic Historical Review*, III (October 1920), 146–69.

many another Irish-American family in Chicago, Peter Dunne's was brought up in a rich atmosphere of partisan discussion.

The boys' mother, Ellen Finley Dunne, was of a background similar to that of her husband. Born in Kilkenny of a less churchly family, she represented a similar Irish-Catholic orthodoxy, although her own mother, Katherine English, had been a Quaker before her marriage. Ellen Dunne shared most of her husband's beliefs and enthusiasms in a milder way, but she was not given to politics or theology. Widely read in English fiction, she brought to the family circle elements which her husband lacked. She was nearly twenty-five years his junior, and as her gayety and youthful freshness increased the contrast, she was nearer to her children in age and temperament than to her husband. Peter Dunne, steadily employed and with some small investments, was a good provider, and the substantial house in which the family lived was well supplied with reading: Chicago newspapers, Irish nationalist weeklies, religious periodicals, and children's magazines — at least *The Youth's Companion* and *St. Nicholas*. Then there were books, some religious, but mostly the standard English authors which Ellen Dunne loved, such as Dickens, Thackeray, and Scott, with various volumes on Irish history and literature. It was an unusually bookish family, considering its background, that grew up on West Adams Street.

The child Peter Dunne was not to be influenced by his twin brother, as the latter died in infancy. But there were the other children, all with ages that were not widely separated. Amelia was the eldest; Patrick, short and stout and nicknamed "Stubby," was next. Then there were Katherine and Mary. After Peter came Leonard, and finally Charlotte, the youngest of those who lived to maturity.

Peter Dunne was the traditional child of literary genius in certain notable ways. He began to talk while very young, and took infantile pleasure in charming adults and older children with his prattle. When he was old enough to sit at the table with the family, he liked to keep attention centered on himself and did so by chattering. When other interests would occupy the family conversation for a longer period than seemed necessary to the child, he would amuse the group by pounding on the table with his spoon, meanwhile crying out: "Why isn't somebody listening to me?" It is a far cry from the Dunne family dining-room in 1869 and its talkative child to the New York clubs and their wit, philosopher, and critic of the nineteen-twenties, but the road from one to the other is straight and direct.

It was not long after this that another mental trait which was equally prophetic made its appearance. While playing on the street with the older children one day, Peter stood long before the window display in the store that specialized in ecclesiastical goods. In the window were pictures representing in exaggerated and gruesome detail the tortures of souls condemned to Purgatory. But to little Peter these were fascinating rather than fearsome, and at the supper table that evening he sent the family into gales of laughter by a pantomime and description of those which had impressed him. All of his life he was to be similarly unawed by the symbols and ceremonies of society, as one of the few observers who insisted on seeing beyond them to the reality which they represented.

The neighborhood of St. Patrick's Church was an excellent place for a realistic education in life. From the very center of respectable middle-class Irish life of Chicago in the late sixties, it underwent a steady transformation into a typical blighted residential area too near the business center to maintain its older character. But its Irish tone hung on to a considerable extent all through Peter Dunne's youth. At a substantial distance south on Archer Avenue was to be found another large group of Irish people, unskilled laborers for the most part, who were to be made famous by Peter Dunne later. But his own immediate environment and the original source of his deep knowledge of the American-Irish was the group about the intersection of Adams and Desplaines streets. Undoubtedly many of the traits of character that were exhibited later in the Dooley articles were memories of his boyhood in this neighborhood.

But the environmental education was wider than the area, because its transitional character was of itself highly illuminating, and its nearness to Chicago's business center brought all the life of the great expanding city within the childhood experience of Peter Dunne. The incredulous horror with which an observer such as Lincoln Steffens was to greet an acquaintance with urban politics, for instance, was impossible to a person with Peter Dunne's background, for he had been familiar with these conditions from early childhood.

To some degree, at least, this was to be the difference between Dunne and his contemporary writers on the American scene. Fortunately, too, these boyhood experiences were not limited to Chicago, for Peter and his brother Leonard spent at least one summer with a relative of their mother's on a farm in southern Wisconsin. From this summer, Peter Dunne gained some of the practical knowledge and more of the point of view which he was to display toward rural life in his subsequent writing. One more obvious result was the injuring of the index finger on his right hand in a piece of farm machinery, which left him to carry through life a stiffened finger that forced him to write in an awkward manner.

All of the children in the Dunne family were mentally alert youngsters, but Peter was the most obviously so, and there is little doubt that he was his mother's delight, if not exactly a family favorite. He impressed outsiders to such an extent that when the boy was about ten years old a visiting clerical relative urged the parents to let him take the boy and educate him for the priesthood. What the mother thought of this is not recorded, but it was unimportant, as the father, in spite of his own deep piety, refused the suggestion. It seemed to offend his sense of fairness, for Peter senior assured the visitor that there would be no " made priests " in his family, meaning, of course, that each child would select his future for himself, and not be forced into a life work that might not be of his own choosing. A few years later a friend took occasion to tell Ellen Dunne that young Peter should learn a trade. The mother repudiated this counsel of safety. Her boy was bright enough to become President and would never need to labor at a trade.

This explains in part why Peter, alone of his brothers, was sent to high school. When he completed the work at the Scammon Public School, he might well have gone to work as Patrick had already done, and as Leonard was soon to do. Instead he went over to the West Division High School to spend four more years in formal education, as his sisters were doing. He had attracted the favorable attention of Mrs. Ella Flagg Young, principal of the Scammon School, who was becoming a close friend of Amelia Dunne's, and with that as an additional argument, his mother and Amelia were able to carry the day in the family circle on the subject of Peter's attendance at high school. Moreover, he enrolled in the classical curriculum as if the intention were that he was going to college at the end of his high school course.

In the meantime changes were developing in the Dunne family. In fact a great tragedy had been hanging over it for several years, as the mother was known by all to be suffering from tuberculosis. This had grown progressively worse each year in the absence of modern methods of treatment; and before Peter had finished at the Scammon School his mother had become bedridden. She had been the great influence which had kept the family circle the jolly, co-operative, and pleasant place it was. And such she continued to make it, although confined to her bed. Amelia succeeded to her place in management of the household, but the mother's own presence was still as pervasive as ever in spite of her illness. Even before her invalidism the children had been accustomed to read to her. It is a family tradition that she had Peter reading Macaulay's *History of England* aloud to her when he was eight years old. After she became bedridden, Peter made reading to her a daily task; each afternoon as he came from school he read to her for an hour or more. Sometimes it was something from a current magazine, but more often it was one of her favorite novelists: Dickens, Scott, or Thackeray. She had already made Amelia and Peter devotees of her favorites. The common interest that Amelia and Peter found in reading was but one of several ties that made them close intellectual companions. They read aloud to each other as well as to their mother, and at one time took delight in Lucretia P. Hale's *The Peterkin Papers*, which was being serialized in one of the juvenile magazines. From its characters they gave each other nicknames: Amelia became "Elizabeth Eliza" and Peter "Agamemnon John," and these they remained to each other as long as they both lived. Amelia retained more nearly her mother's taste in literature, and, as a public school teacher and principal, was to gain considerable distinction as a teacher of literature, a director of children's plays, and a dramatizer of stories for the juvenile stage. Both Mark Twain and Charles W. Eliot were later to praise some of her work, and, after her death, a school in Chicago was named in her honor.[5] As Peter grew older, he grew less and less inclined toward Scott and Dickens and more and more toward Thackeray, who

[5] The Amelia Dunne Hookway School.

became his own literary mentor in so far as he had one. Thackeray was to remain a permanent literary enthusiasm, and his wider reading of later years never displaced the English novelist in his gallery of literary heroes.

The mother died before Peter finished high school, and the blow to the family was immeasurable. The father had never been close to his children. Amelia was a brave substitute, but the father's decreasing earning power was soon to make her and Katherine seek teaching positions in the Chicago schools. Christmas had always been the high time of the year in the family, and as that season approached after the mother's death in September, it seemed that without her presence it would be as naught. The girls even talked of not observing the season, but that sort of melancholia found Peter rebelling. Insisting that such mourning would not have been their mother's wish, he instructed his sisters to prepare the usual good things to eat and promised to see that the boys provided the entertainment. When Christmas Eve arrived, the living-room was cleared for Peter's entertainment, the main part of which was to be a play he had written and named *The Chestnuts.* There were four characters, two of which, the father and the lover, he played himself. Patrick was the villain and the younger Leonard, attired in one of his sister's dresses, was the heroine. It was horseplay comedy, a parody on the sillier melodramas of the day. The high point was reached when Patrick carried the fainting heroine off the stage, said heroine's large feet hanging awkwardly far below the ill-fitting dress.

The children had never heard their father laugh as loud and long as he did at that time. The holiday was saved, and the sense of fun came back to the house.

Peter's work in high school was in poor contrast to that in the grade school. He found little of interest in the Latin course, and developed a positive distaste for the mathematics and textbook science courses. As a consequence he worked hardly at all at these, and wasted most of his time while at school. Universally popular with other pupils, he was a quiet humorist, given to sly witticisms and sometimes to talking back to teachers. The most satisfactory outlet for his energy was found in the debates which were sponsored by the school's literary society, and in writing for the school paper. Many years later, men who had been in other Chicago high schools and who had debated against representatives of West Division High, still had vivid memories of Peter Dunne's impassioned, if not eloquent, arguments.[6] His contributions to the school paper were highly appreciated but seldom printed by the more timid editors who feared that Dunne's characterizations of fellow students and teachers were somewhat libelous. This inability to find a completely sympathetic editor may account for his first venture in journalism. He and his most intimate friend, Arthur Pattison, spent a part of their time one year publishing a hand-written newspaper which they distributed to favored members of their class. *The Missionary*, as they named it, consisted not alone of bits of school gossip and juvenile slander, but also had editorials denouncing the protective tariff

[6] Irene Steyskal in the *Chicago Tribune*, June 6, 1940.

and dealing with other public questions from an angle that reflected some Democratic enthusiasms of young Peter's father. To this enterprise, Peter Dunne devoted most of the energy that should have gone into the mastery of Cicero and trigonometry, according to the plan of the school.

This neglect of high-school work was worse after the death of Peter's mother, and in his last year it brought him close to failure. But he was liked by teachers as well as pupils, and was keenly aware of the degree to which he could neglect his work and still graduate.

One treasured incident in the memory of some of his classmates revolves about an unusually long assignment in Vergil near the end of the senior year. Judging the situation correctly, Peter studied that lesson. Following out his expectations, when class began the next day, the teacher, keenly conscious of past failures, started by calling on Peter to recite. Peter recited. Surprised and incredulous, the teacher kept him reciting, endeavoring to get beyond any accidentally acquired knowledge, but the boy was prepared, and went on with a fine taste for the dramatics of the situation; for the class, which had expected him to fail the course, was hoping he would not, and a teacher who had expected to fail him could hardly believe his ears. For a full half hour teacher and pupil went on, and covered the entire lesson. With the last sentence correctly translated, the teacher threw his book on his desk and shouted "Well done!" — a pun of which Peter was already tired, but which was very pleasant to hear at that particular time.

Peter Dunne graduated in the spring of 1884, the last in a class of over fifty pupils.[7] A few days before the graduation ceremony, Arthur Pattison was at the Dunne home, and Peter's father asked him about his plans for going to college. Pattison was entering a small college outside of Chicago the next fall. "I won't send Peter," Pattison remembered the elder Dunne remarking. "It would be a waste of money, as he would only waste his time as he has done in high school. He is going to work!"

Peter and his father were not very congenial, and were even less so without the mother to keep them from clashing. No doubt the father was proud of his son's fine qualities, but he was now past seventy years of age, and it was difficult for him to understand a lively boy, physically lazy, and not a little independent in his thinking. Perhaps he had an added feeling that the boy's mother had indulged him too much for his own good. At any rate he conceived it his parental duty to keep Peter from becoming proud, and he did it by disparaging his small successes. As long as the father lived he was inclined to minimize his son's work. "I have to come home to have the conceit knocked out of me," was the way young Peter Dunne expressed it.

---

7 Records of West Division High School.

CHAPTER

II

# CHICAGO JOURNALISM FINDS A YOUNG RECRUIT

WHETHER Peter Dunne looked for work on a newspaper or whether he merely sought any attractive job that morning in June, 1884, is not now clear. With some of his friends in the high school he had often talked of newspaper reporting, and once had expressed himself as hopeful that some day he would write well enough to "make" the *Century* magazine. To write well enough to be published in that organ of excellence seemed to him then a goal that should satisfy anyone. Whether by chance or design, he found employment on a newspaper the first day he looked for work.

Peter Dunne had not quite reached his seventeenth birthday when he went to work for the *Telegram* as little more than office boy. He was short and slender, with the light-brown hair, blue eyes, and prominent chin of his father. He dressed in the careless way of a normal boy; for one who had a reputation for making friends easily he had an unusually serious manner, made more noticeable, perhaps, by his defective vision, not yet corrected by eye-glasses. His greatest asset for his immediate work was that he knew the city of Chicago as only one who had been brought up on its streets could know it. He knew his way about the Harrison Street Police Station, the near-by fire houses, and the county and city courts. Brother Patrick had a clerical job in the county court, and Peter had many friends about the other institutions of government as well as in business houses. This circle constantly expanded, for Peter Dunne loved companionship and knew how to enjoy it and profit from it at the same time. While Peter was still in high school, Patrick had taken him to meet his friend, the great policeman John Shea, and Peter, too, became the recipient of Shea's indulgent friendship. This friendship was but typical of many others Peter Dunne was to cultivate throughout the next ten years. Later, when he recalled his days as a young reporter, he thought more often of these friendships than of the work he had done. " Scores of times I have rambled with Jack Shea through the night streets of Chicago, talking ancient Irish poetry, about which he knew a great deal and I was a sort of dab." He told how: " We were sitting over a toddy in the back room of Tom Moran's friendly barroom in Randolph Street, talking about politics and crime, and whether Sullivan at his best could have licked Jeffries and how did Curt Welch compare with Jimmy Ryan as a fielder, and was Finn McCool a fabulous or an historic character, and this and that and the other, and the disgraceful betrayal of Parnell by the Bantry band and their sympathizers. . . ." [1]

Peter Dunne had not been running errands about the *Telegram* office for very long when it was discovered that he could write and that he knew his way about the police department. " Police " became his first reporting assignment, and he did his work with sufficient ability to attract attention. Of course no well-run newspaper, even of that day, would have put such responsibility on a seventeen-year-old boy; but the *Telegram* was the kind of sheet where a bright boy was better talent than any other it could command. It was the poorest of Chicago's numerous journals; it had a meager circulation, and lived precariously from week to week on such advertising as it was able to secure, and, it was commonly believed, on the less ugly forms of blackmail. One of Peter Dunne's earliest witticisms of record concerns his watching a funeral procession from the newspaper's office window, and expressing the hope that the deceased was not the *Telegram's* subscriber.

One of Peter Dunne's news stories caught an eye that knew talent when it saw it. The eye belonged to the managing editor of the evening *News*, Henry Ten Eyck White. White was even then an old hand at Chicago journalism, the author of two books, an expert reporter of horse racing, and a humorist whose work was well known to other newspaper men. Melville Stone and Victor Lawson had hired him away from the *Tribune* a few years before, and he was now in charge of the evening edition of their cheap, re-

[1] Recollections of Peter Dunne.

spectable, and widely read *News*. As an editor he had become a renowned slaughterer of reporter's copy, and in later years many who would not have recognized his full name recalled with neither effort nor pleasure the name " Butch " White.[2]

Peter Dunne had been actually writing for the *Telegram* for only a few months when a *News* reporter told him that White wanted to see him. The result was a new job, with an increase in salary, according to the Chicago tradition, of from five to eight dollars a week. White seems to have put his youthful recruit to work on general reporting, but Dunne hated the routine and liked special features, which the editor tried to give him. In addition, White started to train him to write editorials. White had peculiar ideas about editorial writing, and in contrast to the long, dull polemics of most American papers, he confined the evening *News* almost entirely to short, pithy paragraphs of at most a few sentences. Other editorial pages had a half column or so of these short barbs preceding the longer essays, but White seldom went beyond the short ones. Moreover, as he wanted them to be read, he favored humorous and satirical writing. Peter Dunne had never liked the physical exertion involved in the work of general reporting, and he soon had a desk of his own from which came many of the evening *News's* comments on affairs of the day.

Generally the paper's editorial policy was Republican, but not regularly so, for it supported Grover

---

[2] Charles H. Dennis: *Eugene Field's Creative Years* (New York, 1924), pp. 152 ff.

Cleveland. It was as near an independent paper in politics as Chicago possessed, with strong opposition to Mayor Carter Harrison's organization its most consistent feature. A typical editorial barb is this one-line blow:

> Mike McDonald [gambling king] gets immunity and Carter Harrison gets office. Therefore they cooperate.[3]

At times these shafts might be in the form of verse, as is this example:

> Leaf by leaf the roses fall,
> Drop by drop the spring runs dry,
> Stone by stone the court-house wall
> Tumbles in the street. Oh, why
> Cannot all builders be
> Buried under its debris? [4]

Generally the subjects were political in nature, and usually these were directed at local evils:

> Why isn't Officer Peter Soergel on the detective force? He has been charged at least half a dozen times with brutally pounding inoffensive citizens and it is about time that his qualifications were recognized. He should be either placed at the central station, where his talents would be appreciated, or retired from the police force altogether. He is altogether too ambitious to kill some one to make a good patrolman.[5]

Frequently national politics, and less often international, were the subject of comment:

> The Payne investigating committee of the Ohio legislature was discharged yesterday. That stupendous effort resulted in accomplishing one great good – it furnished work for the

[3] April 3, 1885. [4] April 2, 1885. [5] April 25, 1886.

printers. The evidence was ordered printed. Within a few months those ponderous volumes will find their way to the papermills and the current of Ohio politics will resume its placid course.[6]

And:

Michael Davitt declined to attend a school opening the other day because the queen was to be toasted. Mr. Davitt would not object, however, to toasting Victoria over a warm hard-coal fire.[7]

But politics was not the sole subject by any means, and public figures of all types came in for satirical comment:

Mr. Howells is not content with the honor of founding a new school of romantic literature, but attempts to invade the realm of fashion. He opposes the dress suit. This act commends itself to a large number of young society gentlemen whose resources are severely taxed by the necessity of renting swallow-tails in order to preserve their standing in the highest social circles. Mr. Howells should supplement his works with a thrilling story about "The Old Clo'sman's Charge, or the Rise and Fall of the Clawhammer." [8]

Even such editorial comment needed more than a knowledge of Chicago life to keep it interesting, and this was supplied by Peter Dunne's voluminous reading, for he had acquired a habit of reading whatever interested him. One cannot be sure that this was not, in some part, a means of escaping unwelcome physical exertion. But sheer curiosity was a large factor, and young Dunne was a critical as well as an omnivorous reader. One of his best friends on the *News* was the cartoonist, Art Young, just a year

[6] April 23, 1886. [7] August 19, 1887. [8] April 24, 1886.

older than Dunne. Young recalls stopping in the space Dunne used for an office one day for a chat. "He laid down the book he had been reading — the story of a trip up the Hudson and to New York summer resorts, by Charles Dudley Warner. Looking at me through spectacles set against a bulbous nose, Dunne said, 'I've been wasting my time reading this. Some critics say Warner is a genius. Genius Hell!'"[9]

Dunne made many new friends besides White and Young about the *News* office from the staffs of both evening and morning editions. Charles H. Dennis, editorial writer and later managing editor of the morning *News*, Dr. Frank W. Reilly, the medical journalist of authentic genius, and that remarkable pair of journalists, Robert and Elia Peattie, were soon included in his circle. Not the least was John Devoy, the Irish revolutionist, who had escaped from an English prison and was now foreign editor of the *News*. He taught young Dunne a smattering of French and increased his knowledge of foreign politics immeasurably.

But most important of all was the presence in the same newspaper plant of Eugene Field. Field was on the staff of the morning edition of the *News*, but during Dunne's connection with the paper his very lengthy column "Sharps and Flats" appeared also in the early afternoon editions of the paper. Field's usual copy was not greatly different from the regular editorial matter, although he was a law unto himself, and his column contained poetry, baseball, political

[9] Art Young: *Art Young, His Life and Times,* edited by John N. Beffel (New York, 1939), p. 96.

editorials, or anything that struck his fancy and did not meet the blue pencil of the editors. No close friendship developed between Field and Dunne, but Field's very distinction in Chicago journalism made him an object of emulation, for he was the best-paid newspaper man without executive responsibilities, and everywhere he was hailed as a great writer, as well as the perpetrator of uncouth practical jokes that made him a trial to many of his colleagues. The editorial paragraphs in the *News* during the years Dunne was writing part of them bear the impress of Field's type of comment on the same page.

The peculiarities of the *News* office were not so important in Peter Dunne's life as was the common lot of the Chicago journalist of the lower ranks. For years reporting and even all newspaper writing had been an occupation of Bohemian types, who either graduated quickly into other occupations or into executive positions on newspapers, or remained as a permanent class of poorly paid hack workers who tried to take compensation for their lack of journalistic achievement in riotous living.[10] Thrown with such companions, Dunne was in most ways one of them. With certain individuals he developed strong friendships, especially with Charles Seymour, generally recognized as the greatest reporter of his day in Chicago, and younger brother of the great Horatio Seymour, editorial writer of the Democratic *Herald*. Suffering from the tuberculosis which was to lead him to an early death, Charles Seymour burned the

---

10 Charles H. Dennis: *Victor Lawson, His Time and Work* (Chicago, 1935), pp. 56–57.

candle at both ends in work and recreation. He cared little for money, and was no respecter of his employer, and he was too capable to be seriously questioned by anyone except as he was occasionally incapacitated.

Peter Dunne's first distinction in journalism came to him in company with Seymour. With championship baseball teams in 1885 and 1886, Chicago went baseball mad. The baseball-mad fan was present in the *News* office in the persuasive form of Eugene Field, as rabid as any small-town rooter.[11] Whether due to Field's enthusiasm or to the sport's expected appeal to its readers, the evening *News* decided in the spring of 1887 to print baseball news. Heretofore it had been satisfied to publish the results of yesterday's games without comment. For this task White selected his young — and no doubt jubilant — editorial paragrapher, Peter Dunne, just now turned twenty years of age. To him, covering home games meant the full afternoon at the ball park, telephoning in an inning-by-inning story to follow a lead he had written before he left the office. A running account of the first five or six innings was all that was possible with newspaper printing as it was in 1887, and the scores for the remaining innings were punched into the plate for the six-o'clock edition, which was the final one. When the Chicago team was on the road, it meant travel, fraternization with other newspaper men, athletes, and managers. Stories of the games would be wired back to the *News*, with a maxi-

---

[11] Slason Thompson: *Life of Eugene Field* (New York, 1927), pp. 117–120.

mum of background matter and a minimum on the later innings. To the high-school pupil of a few years before, it would have seemed like paradise, and even to a twenty-year-old it promised almost as much. With Seymour, who represented the *Herald*, and men from each of the other papers, Peter Dunne joyfully took up his new task, continuing at least a part of the editorial paragraphing he had been doing.

The pride of the Chicago fan and the reason for the outburst of enthusiasm was the great team, the Chicago White Stockings, of which Adrian Constantine Anson — " Cap " or " Pop " to all Chicago — was the manager. Although the club had sold Kelly, the greatest of its stars, to the Boston club the year before, it still possessed the great pitcher John Clarkson, and Anson himself, as well as such competent players and colorful personalities as " Old Silver " Frank Flint, Fred Pfeffer, Abner Dalrymple, and the speedy " Billy " William R. Sunday of subsequent revival fame.

In the years just before 1887, baseball reporting in the Chicago papers had been a formal routine of colorless stories that were but a slight expansion of the box score. Newspaper tradition correctly credits Dunne and Seymour with the ending of this condition; for during the season of 1887 they, with perhaps a reporter on the *Times*, established a different type of baseball story. Less concerned with the formal recital of turns at bat, they wrote news stories that gave the rabid fan his kind of news. The high points of interest in the game, the crucial moment, the spectacular play, especially if by one of the

"Chicagos," were treated in colorful language and considerable detail, and eventually all other papers had to follow the lead of the *Herald* and *News*.

Fairly typical of the new style was this from Dunne:

The bravest feat performed in many a day was the phenomenal catch of Tiernan's long fly by Right Fielder Sunday in Saturday's game. There were two out and a man on third when Tiernan came to bat. He lifted the ball high into the air, and it would have been good for a home run had it not been that a gale was sweeping over the grounds from the lake and retarded its flight. Sunday, perceiving this, ran as only the champion sprinter can run, but saw that the ball would light between the club-house and a row of occupied benches about ten feet distant. The score was a tie, and he realized the importance of capturing the fly. The people opened a gap, and with a tremendous leap he cleared the bench, his speed carrying him against the brick wall with great force. Ten thousand pairs of eyes saw him throw his arms above his head, and they were ready to applaud the act, but no one expected that he had caught the ball. As he turned and limped away from the wall, holding aloft the ball for judgment, the shouts of the crowd could be heard for blocks away. He had caught the ball, but severely sprained his delicate ankle, not yet entirely well from a former injury. . . .[12]

The humorous touch had its place too, and was as much used by Dunne as the spectacular incident:

Capt. Anson marched to the bat to the music of rounds of applause, and found a basket of flowers at the home plate. Anson looked a trifle redder than usual, and with his blue suit and white stockings, might have gone to the top of the capitol building as an American flag. He struck out vigorously and the audience laughed him another shade redder.[13]

---

[12] August 8, 1887.

[13] July 11, 1887.

In their work during 1887, Dunne and Seymour are credited with giving currency to a considerable amount of baseball slang that became a permanent part of the technical language of the game. Dunne is credited widely with having coined the expression " southpaw " as a name for a left-handed pitcher, which was a natural one, for in the Chicago park a left-handed pitcher's throwing arm was on his south side. Whether he actually coined this and similar expressions or not will probably never be known, but it is true that Dunne and Seymour were both using it in 1887, before it became common to the newspaper stories of baseball.[14]

Dunne never became a baseball fan like Field, for instance, and that perhaps would have prevented him from ever becoming a great baseball reporter. He was a keen observer of baseball players, and his sympathetic point of view did not keep him from seeing them as the fine physical specimens of ignorant young manhood that most of them were. There are touches in some of his side remarks on players that bring to mind Ring Lardner's baseball stories of a later day. And later, when Dunne had Mr. Dooley summarize the career of a boy who had become a baseball star as " fractions druv him fr'm school, an' th' vagrancy laws druv him to baseball," he was expressing a generalization that came from his season with the White Stockings.

But the most notable thing about Dunne's base-

---

[14] Thomas W. Lawson: *The Krank, His Language and What it Means* (Boston, 1888), does not list " southpaw," and it is in no Chicago papers except the *News* and *Herald* in 1887.

ball stories was not the way they helped Seymour start a new trend in that branch of journalism; it was rather the fact that he could not confine himself to baseball and its attendant concerns. Here was the twenty-year-old boy, whose only experience outside of Chicago had been one summer on an uncle's farm, now traveling for half the long baseball season to Detroit, New York, Boston, Philadelphia, Washington, and the other cities with clubs in the old National League. His great interest in politics, sharpened by his editorial writing, would not down, nor would his interest in human nature. His sense of the ironic, the satirical, and the humorous found expression even in baseball stories. In a report from Philadelphia, Dunne introduced the well-known wit of the Clover Club and editor of the Philadelphia *Evening News*, Moses P. Handy:

> The genial and accomplished editor was in a rollicking mood to-day. The heat opened the pores of his cranium and his humor ran down his face in sparkling and ready profusion. Besides a diagram of the weather and five paragraphs in the column he serves as sauce to the mightier matter on the editorial page, the gifted Handy drops into verse on the same subject. . . . One stanza is a gem that speaks the tender sirloin sentiment of a bosom that yearns for the sufferers who are compelled to live in a city where whiskey sours are 20 cents apiece. The scholarly Handy calls the verse which fled from his over-heated brain " The Weatherman's Pot au Feu." Without violating the copyright law the lines are given:
>
> " Hot " and " hotter " are familiar
> When will " hottest " come?
> Spoke the prophet o'er his pot;
> Then skimmed the seething scum.

After training his brain up to the condition required to conceive the last line, Mr. Handy cantered out to the base-ball grounds and set himself to the task of hoodooing the Chicago Club with his wit. "Not out," he would call in stentorian tones before umpire Connell could open his mouth after a Philadelphian had struck four times at the ball. "Knock it over the fence, Buff," he shouted to the pitcher of the home nine when the latter strode to the home plate.[15]

From the nation's capital he wrote:

During the summer season Washington is deserted, even by the office-hunters. President Cleveland heard that a lot of blue-uniformed people were coming from Philadelphia, and, fearing that some Grand Army posts were on route to raise a row about the battle-flags, fled to New York.[16]

In New York, but lately recovered from a spectacular financial war and in the midst of an exposure of corruption in its municipal government, he found considerable copy outside of baseball.

The politicians enjoy baseball, too, but several vacant chairs were observed in the aldermanic places. Ex-Ald. Jaehne, McQuade, and O'Neil were unavoidably detained at a summer resort up the river. Jacob Sharp was not well enough to attend the game; besides, he was getting ready for a trip into the interior next Monday. Some other enthusiasts were in Canada and didn't want to take any chances on the climate in the neighborhood of the Bartholdi statue. Cyrus W. Field couldn't come. He had to saw wood for Sunday, and now that Mr. Gould owns his elevated road the venerable financier has to pay his fare. A nickel is quite a sum after a fellow loses $5,000,000 more or less. Mr. Gould's elevated roads carried most of the people to the polo grounds where the game was played, and the poor old man sat on his saw-

[15] July 9, 1887.

[16] July 11, 1887.

buck with his suspenders dangling at his side and fanned himself with a rickety straw hat while his trains were luring nickels for his hated enemy.[17]

Dunne had made a place for himself on the *News*, and was able to command as good a salary as journalists much older than he. There were many reasons why he might profitably have stayed with that paper, and his father urged him not to leave. But he did. Sometime shortly after January 1, 1888, he was offered a place on the *Times* where he would do political reporting. That seemed better than editorial writing or baseball reporting, and the salary was much better than anything Victor Lawson's economical management was likely to award to him. Moreover, 1888 was presidential election year, and that increased the desirability of the new position.

---

[17] July 16, 1887.

CHAPTER

III

# PETER DUNNE HAS A TASTE OF SUCCESS AND OF FAILURE

THE *Chicago Times* had been the journal of highly partisan Democracy in the Northwest. Its colorful editor, Wilbur F. Storey — who " wore no man's collar, by Gawd, sir! " — had given sharp partisan opposition to the dominant Republican tone of journalism in Chicago after 1860. Moreover, he was the carry-over from the old-style personal journalism of rural America. In a humorous manner, Peter Dunne was to have Mr. Dooley recall this in later years with regret at its passing:

" Ye don't raymimber Storey's *Times*. That was th' paper f'r ye. What th' divvle did ol' man Storey care f'r th' thrade in pig iron? 'Twas no more to him thin th' thrade in pool checks. He set up in his office with his whiskers thrailin' in an ink pot an' wrote venomious attacks on th' characters iv th' leaders iv high society an' good-natured jests about his esteemed contimprary havin' had to leave Ohio because he stole a cukstove. He didn't have no use f'r prominent citizens except be way iv heavin' scandal at thim. He knowed what th' people wanted. They wanted crime, an' he give it to thim. If they wasn't a hangin' on th' front page some little lad iv a rayporther'd lose his job. They was murdher an' arson till ye cudden't rest, robbery an' burglary f'r page afther page, with anny quantity iv scandal f'r th' woman's page an' a fair assortmen iv' larceny an' assault an' batthry f'r th' little wans. 'Twas a paper no wan took into his house – f'r th' other mimbers iv' th' fam'ly – but 'twas a well-run paper, so it was. . . ."[1]

But Storey had become mentally incapacitated, and brought his journal close to ruin before his death enabled others to secure control. In January, 1888, this control passed to James J. West, who was in no sense a newspaper man, but an able and, it was commonly charged, a none-too-scrupulous promoter. He proceeded at once to build the paper back to its former position in the morning field. He recruited a new staff, bringing some of it in from the outside, but raiding his rivals for most of his talent. Then, by energetic promotion, he quickly regained the lost circulation, and was soon able to claim the largest morning circulation in the city.

In addition to political reporting, Dunne wrote political editorials. The paper was, as before, a partisan Democratic organ. Moreover, the editorial columns were frequently spotted with unfriendly jibes at other publishers, especially those in the competing morning field, such as the great and aging Joseph Medill of the *Tribune*, William Penn Nixon of the *Inter Ocean*, and James W. Scott of the *Herald*. It is impossible to tell whether or not Dunne wrote any

---

[1] *Chicago Evening Post*, June 26, 1897.

FINLEY PETER DUNNE
*when city editor of the* Chicago Times

of these, although some of them read as though he might have been their author.

The principal effect of these barbs was to establish West as the pariah among Chicago publishers, but there is no evidence that he cared so long as he could make the *Times* a financial success. The *Times* enjoyed playing up the disharmonies between the two Republican organs, Nixon's and Medill's. Typical of much of this foolery is this:

> William Penn Nix
> Is at his old trix
> Phonetic Study by J——h M——ll.[2]

More characteristic of Peter Dunne is the jabbing at the *Tribune's* leap-year Republicanism, which consisted of opposition to protection and consequent lukewarmness toward Republican administrations on all except election years. In 1888 that paper had difficulty in coming to the support of Benjamin Harrison, the party's nominee for president. Wrote Dunne:

> The Tribune is doing nobly. The most ultra-republican could find no fault with its editorials on the ancestry of Mr. Harrison. It evidently holds in the highest esteem that sturdy old Englishman, Major John Harrison, who ordered the execution of Charles I, it venerates as a patriot the Harrison who signed the independence declaration, and it regards [highly] William Henry Harrison the hero of the Thames river battle. But what it does not say in favor of B. Harrison, of A.D. 1888, would fill a very large volume.[3]

As the *Times's* political man, Peter Dunne covered the state and national conventions of both parties,

[2] July 24, 1888. [3] July 1, 1888.

work that he found to his liking and for which his talents were of the best. The quality of this news-gathering and comment was one of several reasons for the phenomenal return of the *Times* as an important journal. So pleased was West that he promoted Dunne to the position of city editor, with a salary that was far larger than he had even aspired to while on the *News*. He was just twenty-one, by far the youngest man in such a responsible newspaper position in Chicago. In spite of his lack of age, his equipment for the work was substantial. He had now been active on newspapers for four years, and had proved himself on both the *News* and *Times* as able and dependable, and more than that, as brilliant. Most of all, in contrast to the great majority of outsiders who manned the Chicago papers, he knew the city as they could never know it. The new work meant that he did little writing himself, and that only on special occasions. His work was to direct the staff of reporters, and he found it pleasant.

It was while city editor of the *Times* that Dunne was to score his greatest achievement in news-gathering. That was in the great mystery of the murder of Dr. Patrick Cronin. Dunne's advantages for dealing with it were great; for he knew persons who had bits of knowledge that when assembled together would solve the great mystery of Chicago journalism.

The Clan-na-Gael was a secret Irish organization, working by both legal and illegal means to secure Irish independence. Gradually the control of the local organization came under ambitious leaders who saw other possibilities in it besides its main one — possibilities not directly antagonistic to the original purpose, of course, but somewhat more personal. Alexander Sullivan of Chicago became its dominant leader, and used the organization as a basis for an attempt to swing the Irish vote to the Republican party, especially to James G. Blaine in the campaign of 1884. During the next few years certain suspicious circumstances surrounded the finances of the Clan. It seemed apparent that Sullivan was using part of these for speculations on the Board of Trade. Certain members, especially the popular Dr. Cronin, were suspicious of Sullivan, and began to denounce him and to demand an accounting for the funds. But this was all within the secret brotherhood, and no word of it leaked out, even to the nationalistic Irish who were not members.

Then Cronin disappeared. Little attention was paid to his disappearance, for he had no family in Chicago. Then John Devoy arrived in Chicago. He urged the press and the police to institute a hunt for Cronin, and made public his suspicion of foul play growing out of the trouble within the Clan. Dunne was especially impressed by his friend, and the entire Chicago press began to demand action. Not too vigorous action, it happened, because almost immediately reports began to come from Canada that Cronin had been seen there. Dunne might have believed this, except for Devoy. Dunne appealed to William Pinkerton of the great detective agency, who had private sources of information, to find out where these reports of Cronin came from. He soon was told that they all originated with one man, an employee of the claims department of the Chicago city railway, of which Sullivan was counsel. Pinkerton handed on this information with his conclusion that Cronin had been murdered, but refused to have anything more to do with the case. " Go find the murderer. I'll not help you. I don't care what you Irishmen do to each other. I'm Scotch." [4]

Dunne sent a reporter to see Sullivan, who angrily refused to talk. The police had met the demand for action by turning the case over to one of their best men, Lieutenant Daniel Coughlin. Then Cronin's body was found in a sewer, where it had been thrown after he had been killed. Now Devoy and the press were justified in their campaign, and the police, especially Coughlin, renewed promises of action. Not long after this, Patrick Ryan, a former detective, met Dunne in Boyle's Chop House and teased him about the amateur attempts of the press to solve the crime. As Dunne recalled it later, Ryan revealed the main clue in this way:

" A fine lot of detectives you newspaper fellows are," he said. " Why don't you find out who killed Cronin? "

"We're doing the best we can," I explained. "We're relying a good deal on Dan Coughlin and we turn over to him anything we get."

" Do you ever see Dan? "

" Once in a while."

" Well, when you see him why don't you ask him who it was who tried to get Paddy Guerin and Jack Harvey to beat up Dr. Cronin at an Hibernian picnic last August."

" You mean . . ."

---

[4] Recollections of Peter Dunne.

"On second thought you needn't ask. I'll tell you. It was Dan Coughlin." [5]

Immediately Dunne put men on Coughlin's trail and watched his every move, in the meantime weaving about him an unbreakable chain of evidence. It was clear that Coughlin was a Clan member and a loyal supporter of Sullivan. Dunne was certain that he had killed Cronin, either on Sullivan's orders or on his own initiative, in order to save Sullivan from serious embarrassment. But to prove it was a difficult matter. A missing link in the entire chain of evidence was the white horse which had pulled the buggy in which Cronin had last been seen — ostensibly carrying him to an injured man needing his professional aid.

Then another bit of exclusive news came to the *Times* office. An underworld character who made his headquarters there — he had carried over from the previous management on a contract that could not easily be broken — informed James J. West that he knew the location of the livery stable where the white horse had been rented, and that it had been hired by Dan Coughlin. West called in Dunne, and the story was repeated. Holding the city edition of the paper, they called the Mayor and the Chief of Police, who in turn sent for the proprietor of the livery stable and wrung a confession from him. Then the Chief with two patrolmen arrested Coughlin, and with the fact of arrest settled, the *Times* went on the street at six o'clock, shouting that the crime was solved and the murderer taken. While in no sense a personal tri-

[5] Recollections of Peter Dunne.

umph, it was the biggest news "scoop" in which Dunne played a part. It increased the prestige of the *Times* in Chicago immeasurably.[6]

But neither that nor its remarkable growth in circulation could save the *Times* management. West owned only a minority interest in the paper; the majority interest was owned by persons outside of Chicago. Becoming suspicious of West's efforts to gain control of the board of directors, they put in an entirely new management. Out went James J. West, to retire permanently from journalism, and with him went his city editor Peter Dunne—too close to West to be left in a position of influence. Before he left, Dunne asked one favor of his successor. He wanted his chief reporter and close friend, Charles B. Dillingham, the theatrical producer of a later day, retained. Dillingham continued on the paper.

Peter Dunne returned home from that last day on the *Times* late in the summer of 1889 in a despondent mood. While ordinarily serene-tempered, he was even now capable of the black despair which seems more common among the intellectual Irish than most other groups. But the loss of the city editorship of the *Times* from reasons with which he had no immediate concern, brought on the deepest personal depression that his friends or family had known in him. And not without reason. West's unpopularity with the other Chicago publishers would make his favorite editor *persona non grata* in other newspaper

[6] The memory of John C. Eckel, Dunne's successor as city editor of the *Times*, disagrees with Dunne's regarding the paper and the Cronin case. A careful check of the paper bears out the account as presented here.

offices. Of this Dunne felt certain. He would, he told the family, have to leave Chicago or get out of journalism.

But he was too useful to Chicago papers to remain unattached, and before the following day had passed, he was a reporter on the *Tribune*. His salary and prestige were less than those of the position he had just left, but he was rated and paid with the best of the reporters. It was comforting to him to know that he was good enough to be welcome on any paper.

Dunne was learning that reporting was not a very desirable job for him. He had no love for the physical exertion of the " beat " and, except for rare circumstances, it was exceedingly dull work. To him it must have seemed as it had to Mark Twain at an earlier day, a " fearful drudgery — a soulless drudgery — and almost destitute of interest. It was an awful slavery for a lazy man."[7] Also, there was no future in it for Dunne. He was already at the top as a reporter in Chicago, and that at twenty-two years of age! Except for the political reporting, he was developing an active dislike of the work. The great figures in Chicago journalism were publishers, not reporters nor even editors. The publishers were the ones who made policy and who influenced affairs; they were the leaders in civic life who counted. Joseph Medill of the *Tribune* was the great figure in Chicago journalism, not Eugene Field, the writer, nor even editors such as White of the *Daily News* or Robert Patterson of the *Tribune*. It was Medill who

---

[7] Albert B. Paine: *Mark Twain*, I (New York, 1912), 257.

still wrote editorials occasionally, but who made public policy always. Undoubtedly Dunne's ambition at this time looked toward becoming a publisher. His experience as city editor had given him a definite turn in that direction.

His work on the *Tribune* began as general reporting, and shortly after January 1, 1890, he was made editor of the Sunday edition, a position that relieved him of most of the more disagreeable part of the reporting. But before the next year was over, he accepted an offer from James W. Scott of the *Herald*, a Democratic morning paper for which he would naturally prefer to write political news. The *Herald*, although owned by a local banker and news company owner, John R. Walsh, was published by Scott, who was a highly popular individual among the younger journalists. Scott had gathered together a group of the keenest of the younger men for his staff. Charles Seymour had been with him longer than most of his men and was the best known of the younger group. But he had other men who were bound for distinction. Brand Whitlock, new to Chicago at this time, was one; Charles Lederer, Thomas E. Powers, and Horace Taylor were all cartoonists of great promise. Frederick Upham Adams, genius extraordinary, Wallace Rice, poet and critic — these and many more were on its staff. As Whitlock was later to write: ". . . when they induced 'Pete' Dunne to come over from the *Tribune*, the staff seemed complete."[8] Whitlock and Rice were of the first generation of young college men to go into Chicago journal-

[8] In *Chicago Daily Journal*, April 22, 1924.

ism. They were Dunne's age, and while they had some advantages from their training, his unusual experience in active newspaper work had already placed him among the top reporters.

It was the political reporting that had attracted Dunne to the *Herald*, and for which Scott had hired him. Dunne's growing dissatisfaction with general reporting was evident in his work on both the *Tribune* and *Herald* between 1890 and 1892. Young Theodore Dreiser, who was learning to be a writer on the *Globe*, covered a florists' convention along with Dunne, and noticed that he scorned not only the convention and its copy, but the very fact that he was reporting it.

Once Dunne had to cover an address on " The Royal Leaders of Society " by Mrs. Frank Leslie, who syndicated a column of advice to the love-lorn, and was frequently in the press with silly statements on public affairs, which editors featured with humorous contempt. It was probably with malice aforethought that Patterson had assigned Dunne to cover the address for the *Tribune*. He attended a group interview she gave reporters the day she arrived, and wrote a story in which he played up her statement approving the sentences of the Haymarket anarchists and advising the world at large to " shoot them down like dogs. Treat them like mad dogs. . . . Strikes must be suppressed by law." [9] The evening of the following day, when young Leigh Reilly of the *News* reached the auditorium for the much-publicized address, he found Dunne already there, reclining on the small of his

[9] October 15, 1890.

back and apparently asleep. Dunne would not pretend to listen to such drivel. Reilly felt sorry for Dunne, because he thought prospective boredom had driven him to sleep or drink and that he would fail on his assignment. All through that silly address, Dunne remained in the character of one who would not dignify such nonsense by listening, let alone note-taking. But the following morning the *Tribune* had Dunne's story on the front page, a gem that showed that he had missed not a single thing which had been said.

Mrs. Leslie began her talk with several personal anecdotes concerning Empresses and Queens whose dressmakers she had met abroad. . . . The young Emperor William, she said, had forced his wife to have her gowns made in Germany, with the result that the Empress was, "excepting Queen Victoria, the worst dowd in Europe." This epigram was greeted with riotous applause by the audience, which had evidently a healthy dislike of royalty.

Leaving Queen Victoria for the nonce Mrs. Leslie fluttered back into the reign of Henry VIII. The lecturer seemed to find much to admire in the character of this large fat man, who was, she said, a clever dancer and the author of many bon mots. One of these she repeated.

"When," she said, "this mighty monarch divorced himself from his fourth wife, he said to her, 'I will be a brother to you,' which accounts for the origin of this familiar expression." (laughter) . . .

On the fourth George she lingered cruelly. This unfortunate King Mrs. Leslie lampooned with all the vigor of her brilliant tongue. She showed that he was absolutely unfit to hold his job . . . but that he was certainly a fashionable man.

"Dressed," she said, "in white satin trousers, a white waistcoat, with a great diamond buckle on his shoes and a diamond star in his hat, he must have been indeed a striking figure. He had a most magnificent pair of legs."

Mrs. Leslie spoke feelingly of George IV's shape. . . . She repeated several anecdotes on George IV, which Mr. Thackeray has stolen from her. Coming down to recent days, she spoke of Queen Victoria and Empress Eugenie. . . . She said that either of them was well fitted to rule over a great people, but at the same time, she found much in their character to condemn. Eugenie was frivolous and Victoria's clothes didn't fit her, the stuck-up thing. The Prince of Wales was a bold young man and the Emperor of Germany's trousers looked as though the merchant from whom he purchased them had taken them from the top shelf with a window-pole. Not in these words exactly, but with these thoughts in mind, Mrs. Leslie showed her dissatisfaction with the society conduct of royal persons of England. Her audience was fairly large, among the interested persons in the front seat being the editor whose descriptions of Mrs. Leslie's lingerie have entranced the readers of a morning paper. . . .[10]

While capable of feats of concentration and fabulous stints of writing under the pressure of a great story, Dunne was finding that these opportunities were rarer as he gained more experience. One of the traditions of Chicago journalism is a story which Dunne wrote when his attendance at the Washington Park race track brought him on the scene of a running fight between a raiding police squad and a Texas race-horse owner, Colonel Jim Brown, who objected to being arrested. After following the fight on a run, until its sanguinary conclusion in three deaths, Dunne had hurried back to the *Herald* office and had sat down to a feat of presenting that story for the early

[10] October 17, 1890.

edition. He stuck to his desk for four hours of writing, and produced a graphic pencil-written story of nearly 5,000 words that was still remembered with amazement nearly fifty years later.[11]

He could and did do all types of reporting. For the *Herald* and perhaps for the *Tribune* he covered the hotels. This beat was also trod by Charles Dillingham for the *Times* and Frank A. Vanderlip, the banker of later years, for the *Tribune*. They sometimes traveled in a group, and out of this collaboration grew one of the best known Chicago newspaper stories. It was the habit of the trio to look over the hotel register and select the guests who were newsworthy. Then one of the group would write on cards the names of the reporters and the paper each represented, and send these up to the guest's room. Vanderlip and Dunne had the humiliating experience on a few occasions when an unusually newsworthy personage was available of having him send down word that he would see Mr. Dillingham alone. Becoming suspicious, they waited for an opportunity to seize the cards which Dillingham had written for the group. On them they found:

> Charles Bancroft Dillingham of the *Times*
> Pete Dunne of the *Police Gazette*
> F. A. Vanderlip of the *Salvation Army War Cry* [12]

At another time it was a foursome which included George Ade of the *Record*, as the morning *News*

---

[11] September 7, 1892; statement from Leigh Reilly.

[12] Frank A. Vanderlip and Boyden Sparkes: *From Farm Boy to Financier* (New York, 1935), pp. 46–47. There are several versions of the story differing slightly as to details.

came to be called. A rich western capitalist received them, but would not talk of the large speculative venture about which they wanted information. Instead he made some disparaging remarks about Jews. Ade, who had sized up his man well, interjected: "You shouldn't talk that way in front of Mr. Dillingheimer," at which the capitalist was so apologetic and confused that he gave them the information they wanted before he recovered his caution.[13]

Amusing as some of these anecdotes seem in retrospect, they were only brief highlights in a dull routine. The campaign of 1892 was an exception as far as Dunne was concerned. He covered both conventions for the *Herald*, the Republican in Minneapolis, which renominated President Harrison, and the Democratic in Chicago, which renominated former President Cleveland. The Republicans climaxed their campaign in Chicago with a rally at which Governor Joseph Benson Foraker of Ohio was the orator. Dunne's story, here, was his usual type in reporting a Republican speech for this partisan Democratic paper — he quoted or paraphrased the most unintelligent partisan arguments. He especially dwelt upon Foraker's waving of the bloody shirt:

> While 8,000 democrats were roaring for Altgeld and Cleveland at Battery D last night, Joseph Boomtarara Foraker from Ohio was trying to keep a crowd of republicans in the First Regiment Armory at Sixteenth and Michigan Avenue. He did not have as much success in the task as a man usually has at a republican meeting who can whoop the way Joseph can. . . . Joseph is a whale in the western

[13] Vanderlip and Sparkes, p. 47.

reserve, but last night he went through Chicago without exciting as much attention as a man with side-whiskers would cause at a prohibition meeting. . . .

"Harrison volunteered and went to the front [Dunne quoted], Cleveland volunteered to stay at home. . . . The republican party raised the army without him, got the money to clothe the soldiers without him, and won the glorious victories of the war without him. (cheers) . . . I don't believe any copperhead should be made president of the United States. (applause) I don't believe any man should be elected who would not feel at home in the grand army of the republic. (cries of "That's so.") . . . I appeal to you to stand by the wise policy of protection of American industries and American labor, and I appeal to you especially to stand by that gallant representative of patriotism, heroism and devotion to American institutions without example in the history of the world, Benjamin Harrison."

Then all the people put on their hats and went out to see what news had come from Gettysburg, where a terrible battle is still raging.[14]

That last sentence was peculiarly Dunne's, and no other reporter in Chicago, unless it were Charles Seymour, would have had the audacity to write it.

Immediately after the election Dunne was transferred to the *Evening Post*, published in a different location but owned by the *Herald*. He was no longer a reporter, but was placed in charge of the editorial page.

[14] October 27, 1892.

## A JOURNALIST CONTINUES HIS EDUCATION

WHILE Peter Dunne was on the *Times*, *Tribune*, *Herald*, and *Post*, he was gaining much of the maturity which was to mark his writing of the middle and late nineties. During these years he continued to live at the family home, maintained about the core of still unmarried children, even after Peter Dunne senior died in 1889. That the youthful character of the young journalist had not been changed by his successes is evident in the earliest of his extant letters, written some time in 1887. It is a challenge to his brother Leonard for a boxing match to be held in the basement of the home, with the other members of the family as an audience. He included his own crude sketch of the anticipated result.[1]

More and more Peter Dunne was finding his social life among his fellow journalists. Charles Seymour, now married, lived for a time near the Dunnes, and he

1 Peter to Leonard Dunne, no date. Charlotte Dunne letters.

and the cartoonist T. E. Powers and Horace Taylor were frequent visitors at the Dunne home. But most of this life was nearer the newspaper offices at the center of the business district.

Outstanding in its influence was the group of men who made up the Whitechapel Club. This became a center of social and intellectual activity that was Peter Dunne's first taste of the club life of which he was to become very fond. Organized for no other purpose than the promotion of good fellowship, with good liquor on the table and a good song ringing clear, the group first occupied rooms in the rear of a small saloon on Calhoun Place, " Newspaper Alley," but later in a sudden burst of prosperity it moved into larger and more luxurious quarters on the same thoroughfare. The club had its origin in the summer of 1889, when the Cronin case was the exciting news of the city, and from the hitherto secret mummery of the Clan-na-Gael now being made public, the club travestied its own. The name Whitechapel came from the London site of certain atrocious Jack-the-Ripper crimes also in the press of the day.

The membership was made up for the most part of young reporters and cartoonists with literary and artistic ambitions. In addition to Dunne and Seymour it eventually included such young men as Brand Whitlock, Frederick Upham (Grizzly) Adams, Wallace Rice, Arthur Henry, George Ade, Alfred Henry Lewis, John T. McCutcheon, Opie Read, and Ben King. Besides these, there were a few congenial spirits in other occupations: politicians like Charles Perkins, who was the clerk of one of the judges of a local court, William E. Mason, later an extremely individualistic congressman and United States senator; young businessmen like Robert Hamill and Michael Straus. An honorary member was James W. Scott, the liberal publisher of the *Herald*, which employed many of the newspaper men.

The atmosphere of the club was Bohemian, Rabelaisian, and macabre. The latter was in keeping with the criminal associations of the club's origin, the Cronin and Whitechapel atrocities. The decorations of the club were products of the close association of the reporters with news stories of crime. Weapons used in committing murders and ropes used to hang notorious killers were favorites. Then there was a choice collection of human skulls donated by a doctor at an asylum for the insane. To these and many more of a similar character was added a large coffin-shaped table, which gossip frequently and mistakenly designated as a real burial casket.

In some respects the club was a superior sort of college fraternity, near, perhaps, to what the clownish element in such a group might imagine could be done with a selected personnel and without supervision to hamper it. The legends of the club's escapades are numerous, exhilarating, and sometimes juvenile. Perhaps the height of the latter was reached in the cremation of a tramp suicide on the shore of Lake Michigan with a gaudy ceremony which took its inspiration from Trelawney's account of the burning of Shelley's body, but which was embroidered ingenuously with a procession, odes, "rondelus," orations, and the like. And also an exclusive story, sold to the *Herald* for enough to cover the expenses of the affair! [2]

More typical was the club's entrance into the hysterical mayoralty campaign of 1891, with its own ticket headed by their inventor, novelist, and universal reformer, "Grizzly" Adams, on the platform of "No Gas! No Water!! No Police!!!," with the additional pledges to defend the little red school house against "encroaching polka-dot school houses and those of light blue with vandyke brown shutters," and to abolish "side-whiskers as contrary to the teachings of Washington, Jefferson, and Lincoln." [3]

Politically the club was radical — a place where the young men could talk the realistic politics which they could not write in the conservative Chicago press; for all important Chicago papers were conservative, regardless of whether they were Republican or Democratic. Their tone on public questions took its color from the rapidly accumulating wealth of the city, which in the hands of aggressive businessmen dominated the expression of political opinion in a brutal manner. "Those who conspire to oppose the economic views of its big businessmen," a famous lawyer of the day asserted before the Bar Association, "the law will hang!" In the club complete freedom of expression prevailed; "underlying nearly all their talk was a wholesome cynicism, a ferment of disillusionment." [4] They were intolerant of all pretense, and

---

[2] *Herald*, July 17, 1892.

[3] Wallace Rice in the *Inter Ocean*, March 6, 1892.

[4] Charles H. Dennis: "Whitechapel Nights," *Chicago Daily News*, July 29, 1936.

AT THE WHITECHAPEL CLUB

*where FPD and his Chicago friends came together to roast each other or make merry, Brand Whitlock plays on the piano while FPD leans pensively on the table. Others are Edward Bernard, Dr. Percy L. Clark, Charles Goodyear Seymour, Charles D. Almy, Arthur Henry (on piano), Henry Farnsworth, Wallace De Groot Rice, Charles C. Perkins, and Dr. H. B. Williams.*

here Peter Dunne was in his element. He became the most expert of all in the gentle art of stripping a stuffed shirt of its covering, of gently pricking a balloon of windy conceit. And in the temper of the club, it made no difference whether the wearer of the shirt was a minor politician, a fellow journalist, or the most powerful man in Chicago — all were subject to the same treatment. After George Ade, fresh from college, had listened to Dunne in a flaying mood, he shunned his company, not yet knowing that Dunne's scalpel was reserved solely for fakes and pretenders — "posturers" was Dunne's favorite word for them.

To the young writers the most important feature of the club was the unplanned critical atmosphere which naturally dwelt in the group. The chief interest of the majority was what they and others were writing. In the early nineties Stevenson was the old master of English to most of them, but Kipling was the young pretender whom many tried to emulate. As a source of self- and group-criticism, the club was far more blunt and vigorous than Benjamin Franklin's famous Junto; for these were tough critics with a malicious delight in destructive criticism. During the organization's life, many a newspaper story was written with as much of an eye for its reception at the Whitechapel Club as at the city desk. Mercilessly pounding bad writing, weak reporting, and unrealistic conceptions of life, it helped immensely to develop a sense of quality. But it had its casualties; for huge, kindly, sentimental Opie Read, the club's greatest master of the humorous anecdote, hearing the evisceration of one of his ragged novels, walked out and never came back. Only tougher and less sensitive souls could stand that sun beating down on their daily reporting. "When the heavy firing began across the table," recalls one member, "it was time for the man of weak broadsides to climb a tree. No one had an opportunity to take out his knitting when framing a reply. And the retort always had to be proof against a comeback. Those Whitechapel sharpshooters were the most expert in the business anywhere." [5]

The "five sharpshooters" of the club were its principal wits: Dunne, Seymour, Ben King, Charles Perkins, and a reporter-editor with the least restraint of all, Charles D. Almy.

There were the hilarious nights on which were held "chestnut roasts," when the club entertained noted wits, and usually followed the visitors' best stories with the singing of the song which Ben King, best known as the author of "If I Should Die Tonight," had written for that purpose:

> In the days of old Rameses, are you on?
> In the days of old Rameses, are you on?
> In the days of old Rameses,
> That story had paresis;
> Are you on, are you on, are you on?

But not always; for the eloquent Chauncey Depew was twice the speaker of the evening and twice wore the sword — a decorative lodge piece that had been used to commit a murder — symbolic of a witty victory over the best the club could offer. In more of

---

[5] John K. Prindiville quoted in Dennis: "Whitechapel Nights," *Chicago Daily News,* July 31, 1936.

the spirit of high jinks it once entertained the celebrated wits of the Clover Club of Philadelphia, sang down its wittiest speakers, and finally had the place raided by the police and the visitors carried off in a patrol wagon, which after a tortuous trip dropped the frightened passengers at their hotel.

But there were less spectacular and more memorable occasions, such as the weekly informal entertainments, the evenings of music, liquor, and tobacco, and, on hot summer nights, the sailing on Lake Michigan until nearly dawn, always with intellectual companionship and conversation. Young Charles Hamill, just returned from a year on a graduate fellowship at Yale, sat in the club listening to Dunne and Alfred Henry Lewis, the author of the Wolfville stories, talk most of the night away. It seemed to him that no one had ever been privileged to hear such conversation. Indeed, the first time Arthur Brisbane heard Lewis he was to exclaim: "You ought to talk into a phonograph!" and Dunne was already a youthful Dr. Johnson.

Out of the Whitechapel Club Peter Dunne found some new friends, the most intimate of whom was Robert Hamill, Yale graduate and son of the President of the Board of Trade. Closely associated with both of them was a young Jew, Michael Straus, recently of the grain importing business in Antwerp. Both men had tastes for literature and good living that were shared by Peter Dunne, and the three became close friends. As Robert Hamill moved in Chicago's more select social circles, he drew Peter Dunne into them — slowly, to be sure, for Dunne had a democratic antagonism to formality that was not easily overcome. Then, too, as the reputation of the club grew, its membership tended to expand to include individuals who had few of the common interests of the original group, and its social and intellectual life was less interesting. Dunne tended more and more to find his social life in smaller groups — Robert Hamill, Michael Straus, and one or two others, sitting about a table and talking of the things that interested them.

Peter Dunne also found new intellectual stimulus in his editorial work on the *Evening Post* after November, 1892. This less profitable and less widely circulated part of the *Herald* property had established its own distinct character. It was literary in tone, more so than any paper of the day in Chicago. Its attention to the theater was intensive and intelligent. Music, art, and education were the subjects of wide news coverage and penetrating comment.

Although most of Dunne's intimates were on the *Herald*, still there were new ones here. Maurice Francis Egan, teacher of English at Notre Dame, would occasionally call at the editorial office with a group of book reviews. A young lawyer recently graduated from Harvard, Norman Hapgood, gave up that profession to try his hand at journalism on the *Post*. Cornelius McAuliff, the hard-working managing editor, was a close and stimulating friend as well as an interesting personality. It was he Dunne had in mind when he made Mr. Dooley say: "He swore with th' enthusyasm an' inacc'racy iv an amachoor, though I must say he had his good pints. I wisht I cud raymimber what it was he called th' Czar iv Rooshya f'r dyin' jus' as th' paper was goin' to press. I cud've often used it since."

It was while on the *Post* that Dunne became acquainted with Mary Ives Abbott, who wrote most of the literary reviews. Mrs. Abbott was from a distinguished Massachusetts family, and had spent some years in Calcutta, where her husband had been engaged in trade. After his death she had brought her two children to Chicago to be near her brother, an official of the Burlington Railway, and to find a way to earn a living for her family. Already the author of two romantic novels, it was but natural that she should become the principal reviewer of current books for the *Post*.[6] Some fifteen years Dunne's senior, she possessed a mind stimulated by wide reading and a wit practised by intelligent use. Undoubtedly she was the wittiest woman Dunne had ever met, and he was immeasurably impressed by her. She saw that Dunne was a genius, and determined to make sure that he took advantage of his potentialities, by encouraging him in his writing and by improving his social position. It was noticed that after Mrs. Abbott and Dunne became friends, the latter's appearance gradually improved from the negligent dress which, while never the Bohemian garb of some of his newspaper friends (unlike them, he was living in his own home town), nevertheless was not the kind that would set him off to the best advantage. Unlike his fellow journalists, Peter Dunne became careful and conservative

[6] *Alexia* (Chicago, 1889); *The Beverleys: A Story of Calcutta* (Chicago, 1890).

in his dress. Mrs. Abbott had become a social favorite, noted for her sparkling conversation, which could add the right touch to make a dinner party an outstanding success. Peter Dunne was frequently present at small informal gatherings in her apartment, where wit and intelligence and charm were the common denominator. Mrs. Reginald De Koven, who was an intimate of Mrs. Abbott's, recalls the discussions between Dunne and Mary Abbott at these affairs as marked by " the most sparkling conversations it has ever been my privilege to hear." [7]

To a large extent after 1892 Peter Dunne was outgrowing his youthful life and many of the more rowdy features of the Whitechapel Club. Something of his increasing dignity can be sensed from the changes in his signature. By 1886 he had added his mother's family name to his own to make his initials P. F. Dunne. Two years later he reversed the order to Finley P. Dunne, and then dropped that for the simple initials F. P. Dunne. He now began to see Chicago social life from the inside of its more exclusive circles. Moreover, he was in his own right a person of some importance in the newspaper world and the political life of Chicago. By the time of the World's Columbian Exposition in Chicago in the summer of 1893, Dunne was selected to represent the city on such committees as had an Irish connection, such as welcoming the Lord Mayor of Dublin, and even on occasions of less specialized interest. Once at a public luncheon at the Fair he was assigned the formal toast for the staff of the Governor, mostly

[7] *A Musician and His Wife* (New York and London, 1926), p. 138.

large aldermanic gentlemen of various sedentary pursuits, now dressed in the resplendent uniforms that comic opera and American state government permit to non-military colonels. He arose in his turn, and, lifting his glass, proposed: "To our absent friends, the military!"

## PETER DUNNE WRITES IRISH DIALECT

The *Evening Post* furnished the most satisfactory position Dunne had held up to this time, unless we except the city editorship of the *Times*. There was no more of the strenuous " leg work " of gathering news, and no more of the humiliation of waiting upon self-important individuals for interviews. He was supplied with an office and had to turn out comment on affairs of the day — a great deal of comment, it happened, as he wrote most of the editorial copy himself — but it was pleasanter for him to write editorials than to dig up news. Only on big political stories would he leave the office now.

Cornelius McAuliff was an extremely able managing editor. A strict disciplinarian, he perhaps allowed too little freedom to his writers. But he made an exception of Dunne, chiefly because of his great admiration for what Dunne wrote. A treasured memory among the surviving workers on the *Post* concerns the manner in which McAuliff would go to Dunne's office and come out with an editorial in his hand, chuckling as he read it, and usually stopping to share it with some other staff member before leaving for the composing room. He encouraged Dunne to write satire and humor to avoid the deadly seriousness of most editorial pages. Dunne did not require much encouragement.

Peter Dunne's reaction to the environment of the *Evening Post* resulted almost immediately in his experimenting with Irish dialect humor as an alternative to his regular editorials. One of the reasons was obviously the type of editorial he was writing — witty, ironic, and satirical. Given responsibility for the entire page, he made his daily editorials a local sensation. He had more freedom of expression than he had ever experienced before, for the *Post* officially was independent in politics, and McAuliff saw eye to eye with Dunne on nearly all questions. As both men were Catholics in their religious background and liberals in their thinking, it was natural for them to use the editorial page to support Archbishop Ireland in his controversy with Archbishop Corrigan over an " Americanized " church. Both men were opponents of " fads " in education — especially the teaching of German in the public schools — and these " fads " were frequently damned in the editorial page. And both men were municipal reformers and kept up a constant stream of ridicule against the local machine politicians and their principal source of corruption, Charles T. Yerkes and his street-railway system. Though independent as between parties, the *Post* had been firmly planted in a conservative path by its owner, John R. Walsh.

The editorial page of the *Post* became something different from what Chicago journalism had seen before. In the first place the editorials were short and pithy, without being merely the abbreviated sentences of the old evening *News*. Two or three brief paragraphs became the standard, and the long, windy turgidity of the larger papers was completely lacking. Then they were highly sophisticated and nearly half of them were satirical or humorous. Not that this sophistication was or could be carried beyond certain journalistic limits, but readers who could appreciate that type of writing would understand this. The sophistication was more in the way in which subjects were handled than in the position taken on them. Out from the page went all dully partisan seriousness which characterized the typical editorial page of the day. Out went the elaborate pretense of editorial orthodoxy, whose unreality and intellectual dishonesty were the great shock to the beginning newspaper man.

In its place Dunne gave rein to the humor of which he was the acknowledged master among his colleagues. Mocking satire, joking and waggish in tone, was part of the fare he set before the *Post's* readers. Here was an editorial page that a lively intelligence could read with pleasure and interest. Except for the form and the dialect it had much in common with the Dooley essays of a few years later. None of it was mean, none of it was personal, and none of it was petty. Always it was the intelligent man of the world mocking pretense and sham. It is little wonder that serious-minded Willis Abbot was to complain that its tone was too flippant to be classed as a serious political force.[1]

When President-elect Cleveland announced an appointment which was followed by the usual duty-calls-and-I-cannot-refuse statement from the appointee, the *Post* commented:

> We suppose Mr. Thurber has ordered his wings and his singing robes and that he will begin to tune up his harp for a daily song service and that the oil in the lamp before his picture of the Main Guy has been duly replenished.[2]

But it is a sad mistake to think of the page as flippant. Many subjects treated were of greatest seriousness. Only the expression was comic. After Swift, the Republican, was elected mayor in the spring of 1895, Dunne appealed for fair treatment in a typical plea.

> All blows and no gumdrops make Jack a bad mayor. . . . Mr. Swift makes axle-grease. Mr. Wenter [his opponent] makes rocking-chairs. Dr. Holmes makes pills. They do not belong to the first order of the illuminati. They are human beings, with human resentment for the stick and with human weakness for judicial praise. Every newspaper office in town ought to have this sign over its door: "Do not shoot at the mayor. He is doing the best he can!"[3]

When deeply moved, Dunne could write editorials that lacked his usual light touch, but still reflected his enthusiasm for plain speaking. Governor John P. Altgeld was hated by John R. Walsh, the owner of

---

[1] Willis J. Abbot: "Chicago Newspapers and Their Makers," *Review of Reviews*, XI (June 1895), 646–65.

[2] February 25, 1893.

[3] April 2, 1895.

the *Post*, but Dunne was able to praise him on a non-political occasion. The Governor delivered the commencement address at the University of Illinois in 1893, giving the graduates such simple, unpretentious counsel that Dunne praised it to the skies:

> The class of 1893 . . . listened Wednesday to the truth about life as it has never been told before. . . . We do not know how sufficiently to praise this address of the governor's. . . . It is the best thing of its kind since the appearance of Lord Chesterfield's letters to his son, and is even more valuable . . . because it is addressed . . . to every boy and girl in every station of life.[4]

Many of Dunne's editorials on the *Post* could as well have been written into Dooley essays, as the method was similar:

> Chicago's carnival of crime may be a terrible state of affairs, but she can sympathize with the Irishman in the story. He was digesting his Thanksgiving repast and felt very comfortable indeed. "Mike," he said to his companion, "there's mighty few people that's had a good dinner like this to-day, thank God." New York is not as well off as we are, praise heaven.
>
> . . . New York is so thoroughly wicked and depraved that, as we learn from the *World* of that town, owners of furnished flats are compelled to build pianos into the walls to keep their tenants from stealing them. . . . No Chicago burglar could be so base as to deprive a family of the instrument which, more than any other, makes for æstheticism. Besides, since the hackman's and expressman's trust has been formed, it would cost more than it is worth to move it. . . .[5]

---

[4] June 9, 1893.

[5] December 2, 1892.

Congressman Lawler, political boss in better odor than gambler Mike McDonald, but still a regular, could be treated in this fashion:

Mr. Van Alen has seen the error of his ways. He has retired and the Italian mission still gapes for an American minister. Who will respond? What ails the Hon. Frank Lawler? Body of Bacchus, as they say on the Corso, what a minister to Italy Frank would make! How Rome would howl! What sapient advice concerning "registration" he could give the party by the name of Umberto! We can imagine him dropping in of an afternoon, with his little soft hat on his ear, to see the Pope and cajole him out of a job on the Swiss guard for Mulhearn of the nineteenth ward.

If Lawler got 68,000 signatures on the petition for the postmastership, we are confident he could get 680,000 voters to ask the President to send him to Rome — or further.[6]

One has the feeling that the following editorial would have been a Dooley essay, had its idea been conceived a few years later:

One of the things that keeps congressmen from dying off more rapidly is the fear of what their colleagues will say about them at the memorial exercises. It would require much fortitude or deep distaste with the world to induce a man to shuffle off willingly when confronted with the fact that he might be made the subject of such a funeral oration as the Hon. Elijah Adams Morse, of Canton, Mass., delivered in honor of the late Mr. O'Neill, of Pennsylvania.

Mr. O'Neill was seventy-two years old and a confirmed bachelor. From Mr. Morse's eulogy it appears that Mr. O'Neill's last words were: "Mr. Speaker, I move to strike out the proviso," a sentiment which we believe will be preserved with "Roll up the map of Europe" and "Lay me down and save the flag." . . . Mr. Morse quoted "The Last

[6] December 4, 1892.

Rose of Summer " as particularly applicable to Mr. O'Neill's taking off. He also quoted " The Psalm of Life " which is always nice at funerals. . . .

And yet they ask us to look Death in the eye. They even wonder why men fear to die while Elijah Adams Morse still lives and while there are wax flowers in existence.[7]

In the light of Peter Dunne's greatest achievement, it is malicious, perhaps, to quote his comment on the dialect story, written down within the very week that he wrote his first Irish dialect piece of the Dooley tradition. It adds to the other evidence to show clearly that when he began to write dialect, his purpose was not serious and he did not consider it as anything beyond amusing copy.

. . . There is no doubt that the dialect story is a very bad thing and abundantly deserves every uncomplimentary remark that anybody may find time to make about it. It has filled the magazines so full that we sometimes wonder why they do not explode; it has flooded the bookstands with its pink and yellow covers and its horrid drawings of Dakota farmers and Tennessee mountaineers; in short, it has added an immense weight to the already excessive burden of existence; but we may be pardoned if we say we think it has not perverted literary style or literary taste.

That is our honest opinion of the dialect story. Of course, it might be different if we had ever heard of anybody who had succeeded in reading one.[8]

The tendency for Dunne to attempt Irish dialect was strong as he whetted his appetite on his new editorial freedom. Moreover, a real opportunity was at hand. In their campaign to increase the circulation of

---

[7] April 2, 1894.

[8] December 9, 1892.

the *Post*, Scott and McAuliff planned a Sunday edition. Here were sixteen pages to be filled instead of the daily *Post's* regular eight, and there was room for some experiments. McAuliff asked Dunne to do a humorous piece for each issue in addition to the editorials. He would be paid extra for it. For the very first issue of the *Sunday Post*, Dunne wrote a dialect piece called " Frank's Visit to Grover," in which he pretended to record what an Irishman had said in Alderman John Powers's saloon about the visit of Frank Lawler to President Cleveland, to see about the Chicago post-office appointment. " An' whin Lawluhr wint out Grover an' Bill Whitney wint woud im an' they mopped up a few shells of beer an' Lawluhr bate thim playin' pool by pocketin' th' fifteen balls from th' bust, an' the last thing Grover sez, he sez, ' Raymimber me koindly to little Johnny Powers.' Oi'll take me oath he said it. Oi wuddent loi, Johnny. A bit from th' cooler, Jawn." [9]

There is some good mimicry in this piece, and some high-grade satire in the picture of the little loafer wheedling Powers into giving him a drink. There is also a touch of the high humor that was later one of the finest characteristics of the Dooley pieces in the Archey Road view of the Cleveland household given by the speaker. By all right this is the beginning of the Dooley essays.

But Peter Dunne did not remember it that way when he was to recapitulate the history some years later. Then his memory went back to James Mc-

[9] December 4, 1892. Note Dunne's first attempt at spelling out Irish dialect, especially the " oi " for I, " loi " for lie, and " woud " for would.

Garry and his saloon on Dearborn Street. His recollection here is accurate and worth quoting:

> In Dearborn street near the *Chicago Tribune* office Mr. James McGarry kept an excellent public house. Mr. McGarry, born in the County Roscommon, had lived long in Chicago and both by reason of his natural qualities and his position as presiding officer of what he called "the best club in town, not exclusive minje but refined," had an acquaintance amounting to intimacy with nearly everybody worth knowing in politics, on the bench, at the bar, in trade, on the stage or in journalism. Especially in journalism. I have no hesitation in saying that most of the local copy for the *Tribune* and much for the *Herald* and *News* was written in McGarry's back room. He was a stout, rosy-face, blue-eyed man of sententious speech. He carried himself with dignity as became a personage who was not alone the friend and host of the most brilliant newspaper writers of that period but their counsellor and banker as well. He seldom spoke. "I was," he used to say, "intended be nature to listen not to talk." One of the gayest of our crowd was a reporter who could quote Shakespere for any event or occasion. Leaning easily against the bar he would parry every argument with an apposite line from the poet. This scholar one night found himself financially embarrassed and asked Mr. McGarry for the loan of five dollars "until pay day." Mr. McGarry turned slowly to the cash register, rang up "no sale," took five dollar bills out of the damper, laid them in front of his young friend and said, "Tommy, what does Shakespere say about borryin' an' lendin'?" [10]

There are many tales of McGarry that are legendary in Chicago newspaper circles. He was the first, these all agree, to make the famous remark regarding

---

[10] F. P. Dunne: *Mr. Dooley at His Best* (New York, 1938), pp. xxi–xxii.

saloon credit. His bartender, Mike Casey, stuck his head in the door to the back room and asked: " Is George Babbitt good for a drink? "

" Has he had it? " asked McGarry.

" He has," said the barkeeper apologetically.

" He is," answered McGarry resignedly.[11]

McGarry's dignity was such that his customers all addressed him as " Mr." — all except two privileged ones, Dunne and " Grizzly " Adams, who assumed the familiarity of calling him " Jim." As the saloon-keeper lived on the West Side, it had been a habit of Peter Dunne's when working on morning papers, the *Times*, *Tribune*, and *Herald*, to drop into the saloon early in the morning as he was leaving his work and the two would ride home in the same cab. One of Dunne's favorite stories was of a time when McGarry had partaken too freely of his own stock in trade. When the cab reached his dwelling, McGarry with drunken dignity waved aside the help of the driver and Dunne and staggered up the steps that led from the sidewalk to the porch. When halfway up, he slipped and fell. As they helped him up he glared reproachfully at the journalist. " Dunne, I thought you were my friend. You tripped me."

It was to his old friend McGarry that Dunne always referred as the origin of the Dooley essay. Actually it was the second dialect story for the *Sunday Post*, in which Dunne used a comment of McGarry's. The occasion was the death of Jay Gould, the speculative railroad financier. At the time, Dunne had

[11] John J. McKenna: *Fond Memories of McGarry's Place* (no place, no date [1923]).

commented on his passing in an editorial that was typical of his usual intelligent point of view:

> Jay Gould was the ultimate product of the civilization of his time. In a money-making country and generation, he was the prince. No other country could have produced him; no other country ever will. Be this high praise, or deep dispraise, for Gould and America, it is true. . . . He was hampered by no inconvenient scruples. . . . In the presence of the unburied dead it is ill to withhold praise when praise is due. Gould's private life was deserving of all praise. He had no vulgar or vicious tastes.[12]

Later that day or the next Dunne heard McGarry make some observations on Gould's death. "I thought they were funny enough to quote and I put them in a little piece for the *Sunday Post.*"[13] It was so near the form and type of the Dooley essays that it is not strange that Dunne recalled it as the first of the dialect pieces. In this second essay there was not only McGarry, called Colonel McNeary because Dunne well knew the saloon-keeper would object to seeing his name in the piece, but another who is every bit as important as the saloon-keeper in the early Dooley essays. This was John J. McKenna.[14] McKenna was a small-time Irish politician, honest, friendly, likable, and possessed of considerable earthy humor. He was a Republican from the Democratic stronghold of Bridgeport on Archer Avenue, and secured his living out of small political jobs that were the

---

12 December 2, 1892.

13 *Mr. Dooley at His Best*, p. xxiii.

14 John J. McKenna: *Stories by the Original "Jawn" McKenna from "Archey Road" of the Sun Worshippers Club of McKinley Park* (Chicago, 1918).

reward for leading his party's forlorn hopes in that area. He liked to bait McGarry, and as a reward he was frequently the object of the saloon-keeper's not inconsiderable anger and contempt. McKenna did not object to seeing his name in print, and Dunne kept it there. As the Dooley essays developed, McKenna became the one active character unquestionably drawn from life and traveling under his own name. The inactive characters were also real. Casey was McGarry's late barkeeper, Gavin was a well-known undertaker, and Boyle was the proprietor of the popular chophouse near by.

"I see our friend Jay Gould is dead," said Colonel McNeary, turning from his regular noonday survey of the procession of fair ones on Dearborn street. "Jay Gould is dead, Vanderbilt is dead, Mike Casey is dead. They're all dead and gone, poor men, and none of them took his money with him. Jay Gould had no fun in life. My friend there, little Johnny McKenna, would have more fun at a dance at Brighton Park, ten times over, than Jay Gould had all his lifetime with $100,000,000. Ten times over, for McKenna could get up the next morning and eat a side of bacon, cabbage and boiled potatoes, put on his cambric shirt and come down town as fresh as e'er a man you know, while Gould, sure, the poor little wisp of a man if he ate one egg for breakfast, he'd be doubled up with sorrow in his stomach. Besides, McKenna never had fear of mortal man nailing him with a bomb. The worst he ever got was some friend of McElligott's soaking him with a brick, and divil a bit they care for that in Bridgeport. It's a mere diversion, but Gould, the unhappy divil, the minute he poked his whiskers out of his office some crazy arnychist was liable to crack away at him with a gas-pipe bomb full of dynamite, or some strong-arm man toss him into a coal hole. Now he's dead, and what of it? He has a fine box and a mausolyum, but manny's the boy I've seen as contented and gay in one of Gavin's old crates as if he was laid out in a rosewood casket, with a satin pillow under his head; and making no more kick to be dumped into a hole in Calvary than if he was put on a shelf in a vault like a jar of pickles. It's little difference it makes to a man when he's dead. He didn't take anything with him barring a new suit of clothes. He had to leave all the coin behind. I see he left his son George only $5,000,000 for the three years' work. It's a burning shame. Faith, I hope the lad will be able to get through the winter on it, though its little enough with hard coal at $8 a ton and Boyle contemplatin' a lift in the price of steak; and an actress for a wife, at that. Them actresses is spenders. I wonder if the boy will ever think of his father or will he think of the money all the time. Aha! it'll be little pleasure he'll take from pondering on the old man if what Shakespeare says is true — that it will be easier for a camel to go through the eye of one of them little cambric needles than for a rich man to enter the kingdom of heaven." [15]

We do not need to take Dunne's statement that these were McGarry's remarks too literally. That was his spring-board, and the tricks such as " Gould . . . Vanderbilt . . . Mike Casey . . ." and introducing a Biblical quotation with " as Shakespeare says " reveal all too clearly the hand of Peter Dunne.

For the third Sunday issue Dunne used a recent statement of the English actor Wilson Barrett that American actors lacked imagination, as a starting-place for a discussion of the theater. While it is possible that another chance remark of McGarry's suggested the piece, it is much more likely that it had no connection with that worthy. One section of the article is an oft-told recollection of Dunne's relating to Edwin Booth's acting in *Richelieu*. But the im-

[15] December 11, 1892.

portant thing was that Dunne, instead of using new characters to make this story, as he had when he dropped the unnamed loafer in Powers's saloon and took up McNeary, kept the Colonel and John McKenna as the characters in the new piece, and thereby established the form of all his future dialect essays.[16]

The McNeery articles (the spelling soon changed) continued to be a regular feature of the *Sunday Post*, Dunne being paid ten dollars extra for each one. They were read with amusement all over Chicago and served as a stimulus to the new Sunday paper's circulation. Part of the humorous appeal was in the brogue and idiom, and part of it lay in the use that was made of well-known local characters' names. McNeery was easily recognized by the many who knew him as McGarry, and nearly all of the other names were of local celebrities. Other than this there are only occasional flashes of the wit and satire that were to make Mr. Dooley famous. The subjects treated were extremely varied, as if Dunne were seeking experimentally to find the best type. They had started with politics, but it was not easy to place opinions on politics in the mouth of a recognized character. Certainly that would never do for McGarry, whose announced business practice was to " find out what the other fellow thinks and then agree with him. It pleases him and saves a lot of foolish argument." [17] As spring arrived, with the excitement and color of the World's Fair ever present, that furnished suitable

[16] Another real person, John O'Connor, was also present in a few of these early essays.

[17] Charles H. Dennis in the *Chicago Daily News*, April 27, 1936.

subjects, and McNeery commented upon its notable visitors, special days, and exhibits. Perhaps the high point of the Fair was the visit of Princess Eulalia of Spain, which rocked high society in the city by the Lake to its foundations. Never before had Chicago entertained such a visitor, and the bowings and scrapings of the socially elect and politically and commercially successful reached an all-time high. It was an affair made for Dunne's pen.

"Well, sir," said the colonel, "I was disappointed an' I wasn't. I never seen a princess before, Jawnny, because, ye know, they ain't in moy set an' I suppose I must'v had the idea that a princess to be right ought to be as high as th' dure there, wid a gold petticoat an' a crown of dimons an' jools on her nut. Annyhow, I was disappointed, Jawnny, in my own secret mind tuh see a little red-haired slip 'v a woman, with big blue eyes an' a mouth as full 'v smiles an' kisses —,"

"Who-ho there!" said Mr. McKenna. "Back up, ye've thrun a shoe."

"— as full 'v smiles an' kisses as that there dish was full 'v cheese before ye come in, Jawn McKenna," continued Colonel McNeery with sudden severity. "Not a pretty woman, mind ye," he continued, "but a nice, clane-lookin' party, Jawn, with a smile that melted me heart. She's a woman that I'd like to know better, an' th' nex' time I go through Madhrid 'tis me intintion to dhrop in on her an' make her a call.

"She's a sinsible lookin' woman, too, Jawnny, an' between we two, if she isn't sick an' tired 'v all this palaver, I don't know nothin' about women. Her husband, he don't try to conceal his onyou, as we say in French. Ye never saw a more onyoued man in all ye'er born days. He keeps ye wondhrin' who does his thinkin' f'r him. There's a man I don't suppose never did a lick 'v work in his life an' he's as tired lookin' as a doctor's horse in measles time. He is so he is. Aulooly — "

"Ay-oo-lah-le-ah," interjected Mr. McKenna.

"Oh, Alatooralah," the colonel went on, "thries to luk pleasant, but a man with half an eye could see her heart is gray with all this hand-kissin' an' bowin' an' scrapin', an' will ye'er royal highness pass th' butther an' can't I help ye'er royal highness tuh another plateful of this spinach? Think o' it — old [Mayor Carter H.] Hahr'son bendin' his back till his joints creaked like a cellar dure an' kissin' her hand, with Bath House Jawnny Coughlin standin' prisint arms and Jack McGillen a crookin' his knee that never was crooked in prayer, I promise ye. What does it all mean, I dunno? Sometimes I do be thinkin' all th' speeches we hear Macchew P. Brady an' Finerty an' Luther Laflin Mills makin' an' th' Fourth 'v July an' Patrick's day an' other na'chunal holidays is no more than a mere bunco game for to hide th' people from th' real facts — like they put out th' lights in th' theaytre so's th' stage'll look brighter whin th' corpse de bally comes out. D'ye suppose poor old George Washington an' Patrick Hinry an' Andrew Jackson afightin' amid th' blood an' murdher 'v Bunker Hill ever thought th' counthry they were takin' th' long chance f'r wud come to a stage where big amolooks 'v aldermen would be takin' off their hats an' breakin' their backs in honor of a princess? D'ye think that old Benjamin Franklin would 'v died happy if he'd knowed that women'd jam into th' streets t' touch th' dress of a princess as she passed? 'All men an' women are created free an' akel,' says Brady in his speech at Ogden's Grove. They are, like hell, 'created free an' akel.' It's over th' left, this free an' akel talk. It goes with th' droopin' eyelid. If there was a man or woman in that push that considered himself th' akel of Oooloolah I'll take an' eat that there cat, I will, so I will. There was men in that crowd that'd give their right eye to take th' place 'v Mrs. Patther Pammer's hackman an' drive th' horses before th' princess. Why, sir, after she'd passed over th' carpet in th' big buildin' at th' fair old gray-headed men an' women lams over an' likes to break their necks pickin' up th' pansy flowers she'd stepped on. Th' princess seen thim, too, an' she looked sore. She wint right up tuh her room an' sint over for refreshments. What d'ye suppose th' waiter brought back on th' thray? "

"Ice cream sody? " said Mr. McKenna, whose notions of the royal tipple are not very clear.

"Dom'd th' bit," said the colonel. "A bottle 'v th' good old stuff — one quart 'v lush, with a package 'v cigaroots on th' side."

There was a pause after this, which was broken by Mr. McKenna asking: "Where'd you get th' pansies? "

"Thim pansies," said Colonel McNeery in a proud tone, "is none other than some that was shtepped on by her royal highness th' Princess Hallaluliah 'v Spain. There's no con about thim. Some 'v th' silly people tuk those that old Hahr'son planted his big fut on, but I copped only thim that her royal highness touched. I had to poke a Jew man in th' oye to get thim, but it'd be a could day before th' likes 'v him'd get th' best 'v th' likes 'v me." [18]

The McNeery articles were gaining an ever expanding circle of readers, and McAuliff used them in his advertising to attract readers to the *Sunday Post*. But they were not enough to carry the new venture, and in August the edition was given up with the explanation that the public seemed to want the large blanket Sunday paper instead of the condensed journal which the *Post* had introduced. However, the McNeery articles were too popular to be lost, and they continued in the Saturday edition of the daily.

In spite of this recognition of their popularity after they had been published less than nine months, the

[18] June 11, 1893.

articles had certain inherent weaknesses. The closing of the World's Fair would end the most available source of topics. Moreover, some of the characters might object to what was written about them. John McKenna would not; he gloried in the attention. And the public figures such as Mayor Harrison, the wealthy Potter Palmer, Lawler, Coughlin, Powers, and the other politicians whose names were merely mentioned could not admit they objected to such good-humored dialect from comic Irishmen, even when it cut a little. But the one traveling under a false name did. Jim McGarry's tolerance had limits and his personal dignity became affronted as more and more people called him McNeery and he began to think they were laughing at him. The limit of his patience was reached in September, 1893, when a Swede, the traditional enemy of the Irish in all American-Irish humor, and a common laborer at that, entered McGarry's place and bought a drink. He gazed long at McGarry with a wide grin on his face, and finally said: "Aye tank you been very funny feller." It was more than the old man could stand. "If the Swedes are on, everybody is on!" he exclaimed. Peter Dunne recalled later what happened:

I was going on well and enjoying myself until one afternoon when I happened in at Jim McGarry's. My friend scarcely spoke to me. I tried various topics of conversation. He would have none of them. Suddenly he shook his finger under my nose.

"You can't put printer's ink on me with impunity," he cried.

"But, Jim, what have I done?"

"I'll see ye'er boss, young man. I'll see Jawn R.," he said and turned away.

Sure enough, the next day I had a visit from John R. Walsh, the banker who owned the *Chicago Herald* and the *Evening Post*. I knew him well and liked him, even if he was a pirate over-punished through President Taft's malignant hatred of him. Walsh said he had a favor to ask of me. I knew at once what it was.

"Jim McGarry has been to see you," I said.

"That's it," said my Boss. "You know the old fellow is broken up over those McNeery articles. His friends are laughing at him. Can't you change the name?" [19]

And so Colonel McNeery passed out of existence.

---

[19] *Mr. Dooley at His Best*, p. xxiv.

## CHICAGO WELCOMES MR. DOOLEY

THERE was no suggestion that Dunne should stop writing his dialect pieces, but merely that he change the name so that McGarry would not continue to be offended. Changing the pseudonym would not be enough, though, as people would still identify the soliloquizer as McGarry. Consequently, Dunne had to move the saloon from Dearborn Street, because the form — the saloon-keeper talking to his customer — must be retained. It was but natural that Dunne should follow John McKenna out to Archer Avenue and its center of suburban Bridgeport, where the largest group of Chicago Irish lived. Such a location had other advantages too, for along Archer Avenue lived the unsophisticated people who were comic to other Chicagoans, as the residents of near-by rural towns are to the residents of Manhattan. Surely no "stately liquor merchant" such as McGarry would place himself there. Colonel McNeery once made an Easter call on McKenna, and described Archer Avenue in this way:

"Did ye ever go to McKenna's? No? Well, sir, of all th' places! Ye go down Madison street to Halstead an' down Halstead to Archey road an' out Archey road past packin' houses an' rollin' mills an' th' Healy slew an' potato patches till ye get to McKenna's." [1]

There lived the "shanty Irish," with potato gardens, pigs, goats, and one-story stores and saloons. Perhaps one should say the community had been Irish, for already the original Irish were heavily diluted with peoples of other extractions. But the Irish whom Dunne loved were dominant: "knowing and innocent; moral, but giving no heed at all to patented political moralities."

On October 7, 1893, Dunne introduced his readers to the change. McKenna, "exceedingly restless since Colonel McNeery went home to Ireland, and on his way out to Brighton Park for consolation, had bethought himself of Martin Dooley. The lights were shining in the little tavern. . . ." [2] And the great character was born. Not born in his full glory by any means, as Dunne could not evoke such a rich character immediately, even after nine months of practice on Colonel McNeery. It would be better to say the evolution of Mr. Dooley began. He is not always in character here at first, but as the weekly stories continued, the character emerged. Superficially, at least, he was like McGarry in that he was a bachelor, a saloon-keeper, and a Roscommon Irishman.

The question of the real prototype of Mr. Dooley, if any, has been answered in every imaginable way by commentators. Except for the connection with Mc-

---

[1] January 1, 1893.

[2] October 7, 1893.

Garry, Dunne refused to designate any. Traditions active in Chicago in 1940, however, offer a wide range of possibilities. Among those suggested, in addition to McGarry, are Peter Dunne's own father, his Uncle William, and John McKenna. After the Dooley stories became popular on Archer Avenue, many of the Irish there identified the original with a certain Dennis Dooley who loafed at Murphy's saloon and maintained a reputation as a wit, until he fell from his porch one New Year's day and was killed. One finds many defenders of this identification along the " Road " today. Charles Dana Gibson thinks that the comedian J. W. " Rolling Mill " Kelly was a character very near to Mr. Dooley. Some evidence for this identification might be found in Kelly's appearance with Tony Pastor's entertainment features at the World's Fair in September, 1893, just before Dunne changed McNeery to Dooley. Considering Dunne's fondness for all sorts of theatrical entertainment at this time, it would be strange if he had not seen Kelly. However, Dooley was more like McNeery, whom Dunne had created out of his own imagination, and Jim McGarry, than he was like any of these. He had no single prototype. Dooley was compounded of the qualities of many real men, not the least of whom was Peter Dunne.

As he began to write of Mr. Dooley, Dunne found that he needed a better acquaintance with Archer Avenue, and in company with John McKenna he made several visits there, going the rounds of some of the saloons, meeting many Irish characters and listening to their talk. With these superficial things to use, and his own good memories of the Irish of St. Patrick's Parish to draw upon, he had what he needed for his work. Why he chose the name Dooley is impossible to discover.[3] As a boy Eugene Field had given that name to a dog which he liked to think had something Irish about his face. There were four saloons owned by Chicago Dooleys in 1893 when Dunne started using the name, but none of these was on Archer Avenue and there was no Martin Dooley in Chicago. There were more Hennessys — one liquor dealer by that name employed a Mr. Dooley — but as yet that famous listener was unborn to journalism and literature.

If we suppose that Dunne was now consciously planning a great work that would show the human race as it was represented in the very human Irish of Archer Avenue, we are reading into the record something that is not there. True, all of his essays, the older McNeery and the current Dooley sketches were designed according to the Thackerayan standards: a realism that went beneath pretense and humbug but which did not eliminate the elements of human sympathy and decency. These standards were well known and heartily approved by Dunne, but it seems more probable that as yet he was meeting his weekly deadline without much consideration of his ultimate purpose. A few years later he was to tell

[3] Brand Whitlock is authority for the statement that Dunne had sometimes written imaginary interviews with Colonel Thomas Jefferson Dolan, and that these were forerunners of the dialect essays. The writer could find none of these in the *Herald* or *Post,* although Dolan was in the news from time to time. If Whitlock were correct, Colonel Dolan, Colonel McNeery, Mr. Dooley would be a suggestive sequence. *Forty Years of It* (New York, 1914), p. 46.

Michael Straus that he wanted to make the world see itself through a picture of the simple life of the Irish immigrant in Chicago — " simple like th' air or th' deep sea " — but he then conceived of doing it in some other form than the dialect essay. For the present, at least, the Dooley pieces were merely other editorials in which Dunne could often express ideas and urge points of view that it was not easy or even possible to put into the regular editorials.

The most distinctive change in the Dooley essays as contrasted with the McNeery pieces was that as Dunne began to picture the life of Archer Avenue and, through that, hold up a mirror in which humanity might see itself, he found himself frequently deserting satire and comic humor for pathetic and tragic sketches that were necessary to his total picture. The first of these touches came when during a bitter cold evening Dunne had the little Grady child come shivering to Dooley's door with a can for beer for her father, and Dooley returned home with her to whip her sodden parent into some decency. It has a ten-nights-in-a-barroom touch that was a long way from the tone of the Whitechapel Club. For the Christmas piece, too, Mr. Dooley related a sentimental recollection of Christmas in Roscommon which privately reduced him to tears. But it was in the spring of 1894 when Dunne produced his first wholly tragic essay. Croker, the great Tammany boss, had fled the country to escape the finally aroused law, and Dooley took off from there to tell a stark tragedy of another boss named Flannagan, whose power-mad mind drove him from one cruelty to another political success until his very soul became identified with the evil one. There was not the faintest trace of a smile in the awful horror, and it must have been with some doubt as to its reception that Dunne and McAuliff used it. But thereafter these varied the usual humor with memorable regularity. Essays such as " The Trust at Work," " The Idle Apprentice," or " Shaughnessy " are as effective evocations of simple human tragedy as English literature affords. An occasion like the death of four heroic firemen in the line of duty would bring on a piece about another heroic fireman who went to his death bravely; for no obvious reason, the problem of rearing boys on the city streets was a frequent and usually tragic topic. Any occasion of unusual human misery was likely to call for such a piece, frequently a perfect sermon. As a matter of fact, one of them, " On Criminals," tracing the story of a killer from his boyhood in a quiet, pious family until he is finally taken by a squad of police, was read annually in one of the Catholic churches in the city for several years.

But the great majority of the pieces were humor, pure, simple, and great. The comedy and irony of life on Archer Avenue was the usual subject, varied occasionally by a glimpse via the newspaper into houses on Michigan Avenue, the home of one of the Vanderbilts, or Buckingham Palace. A popular novel or a play, or a trial or prize-fight were all probable subjects. Sometimes a piece would be built about one or more humorous anecdotes, or it would be based upon some happening in the news that could be made to yield laughter by presentation with the salt of wit and satire. Not often, but now and then, a tall tale would be produced that had all the characteristics of a Paul Bunyan exaggeration. Like all writers of importance, Dunne knew how to treasure a good story or an incident until he found an opportunity to use it, and into these essays came memories of his own childhood, stories which his older relatives and their friends had told of Ireland and an earlier Chicago, incidents by the hundreds which he had picked up all over Chicago during the past fifteen years, and innumerable bits from his reading. A humorous story from St. Louis telling how a ballot box was " stuffed " by feeding the opposition ballots to a convenient goat, which appeared in the *Post* soon after Dunne began his work there, turned up later in a Dooley essay as part of that philosopher's memories of " Archey Road."

In his more serious pieces Dunne liked to attack local evils which aroused his indignation. Here he was much freer than in a regular editorial and much more effective. Unfeeling organized charity would frequently bring on a blast. " Why don't they get th' poor up in a cage in Lincoln Park an' hand thim food on th' end iv a window-pole, if they're afraid they'll bite." [4] When the Illinois Central Railroad fenced off a large section of the Lake front, which had been a common refuge for Chicago people in hot weather, Dooley sprang to the attack with a withering blast that was long remembered.

The summer of 1894 was one of the great crises in Chicago's life, with unemployment acute and dire want on every hand. The climax was the Pullman

[4] January 30, 1897.

strike and its suppression by Federal troops. With the *Post's* ownership where it was, there can be little surprise that its editorial policy was completely opposed to the strike, to Eugene Debs, and to the American Railway Union. In his Dooley essays Dunne showed no partisanship toward the main labor struggle, limiting himself to satire on some of the excesses of both sides. But regarding the inhumanity of Pullman's policy and his cowardly flight from the scene of action, Dunne laid on with vigor.

"This here Pullman makes th' sleepin' cars an' th' Constitootion looks afther Pullman. He have a good time iv it. He don't need to look afther himsilf. . . . He calls out George Wash'ngton an' Abraham Lincoln an' Gin'ral Miles an' [police officer] Mike Brinan . . . an' thin puts on his hat an' lams away. 'Gintlemin,' says he, 'I must be off,' he says. 'Defind th' Constitootion,' he says. 'Me own is not iv th' best,' he says, 'an' I think I'll help it be spindin' th' summer,' he says, 'piously,' he says, 'on th' shores iv th' Atlantic ocean.'

"That's Pullman. He slips out as aisely as a bar iv his own soap. An' th' whole wurruld turns in an' shoots an' stabs an' throws couplin' pins, an' sojers march out an' Gin'ral Miles looks up th' sthreet for some man to show that he can kill men too." [5]

After the strike had been suppressed and the suffering of the unemployed increased, with actual starvation in the village of Pullman, Dunne cut loose with unaccustomed fury.

What Does He Care?

"Jawn," said Mr. Dooley, "I said it wanst an' I say it again, I'd liefer be George M. Pullman thin anny man this

[5] July 7, 1894.

side iv Michigan City. I wud so. Not, Jawn, d'ye mind that I invy him his job iv runnin' all th' push-cart lodgin'-houses iv th' counthry or in dayvilopin' th' whiskers iv a goat without displayin' anny other iv th' good qualities iv th' craythur or in savin' his taxlist fr'm th' assissor with th' intintion iv layin' it befure a mathrimonyal agency. Sare a bit does I care f'r thim honors. But, Jawn, th' lad that can go his way with his nose in th' air an' pay no attintion to th' sufferin' iv women an' childher — dear, oh, dear, but his life must be as happy as th' day is long.

"It seems to me, Jawn, that half th' throuble we have in this vale iv tears, as Dohenny calls Bridgepoort, is seein' th' sufferin' iv women an' little childhern. . . .

"But as I said, Jawn, 'tis not th' min ye mind; 'tis th' women an' childhern. Glory be to Gawd, I can scarce go out f'r a walk f'r pity at seein' th' little wans settin' on th' stoops an' th' women with thim lines in th' face that I seen but wanst befure, an' that in our parish over beyant, whin th' potatoes was all kilt be th' frost an' th' oats rotted with th' dhrivin' rain. Go into wan iv th' side sthreets about supper time an' see thim, Jawn — thim women sittin' at th' windies, with th' babies at their breasts an' waitin' f'r th' ol' man to come home. Thin watch him as he comes up th' sthreet, with his hat over his eyes an' th' shoulders iv him bint like a hoop an' dhraggin' his feet as if he carried ball an' chain. Musha, but 'tis a sound to dhrive ye'er heart cold whin a woman sobs an' th' young wans cries, an' both because there's no bread in th' house. Betther off thim that lies in Gavin's crates out in Calv'ry, with th' grass over thim an' th' stars lookin' down on thim, quite at last. An' betther f'r us that sees an' hears an' can do nawthin' but give a crust now an' thin. I seen Tim Dorsey's little woman carryin' in a loaf iv bread an' a ham to th' Polack's this noon. Dorsey have been out iv wurruk f'r six months, but he made a sthrike carryin' th' hod yistherday an' th' good woman pinched out some vittles f'r th' Polacks."

Mr. Dooley swabbed the bar in a melancholy manner and

turned again with the remark: "But what's it all to Pullman? Whin Gawd quarried his heart a happy man was made. He cares no more f'r thim little matthers iv life an' death thin I do f'r O'Connor's tab. 'Th' women an' childhern is dyin' iv hunger,' they says. 'Will ye not put out ye'er hand to help thim?' they says. 'Ah, what th' 'ell,' says George. 'What th' 'ell,' he says. 'What th' 'ell,' he says. 'James,' he says, 'a bottle iv champagne an' a piece iv crambree pie. What th' 'ell, what th' 'ell, what th' 'ell.'"

"I heard two died yesterday," said Mr. McKenna. "Two women."

"Poor things, poor things. But," said Mr. Dooley, once more swabbing the bar, "what th' 'ell." [6]

When the typesetter ran off his proof of this piece he passed it about the composing room, and later when Dunne stepped into the room for a moment, the typesetters started to drum their sticks on their cases, and then broke into the more customary applause of handclapping. It was painfully embarrassing because it was so unusual and yet so natural, and Dunne remembered it as one of the great thrills of his life. The essay was read and reread all over Chicago and most of Illinois. It was memorized and recited in Chicago. It became a highly important factor in rousing public sentiment to the reality of suffering in Pullman, and in bringing into being a relief fund that aided the worst cases. While an extreme instance, its method is reasonably typical of the influence of the Dooley pieces on affairs in Chicago.

During the first year of the Dooley articles, less than half of the topics were political. Politics was then a topic only because it was the main interest of

[6] August 25, 1894.

the Irish on Archer Avenue. But as the didactic aspects of the essays grew, politics began to play a larger and larger part in them. Probably no other American city ever presented a more corrupt Common Council than the city of Chicago. The worst evils of the city could be traced directly to it and the forces and men who controlled it. The public was lethargic — " corrupt and contented " describes the city very well. Over the eight years from 1892 to 1900 there was no single force for improvement more effective than the Dooley essays.

Dunne usually made an exception of the police department. Mr. Dooley would refer to the patrolman who " dhrinks this beat," but in general, either out of respect for his many friends such as John Shea or because the department was as good as it was reasonable to expect, considering the Council, he let it off easy. Not so the corrupt members of the gang which dominated the Council, including O'Brien, who represented Bridgeport and Archey Road. Mr. Dooley described the life of a member of that dignified assembly to John McKenna.

" No work or worry. Nawthin' but sit down with ye'er hat cocked over ye'er eye an' ye'er feet on a mahogany table an' let th' roly-boly [easy money] dhrop into ye'er mit. Th' most wurruk an aldherman has to do is to presint himself with a gold star wanst a year so he won't forget he's an aldherman. . . . 'Tis good f'r annythin' fr'm a ball to a christenin' an' by gar Billy O'Broyn wurruked it on th' church. He went to mass over by Father Kelly's wan Sundah mornin' to square himsilf, an' whin Dinnis Nugent passed th' plate to him he showed th' star. ' Are ye an aldherman? ' says Nugent. ' I am that,' says O'Broyn. ' Thin,' he says, stickin' th' plate under his nose, 'thin,' he says, 'lave half f'r th' parish,' he says." [7]

It was not alone a matter of being able to say safely in dialect what one dared not write in regular editorials, for in the latter Dunne could be equally direct. When the notorious alderman, Bathhouse John Coughlin, proposed to exterminate Chicago's opium dens by increasing the penalty for their conduct from a fine of three dollars to one of a hundred, Dunne quoted it in an editorial and added:

> We welcome this amiable statesman to the army of reform. We commend his illustrious enterprise. But we should be more enthusiastic in our applause if we were sure that the statesman was unselfish in his undertaking – that he was not indirectly aiming to divert the drab procession of vice from the hop to the hot room.[8]

But the Dooleys were far more effective, and no one knew that better than Dunne. He never dignified the Council by treating it as seriously as he had Pullman; always his weapon against this body was comic, witty satire. And he kept at it persistently. Much less frequently he dealt similarly with the Illinois Legislature, partly because it was less regularly corrupt, and partly because he felt less free to do so in view of the editorial policy of the *Post*.

When the Legislature passed a law, over the protests of the German Lutheran Church, requiring all schools to display the American flag, Dooley discoursed on the values of patriotism.

> "Did ye iver see a man that wanted to free Ireland th' day after to-morrah that didn't run f'r aldherman soon or late?

[7] February 10, 1894.

[8] May 14, 1894.

Most iv th' great pathriotic orators iv th' day is railroad lawyers. That's a fact. . . . Well, 'tis th' Lutheryans that are roarin' again puttin' flags on th' schoolhouses. Th' legislature that stole ivrythin' in sight fr'm th' money iv poor Hankins to th' inkwells in their desks wants to make thim hist flags on their schools to show that they're pathriots enough not to care whin they're robbed, an' th' Lutheryans are fightin' it because it ain't th' German flag. An' — " here Mr. Dooley paused for thought.

" Well, what is it? " Mr. McKenna asked briskly.

" I was on'y wondhrin'," said Mr. Dooley, " if there ain't some money left in th' gold brick game." [9]

Dunne reserved his wittiest scorn for the source of the corruption of both the Council and the Legislature, Charles T. Yerkes — " Yerkuss," he always had Dooley pun. Yerkes was a buccaneer promoter, who had reached Chicago in the eighties and was now in control of most of her street-railway system, the City Council, and such other instruments as he could use in his peculations. No city ever suffered from a more unscrupulous pirate than Chicago did from Charles T. Yerkes, who is adequately characterized in Dreiser's *The Titan* and *The Financier*. Dunne usually attacked Yerkes with stiletto-like side remarks while descanting upon humorous or pathetic aspects of life on Archey Road. In recounting a suicide resulting from the failure of market operations in Yerkes's traction shares, Dooley remarked:

" Now, Jawn, I don't know Yerkuss. He doesn't do his dhrinkin' here an' he's no more to me thin I am to him. But if iver I go out f'r to rob annywan I'll make arrangements with Yerkuss to divide up th' territory an' thin I'll wait till he's out iv town." [10]

[9] August 17, 1895.

[10] September 28, 1895.

Mr. Dooley did not wholly approve of the ceremonies commemorating the Chicago fire of 1871:

"We've had manny other misfortunes an' they're not cillybrated. Why don't we have a band out an' illuminated sthreet cars f'r to commimerate th' day that Yerkuss came to Chicago? An' there's cholera. What's th' matter with cholera?" [11]

When the traction magnate purchased control of the *Inter Ocean* in order to have an organ of his own, Dooley pointed out that Yerkes wanted to reform the Chicago press. "He's a great journalist. All he needs is a bald head an' a few whiskers an' principles to be a second Horace Greeley." [12]

Moreover, Dunne was not willing to stop with satirizing the boodlers on the Council and their principal employer, Yerkes, but he extended his bombardment to all those elements of respectability in the city who profited from the system. Shortly before he took the Dooley essays from the *Post*, he put it all in one essay in defense of John Powers, leader of the corruptionists on the Council. After detailing the story of Powers's youth and young manhood in the tough Nineteenth Ward, Mr. Dooley continued:

"They raise no saints in that part iv th' nineteenth ward, an' they was nawthin' Jawnny Powers seen afther he got into th' council that'd make him think th' worse iv Alick Swan iv Law avnoo. He didn't meet so manny men that'd steal a ham an' thin shoot a polisman over it. But he met a lot that'd steal th' whole West Side iv Chicago an' thin fix a grand jury to get away with it. It must've been a shock to

[11] October 9, 1897. [12] November 20, 1897.

Jawnny Powers, thim first two years in th' council. Think iv this quite, innocent little groceryman that knew no thieves but thim that lurked along alleys with their hats pulled over their eyes, bein' inthrojooced to bigger thieves that stole in th' light iv day, that paraded their stovepipe hats an' goold watches an' chains in Mitchigan avnoo. Did ye iver see an aldherman go by th' Chicago Club? He looks at it as if he ownded it.

" Whin Jawnny Powers wint into th' council I don't suppose he had anny idee what a great man he'd make iv himsilf. He thought iv most all th' wurruld except th' nineteenth as honest. He believed that th' lads that presided over th' municipyal purity meetin's was on th' square an' he hated th' ladin' mimbers iv churches an' th' boys that gives money to home missions an' thrainin' schools because he thought they were inhumanly honest. It didn't take long f'r to make him see diff'rent. Inside iv his first term he begun to undherstand that they was rale, flesh-an'-blood, bribe-givin' men. They was good fellers, th' same as Chick McMillan, an' betther to dale with because if things didn't go right they'd not be apt to come down an' shoot bullets through th' sawdust ham in front iv a man's grocery store. An' whin wanst he got their measure he knew how to threat thim. He's quick to larn, Jawnny Powers is. None quicker. But I wudden't iv had his expeeryence f'r twict his money. I'd rather set back here an' believe that whin a man dhresses dacint he's respectible an' whin he has money he won't steal."

" Somethin' ought to be done to rayform th' rayformers," suggested Mr. Hennessy.

" Thrue," said Mr. Dooley. " I'm thinkin' iv gettin' up an organization to do th' wurruk. I'd attimpt to put a branch in ivry church an' charitable society in Chicago an' in ivry club. An' whin anny man that abuses Jawnny Powers an' Yerkuss while buyin' th' wan an' guaranteein' th' bonds iv th' other'd come up f'r Main Shepherd or Chief Angel I'd agitate again him. I wudden't let him set by while Jawnny

Powers was bein' done up an' purtend he was in on th' play; I'd get afther him.

"Thin I'd put up a social colony like Hull House down town near th' banks an' th' boord iv thrade an' th' stock exchange. I'd have ladin' citizens come in an' larn be contact with poor an' honest people th' advantage iv a life they've on'y heard iv. I think th' Hull House idee is right, but I'd apply it diff'rent. A man wurrukin' in a bank all day thryin' to get money anny way he can, how's he goin' to know anny diff'rent? What he needs is to be cheered up, have th' pianny played to him be nice-lookin' girls, an' find out somethin' iv th' beauties iv honest poverty be convarsin' with poor an' honest people."

"But where'd ye get th' lads to run it?" asked Mr. Hennessy.

"That's easy," said Mr. Dooley. "If ye'll get th' bankers I'll get th' others. I know thousands iv poor but honest men that are on'y waitin' f'r th' chanst to get wan crack at a banker." [13]

Along with the Dooley articles, Dunne was keeping up a steady fire in his regular editorials against the corruptionists, directed here, it must be admitted, more at Yerkes and Powers. Dunne had welcomed a Municipal Reform Association which had been organized in 1895 under the leadership of the banker, Lyman J. Gage. With this as a rallying-point, and with the support of most of the press, a sustained effort was made to drive Yerkes and his agents out of control of the Council. Dunne was on friendly terms with the reformers, especially a young alderman, William Kent, who for a time was the spearhead of the movement in the Council. He advised with them regarding strategy, suggested means of uncovering cor-

[13] January 15, 1898.

ruption, and arranged publicity for what was found. By the time success was achieved, Dunne had moved to the *Journal*, and was using its editorial page and news policy to push the cause along. In the crucial Council election of 1898, his editorials were more than usually effective. Early in the race, he took his text from a speech of Jane Addams and enlarged upon it to advise the reformers on political strategy. After describing in realistic terms how Powers kept his hold on the voters of his ward, he went on to describe how he might be beaten:

> If he is defeated it must be by the use of weapons similar to his own. The candidate who beats him must be:
>
> A friend of the poor.
>
> One whom the people can trust to make reform a perceptible benefit.
>
> One who won't make reform an affliction and a restraint on personal liberty.
>
> A candidate who can conform to these specifications may beat Powers. For any one who can't, to try to beat him will be a waste of effort.[14]

With the issue drawn, Dunne added good measure to his editorial pages from the rich supply of humor. Hinky Dink and Bathhouse John were Yerkes's two aldermen from the First Ward.

> Mr. H. Dink, otherwise known as Michael Kenna, of the First Ward, has as able an estimation of a statesman as ever graced the inside of a head. But he has applied it to the Hon. Bath-House John Coughlin, also of the First, whose extended arms welcomed H. Dink to the Chicago Common Council, and he has found that Hon. Coughlin fits the ideal like a cork fits a bottle, with one single, sad exception.

---

[14] January 24, 1898.

"He is a great man," says Mr. Dink, referring to Hon. B.-House John. "He's got the grit and the gall, and if he only had the grammar, he'd be a statesman, and don't you ever forget it."

So please to you Mr. Dink we shall not forget it. But do you really think he needs the grammar? . . . Isn't your colleague a statesman without the grammar? Does he ever have any difficulty doing a statesman's work simply on the grit and the gall?

. . . Mr. Dink's definition is too narrow as long as it excludes, for mere lack of grammar, a statesman of such transcendent attributes as the Hon. B.-House Coughlin. He is a complete statesman with just the grit and the gall.[15]

When an alderman pledged to reform was brought to Powers's heel by a job for a son in the city hall and a few railroad passes, Dunne's scorn was unrestrained:

Some people in Ald. Powers' ward may be had for turkeys, but not reformers. Reformers come higher. And when a reformer who is at the same time an Italian patriot may be had for a few passes the price is cheap enough. Only the question remains, "Why did Signor O'Hanion desert his benefactor in the first place?"[16]

Although Powers himself was returned to the Council, the machine's majority was at last broken, and the decline of Yerkes's power in Chicago had begun.

The Chicago newspaper-reading public of the nineties had been used to solemn editorial denunciation of the city's crooks and boodlers for years, and it had developed a partial immunity to such attacks. After 1893, Dunne had, in Mr. Dooley's utterances, a different type of polemic, one that would be widely read

[15] February 7, 1898.

[16] March 22, 1898.

and then memorized by amateur elocutionists who could recite Irish brogue. Declaiming essays like those on Pullman and Powers, or stories like that quoted on O'Brien, or remarks like those on Yerkes, was a common method of entertainment wherever men were congregated. These, with his satirical editorials, made Dunne a vital factor in the situation. We can be sure that no editorial page in the city was more effective in bringing home the real corruption. Not the least element of its strength was that Dunne, in the Dooley essays as well as his editorials, cast the same skeptical eye on most reform movements, and presented them truthfully for what they were — another method of political promotion. "Jawn, niver steal a dure mat," said Mr. Dooley. "If ye do ye'll be invistigated, hanged, an' maybe rayformed. Steal a bank, me boy, steal a bank."

In his later years Dunne liked to recall that as a young man he had been a radical social reformer. If his memory was accurate, that period must have been before the development of the Dooley articles. Although it is dangerous to generalize from the writing he did for conservative newspapers, still the Dooley essays often expressed a profound fatalism which was saved from becoming defeatist cynicism only by an intensely emotional sympathy for the under-dog, and a love of humanitarian values. Some of Dunne's essays implied ideas that were close to philosophical anarchism, but he made hilarious fun of the solemn anarchists of Chicago, and satirized as well the socialists with their dull oratory and fuzzy ideas of political strategy. Too many of the leaders of such movements whom he met were poseurs for him to take their programs seriously. But his distrust of government was certainly no greater than his distrust of business or any other method of control. When municipal ownership was proposed as a solution of the "Yerkes problem," Mr. Dooley looked at the City Council and told Mr. Hennessy " 'tis only a question iv who does th' robbin'." [17]

The Dooley essays were a treasured Chicago institution after 1894. Their author was, of course, not generally known, even though some fan mail came to the *Post*. There never was a name nor initial signed to them. However, the newspaper men in the city knew they were Peter Dunne's work. One of these, signing himself with the initials E. M. L., celebrated Mr. Dooley in verse which found its way into print:

> There's been tellin' sthrokes in Dooley's speechin' —
> Didn't Pullman squirm at things he said?
> And others thank him for thoughts as tindher
> As a mother's glances at her baby's bed.[18]

But the Dooley stories were a small weekly assignment, while Dunne's work was the editorial page of the *Post*, to be prepared daily. Into this he was putting his best work, and the results were highly pleasing to McAuliff and Scott. Prospective changes in the spring of 1895 were to their liking, as Scott, the popular and liberal publisher, was at last in a position to buy out Walsh's interest in the *Post* and *Herald*. This he did, and immediately united the *Herald* with the other Democratic morning paper, the *Times*.

---

[17] *Post*, October 16, 1897.

[18] January 26, 1895.

Here was a great journalistic venture, exciting in prospect to Dunne, McAuliff, and others of like mind on the staff. The union of two strong morning papers gave them a great advantage in the morning field; the union of the two most popular Democratic dailies in the Northwest promised a wide circulation; and the continuation of the scholarly *Evening Post* as the afternoon adjutant assured it of a stable future. With Scott in complete control, an independence of position was possible which seemed to promise a paper that would become one of the great traditions of American journalism. But within two weeks, Scott, who was only forty-six years of age, had died of apoplexy and his majority interest in the papers was for sale.

It was purchased by Herman Kohlsaat, owner of a chain of bakeries and restaurants, and but recently a part-owner of the solid Republican *Inter Ocean*. Among the reasons for his purchase was an ambition for political power and social prestige. Already he was heavily involved in the campaign to make William McKinley the next President. Honest, forthright, and generous, Kohlsaat, with his political ambitions and limited knowledge of public affairs, would make a problem for any newspaper management where he was the determining factor. At an early editorial conference it was pointed out to him that because the *Times-Herald* was a combination of the two most partisan Democratic papers in the Northwest, and the only important Democratic paper in Chicago, its editorial policy should be considered seriously before being changed materially. " Oh," the new owner declared, " this paper is going to be strictly independent, except that it will be for protection, for William McKinley, and for anything he wants." Thereafter both the *Times-Herald* and the *Post* were just that. Beginning in May, 1895, the *Post* lost its boasted independence from partisan politics. Only in municipal affairs, where Kohlsaat was as opposed to Yerkes and the racketeers on the Council as was anyone else, were the old policies to continue. McAuliff was moved over to the *Times-Herald* as managing editor of the larger paper, and Sam T. Clover replaced him on the *Post*. Dunne stayed in charge of the editorials on the *Post* for a time, and then McAuliff moved him over to the *Times-Herald* to add to an editorial staff which included such stars as Moses P. Handy, the Philadelphian whom Dunne had satirized years before, and Margaret Sullivan. In spite of this talent, the tradition of Horatio Seymour dominated the page, and a heavy tone of deadly seriousness gave Dunne little room to exercise his real talents.

Mr. Dooley continued to appear in the Saturday issue of the *Post*. This was now the only real outlet for Dunne's gift of witty and satirical writing, and even here it was restricted by the more partisan character of the paper. Dunne covered both national conventions for the *Times-Herald* in 1896, in addition to his editorial writing. This campaign made one important change in the Dooley essays. McKenna, in his true character of the Irish Republican, did not permit Mr. Dooley to use him as a foil for his wit, now to be exercised on a Republican gold-standard paper. Consequently the great listener, Mr. Hennessy, typical Irish Democrat of Archey Road, was created and introduced to McKenna by Mr. Dooley. During the campaign the arguments of the three characters satirized that hectic contest; for, unlike the editorial pages of Kohlsaat's newspapers, Dunne did not use the Dooleys to make votes for McKinley. These pieces made about as much sport of Mark Hanna as of Bryan. And as the campaign increased in intensity and in partisan blindness, the Dooley essays took on a tone of resigned sorrow that such nonsense could be taken seriously by adult citizens. When Yale students rioted at a Bryan meeting in New Haven, Dooley remarked: "I don't mind th' rah-rah lads at Yale. What can ye ixpict fr'm a thribe iv young chimpanzees whin th' paternal apes is hangin' fr'm th' trees be their tails an' callin' upon hivin not to cut th' bough." [19]

After the campaign, Hennessy replaced McKenna in the sketches. There were good reasons for this. Dooley needed a foil to talk to, and the character which Dunne had made for Hennessy was a better one for that purpose than McKenna. Moreover, as a day-laborer with a large family, Hennessy was more characteristic of Archey Road. Most important of all, perhaps, he was pseudonymous and thus could be abused in ways Dunne would not treat McKenna. Thus, after being a regular character of the dialect pieces for four years, with both Colonel McNeery and Mr. Dooley, John McKenna, to his own sorrow, passed out of the stories except for very infrequent mention.

[19] September 26, 1896.

Dunne remained with the *Times-Herald* through most of 1897, but he was not well pleased with the new ownership. To Hamill and Straus he would occasionally mimic the editorial conferences at which Kohlsaat decided on policies. Although intimate friends such as Mary Abbott, Horace Taylor, and McAuliff were also with the paper, the stimulating group of young men that had been on the old *Herald* was now scattered to other parts of the world. Dunne was ripe for a change.

Detroit newspaper interests, represented by George G. Booth, came into Chicago and purchased the aged and respectable *Chicago Journal* in 1897, placing Willis H. Turner in charge to build it into a cheap, popular afternoon journal by methods similar to those which Pulitzer and Hearst were using so successfully in New York. After Turner had studied the local situation, he asked Dunne to become the *Journal's* managing editor, with charge of the editorial page. Turner could promise that the paper would be truly popular and independent in politics. Dunne accepted, and moved over sometime in the late fall or early winter of 1897–98, transferring his Dooley essays to it after the first of the year. Dunne had now nearly completed the circle of the important papers in Chicago. He had worked on all of them except the *Inter Ocean*.

A few months later Dunne's work on the *Journal* was hailed with delight by Frederick U. Adams in his muckraking periodical, *The New Times*. He declared that Dunne had " wasted several years of his newspaper life on the *Chicago Times-Herald*. . . . In two months he has lifted the *Journal* from comparative obscurity to national importance." [20] It was the judgment of a very partial friend.

[20] II (May 1898), 340.

# MR. DOOLEY BECOMES A NATIONAL SENSATION

WHEN Peter Dunne started writing Irish dialect he was but twenty-five years of age; when employed by the *Journal* he was thirty. Excepting for the Dooley essays, there was little in the purely professional sense that indicated any great growth over the period. True, the managing editorship of the *Journal*, which placed him second in command to Turner, was more important than editorial writer for the *Post*, but it was not enough more, considering Dunne's reputation as a political reporter in 1892, to indicate any very notable achievement. The difference was chiefly in the dialect essays, of which relatively few people in Chicago knew the author. Dunne himself was not inclined to admit that he thought highly of them. Chance acquaintances sometimes heard him disparage them with more than superficial modesty. Shortly before his death in 1895, Eugene Field, in one of his infrequent contacts with Dunne, urged him to make a book of the articles, but

Dunne refused to consider it. The praise that came to him from his friends was treated in a like manner, however gratifying it may have been to him privately.

The reasons for this attitude are not easy to understand. It seems clear that he did not want to be known as a humorist. In spite of his frequent resort to humor in his editorials, he considered himself a serious writer and not a wit. His own subsequent explanation was that his ambition was to become a publisher, and hence his desire to establish himself as a newspaper executive. His move to the *Journal* was in that direction. On the other hand, he had made no attempt whatever to accumulate any capital of his own, and fatalistically lived up his substantial salary. Still, if we accept his own memory of his ambition, it is hard to escape the conclusion that during his years as an active newspaper man in Chicago, he visualized his ideal future as something on the order of Joseph Medill's, although with a far different social and political philosophy.

Dunne had few associations with the professional literary people of Chicago, although some of them found their way to Mary Abbott's informal gatherings. It is doubtful that he more than knew by sight the novelist Henry B. Fuller, who was Chicago's foremost writer in the minds of many critics. Hamlin Garland saw Dunne occasionally, and his own seriousness had its reflection in the editor. Garland's recollection is specific on this point. "He had the somber temperament of the Celt. I felt in him a sadness of outlook, a fatalistic philosophy which was curiously at variance with his writing. He was very serious in his talks with me, perhaps because he felt something depressing in me. We discussed weighty things most weightily." [1]

With the more popular writers having a journalistic background, Dunne was on more intimate terms. George Ade had been writing his "Stories of the Streets and of the Town" in the *Record* as long as Dunne had been doing his dialect pieces, and Ade had published his books *Artie* and *Pink Marsh*, and was soon to bring out *Doc' Horne* from sketches that had been used in that paper. These and the Dooley series had more than a superficial resemblance in that both writers pictured with objective realism and sympathetic understanding aspects of Chicago life. The most obvious difference was that Ade wrote of the young men from the towns about Chicago who were working in the city, and the life about their places of labor and play, while Dunne wrote of the community life of Archer Avenue. Dunne and Ade continued to be close personal friends, and that friendship included Ade's most intimate associate, John McCutcheon, a writer of ability whose great talent lay in graphic humor. Other friends from the old Whitechapel Club, such as Wallace Rice and Frederick U. Adams, were active writers. Rice was a poet of considerable merit, and a critic and editor of ability. Adams published his first novel in 1897, but most of his writing at this time went into the small muckraking periodical which he edited.

Additions to the group of Dunne's intimates had come from a younger group of writers. Melville

---

1 *Roadside Meetings* (New York, 1930), p. 280.

Stone's eldest son, Herbert S. Stone, and H. I. Kimball had started a literary review, *The Chap Book*, while at Harvard, and after graduation brought it back to Chicago with them. There, aided by Harrison Rhodes and Wallace Rice, they began a significant publishing venture in which they brought out important essays, stories, and poetry. H. G. Wells, Henry James, Norman Hapgood — who had left Chicago — Stephen Crane, Harold Frederic, John Fox, Jr., Bliss Carman, Arthur Morrison, Elia Peattie, and many other Americans and foreigners were among the contributors to the unique journal. The book-publishing concern which Stone and Kimball erected about their review pioneered significantly in introducing George Bernard Shaw to American readers, as well as many midwestern authors such as Ade and George Barr McCutcheon. Dunne, Mary Abbott, and Robert and Catherine Hamill were all intimates of this group of editors and publishers, and with the growing tide of appreciation of the Dooley stories as a guide, Rhodes and Stone urged Dunne to let them make a book of the essays. But he doubted the wisdom of the idea, or at least let an excessive modesty lead him to use that as an excuse.

Dunne was not an easy writer in spite of almost fifteen years of daily newspaper work. He could turn out straight news like any good reporter, and even the usual run of editorials. But when it came to an essay of more than ordinary importance, he could easily work himself into a mental fever over the problem of writing, to say nothing of the problem of reasoning. The dialect articles were in this class, at least after

McNeery was changed to the more serious and didactic Dooley. Dunne's chief problem seemed to be finding a suitable subject and planning its development; the actual writing did not seem difficult for him. A procrastinator by nature, he seldom had an essay done ahead of time. The deadline was late Saturday forenoon, and the end of the week frequently found him disinclined to work. If he had his piece well thought out after discovering something during the week that could be used as a basis, he then could sit down Friday night or early Saturday forenoon, and put it into shape in from thirty to sixty minutes. If he had no stimulating subject at hand, he rebelled at writing, and it took McAuliff's — and later Clover's — pleading to get him to produce a Dooley article. Sometimes he refused, and the space had to be filled with a substitute, but more often he let it go until near press time, and then he would produce it under pressure with a copy boy carrying a few sentences at a time to the typesetters. Some were published without any revision, and several had only a superficial proofreading. But it is another evidence of his genius that these frequently will stand comparison with his best.

Perhaps the process was not made easier by the fact that Dunne was paid extra for the Dooley essay each week, while his regular salary was adequate for his living expenses. Consequently it worked out that the extra ten dollars that came on Saturday was spent on a dinner for a few intimate friends, and was not always needed. But sometimes circumstances conspired toward the end of the month so that the extra ten was desired before Saturday. Clover, who was managing editor of the *Post* after 1895, preserved some intimate notes which indicate that at times Dunne collected in advance.

Dearest Sam'l: The article for Saturday will be such a prose poem that I feel warranted in asking for payment in advance. Couldst do it, dear child-poet, traveler, guide, philosopher and friend? Dooley D.[2]

Dunne's personal and social life had changed but little in the past five years. A larger income enabled him to live better, with membership in a few good clubs, including the new and increasingly popular golf club at Wheaton, where Chicagoans were learning to play that ancient game under the inspiration of Britishers in the city. When the Dunne family had moved farther out on the West Side, Peter Dunne had left the group for the fashionable Virginia Hotel, where he and John Grier, a likable young broker from St. Louis, had adjoining quarters. Dunne dressed well and so conservatively that it was often remarked that he looked like a clergyman or a theological student. He was never anything of a clown, and to most mere acquaintances he seemed as he had to Hamlin Garland, rather sad and serious. The effect of flashing wit which he could produce at a moment's notice was greater for this background of solemnity. He was never a raconteur who would relate humorous anecdotes without end. Rather his was the type of humor which found its expression in the witty characterization of institutions and individuals. Under provocation he could still be as vicious as in the days of the Whitechapel Club. One famous Chicago story is of

[2] Quoted by Clover in *Evening Post,* April 29, 1915.

a group, playing golf one afternoon at Wheaton. Included were Peter Dunne and Chicago's richest man, Marshall Field, noted both for his economy and his intimate knowledge of everyone's financial standing. A lady in the party offered to bet Dunne that he could not drive the pond hole with a mashie. As he prepared to try, Field called out: "Better make him put up his money first." The ball went directly in the pond. At the next tee, Field complained that he had "lost his drive," no great loss, perhaps, but the merchant disliked to lose anything. "Why don't you try putting a dollar on the ball?" asked the innocent Peter Dunne. "What good would that do?" replied the merchant. "Well, all Chicago believes that you can make a dollar go farther than anyone in the world," answered the revenged journalist. And he watched Field make a mighty assault on the ball that propelled it some three feet from the tee.[3]

The management of the *Journal* was a pleasant task to both Turner and Dunne. Turner had a considerable wit and a real gift of repartee, and he and Dunne kept the staff on an intellectual edge. The two men had opportunities for experimentation on the paper, and they took advantage of it. They introduced and tried several different types of "columns," which they wrote or turned over to other members of the staff on trial. One of these was a column, "A Little About Everything," which was kept on the front page. Both Dunne and Turner wrote for it, as did several other members of the staff. It contained odd

[3] Charles Blair Macdonald: *Scotland's Gift, Golf* (New York, 1928), pp. 95–6.

bits of information, humorous remarks, and miscellaneous observations. One writer who had come from Duluth to take a place on the *Journal* proved so able at supplying sparkling material for it that soon the editors put him in sole charge, and thus Bert Leston Taylor found his place in journalism and began a career that made him the great columnist of his day.

Dunne's editorials in the *Journal* were like those he had written for the *Post* before he had been moved to the *Times-Herald*. Among the regular short polemics was mixed a large proportion of humorous and satirical paragraphs very close to the dialect essays in their essence. One that deserves recording is a tribute to Chicago's most important German-language paper on its fiftieth anniversary:

Best Wishes to the Staats Zeitung

It gives reason of congratulating Staats Zeitung by its jubilitiveness after this fifty yearen of loftyrightstruggle. The heart to us shimmers after incandescencehelt like a notimitation Halbach coalvaporlamp with the grosse noblefeelung from our kostbar neighbor. We to her through this one hoping of in comingtime cordialityheit, extend our magnanimity and burn with admirable wishes after her evergreathood and prosperity. May she great be and much money make.

. . .

The above has suffered somewhat by the Swedish galley boy's translation from our pure and idomatic German, but it still expresses our sentiments.[4]

The excitement of the approaching war with Spain and the *Journal's* sponsorship of a belligerent attitude helped to double the paper's circulation within three

[4] April 21, 1898.

months after Dunne joined the staff. In addition to being enthusiastically for aid to the Cubans, the *Journal* was aggressively opposed to the McKinley administration. How much of the policy on national affairs was Dunne's own, one cannot now discover. It had assumed its general form under Turner's direction before Dunne joined the staff. But during the first half of 1898 the Dooley essays were more partisan in a narrow sense than at any other time. They damned with vigor the seeming financial domination of McKinley's policy toward Cuba. In February, Mr. Dooley tells Hennessy: "Ye cud niver be a rale pathrite. Ye have no stock ticker in ye'er house." [5] As the *Maine* disaster increased the danger of war many-fold, someone suggested an indemnity as compensation. Dunne compared its supporters with O'Connor, the money-lender:

> "O'Connor's idea iv things is diff'rent. O'Connor believes in indemnity. If a man was to kick O'Connor — an' manny's th' time I've wanted to — all he'd have to do wud be to give him $5 — three kicks f'r tin, rayjooced rates f'r clubs iv more thin twinty, genteel business solicited. That's O'Connor." [6]

And that, he implied, was also Mark Hanna and the McKinley administration.

These new Dooley essays were attracting attention outside of Chicago, and as they dealt more with national affairs and less with local Chicago politics, they were reprinted in outside papers. The *Boston Globe* was the first to begin regular reprintings, and although the articles were not copyrighted, Dunne was paid

[5] February 19, 1898.

[6] March 26, 1898.

by the *Globe*. Soon, too, he was being paid by a Buffalo paper, where there had been competition in republishing the Saturday articles, and one paper offered a fee for an advance copy.

These early intimations of the appeal of the Dooley stories were but faint indicators of the pending national audience. This last was not to become clear until the Spanish War itself led to a series that swept the country like a prairie fire. The sheer excitement of the war was partly responsible; but more important was the natural way in which the humor and philosophy of Mr. Dooley suited the public temper of the day. The excess of emotionalism, the examples of bombast and bluff, the wartime oratory and journalism, and the striking cases of incompetence in Washington, all lent agility to Dunne's imagination. Satire, droll mimicry, tall tales, and rollicking comedy resulted. Once Dunne had made the transfer of Mr. Dooley's attention from Chicago to national and international affairs, that gentleman trod the new paths with all of the sure-footedness he had displayed on Archer Avenue. As before, he reduced all questions to the unique terms of Archey Road, and provided the needed balance to keep a measure of sanity in his readers. His comment on President McKinley's seeming failure to score a diplomatic victory over the Spanish premier, Sagasta, is typical of all this series, and represents Dunne's facility for mimicry and tall humor:

"I'll explain it to ye," said Mr. Dooley. "'Tis this way. Ye see, this here Sagasta is a boonco steerer like Canada Bill, an' th' likes iv him. . . . He's been up again Gladstun an'

Bismarck an' ol' what-ye-call-'im, th' Eyetalian, — his name's got away fr'm me, — an' he's done thim all.

" Well, business is bad. No wan will play with him. No money's comin' in. Th' circus has moved on to th' nex' town, an' left him without a customer. . . . Whin, lo an' behold, down th' sthreet comes a man fr'm th' counthry, — a lawyer fr'm Ohio, with a gripsack in his hand. Oh, but he's a proud man. He's been in town long enough f'r to get out iv th' way iv th' throlley car whin th' bell rings. He's larned not to thry an' light his seegar at th' ilicthric light. He doesn't offer to pay th' ilivator man f'r carryin' him upstairs. He's got so he can pass a tall buildin' without thryin' f'r to turn a back summersault. An' he's as haughty about it as a new man on an icewagon. They'se nawthin' ye can tell him. He thinks iv himsilf goin' back to Canton with a red necktie on, an' settin' on a cracker box an' tellin' th' lads whin they come in fr'm pitchin' horse-shoes what a hot time he's had, an' how he's a seen th' hootchy-kootchy an' th' Pammer House barber shop, an' th' other ondacint sights iv th' great city.

"An' so he comes up to where Sagasta is kind iv throwin' th' cards idly on th' top iv th' bar'l, an' Sagasta pipes him out iv th' corner iv his eye, an' says to himsilf: ' Oh, I dinnaw,' an' thanks hiven f'r th' law that has a sucker born ivry minyit. An' th' lad fr'm Canton thinks he can pick out th' Jack, an' sometimes he can an' sometimes he can't; but th' end iv it is th' Spanyard has him thrimmed down to his chist protector, an' he'll be goin' back to Canton in a blanket. Ye see it ain't his game. If it was pitchin' horse-shoes, 'twud be diff'rent. He cud bate Sagasta at that. He cud do him at rasslin' or chasin' th' greased pig, or in a wan-legged race or th' tug-iv-war. He cud make him look foolish at liftin' a kag iv beer or hitchin' up a team. But, whin it comes to diplomacy, th' Spanyard has him again th' rail, an' counts on him till his arm is sore."

" Why don't he turn an' fight? " demanded the patriotic Mr. Hennessy. . . .

In June Dunne wrote a satire on a meeting of the President's Cabinet, which the Chicago member, Secretary of the Treasury Lyman J. Gage, sent around to his colleagues. John D. Long, Secretary of the Navy, wrote back to Gage:

> I suppose it is fair to say that he does not get correctly the exact topics of our Cabinet meetings, but can you deny that he gets a fair measure of their importance? . . . I have conferred with the Secretary of War and several others of the Cabinet and . . . we have come to the conclusion that Dooley is a fictitious name for somebody very near the scene of action and more familiar than any outsider can be with the internal proceedings.[7]

The piece that made Mr. Dooley a national hero almost overnight was an essay on Admiral Dewey's destruction of the Spanish fleet at Manila. Back of its reception was a period of general excitement seldom equaled in American history. To a public already agape beyond present-day comprehension with wild tales of the prospective bombardment of the cities on the Atlantic coast by a mythical Spanish fleet came the news that Dewey had led the Asiatic squadron to Manila, that a battle had been fought there, but that, because of a cut cable, there was no news of its result. Rumors and fears of defeat during a period of suspense were relieved by the sudden announcement that the entire Spanish fleet — dangerous only in the eyes of the readers of excited newspapers — had been destroyed by Dewey's squadron. But still there were no details from Dewey, and enthusiasm was mixed with speculation as to his eventual fate. Into that mood

[7] June 29, 1898. Charlotte Dunne letters.

fitted more than one bit of journalistic writing, but none as effectively as Dunne's piece " On His Cousin George " :

" Well," said Mr. Hennessy, in tones of chastened joy, " Dewey didn't do a thing to thim. I hope th' poor lad ain't cooped up there in Minneapolis."

" Niver fear," said Mr. Dooley, calmly. " Cousin George is all right."

" Cousin George? " Mr. Hennessy exclaimed.

" Sure," said Mr. Dooley. " Dewey or Dooley, 'tis all th' same. We dhrop a letter here an' there, except th' haitches, – we niver dhrop thim – but we're th' same breed iv fightin' men. Georgy has th' thraits iv th' fam'ly. Me uncle Mike, that was a handy man, was tol' wanst he'd be sint to hell f'r his manny sins, an' he desarved it; f'r, lavin' out th' wan sin iv runnin' away fr'm annywan, he was booked f'r ivrything fr'm murdher to missin' mass. ' Well,' he says, ' anny place I can get into,' he says, ' I can get out iv,' he says. ' Ye bet on that,' he says.

" So it is with Cousin George. He knew th' way in, an' it's th' same way out. He didn't go in be th' fam'ly inthrance, sneakin' along with th' can undher his coat. He left Ding Dong, or whativer 'tis ye call it, an' says he, ' Thank Gawd,' he says, ' I'm where no man can give me his idees iv how to run a quiltin' party, an' call it war,' he says. An' so he sint a man down in a divin' shute, an' cut th' cables, so's Mack cudden't chat with him. Thin he prances up to th' Spanish forts, an' hands thim a few oranges. Tosses thim out like a man throwin' handbills f'r a circus. ' Take that,' he says, ' an' raymimber th' Maine,' he says. An' he goes into th' harbor, where Admiral What-th'-'ell is, an', says he, ' Surrinder,' he says. ' Niver,' says th' Dago. ' Well,' says Cousin George, ' I'll just have to push ye around,' he says. An' he tosses a few slugs at th' Spanyards. Th' Spanish admiral shoots at him with a bow an' arrow, an' goes over an' writes a cable. ' This mornin' we was attackted,' he says.

'An',' he says, 'we fought th' inimy with great courage,' he says. 'Our victhry is complete,' he says. 'We have lost ivrythin' we had,' he says. 'Th' threachrous foe,' he says, 'afther destroyin' us, sought refuge behind a mud-scow,' he says, 'but nawthin' daunted us. What boats we cudden't run ashore we surrindered,' he says. 'I cannot write no more,' he says, 'as me coat-tails are afire,' he says, 'an' I am bravely but rapidly leapin' fr'm wan vessel to another, followed be me valiant crew with a fire-engine,' he says. 'If I can save me coat-tails,' he says, 'they'll be no kick comin',' he says. 'Long live Spain, long live mesilf.'

"Well, sir, in twinty-eight minyits be th' clock Dewey he had all th' Spanish boats sunk, an' that there harbor lookin' like a Spanish stew. Thin he run down th' bay, an' handed a few warm wans into th' town. He set it on fire, an' thin wint ashore to warm his poor hands an' feet. It chills th' blood not to have annythin' to do f'r an hour or more."

"Thin why don't he write something?" Mr. Hennessy demanded.

"Write?" echoed Mr. Dooley. "Write? Why shud he write? D'ye think Cousin George ain't got nawthin' to do but to set down with a fountain pen, an' write: 'Dear Mack, — At 8 o'clock I begun a peaceful blockade iv this town. Ye can see th' pieces ivrywhere. I hope ye're injyin' th' same great blessin'. So no more at prisint. Fr'm ye'ers thruly, George Dooley.' He ain't that kind. 'Tis a nice day, an' he's there smokin' a good tin-cint seegar, an' throwin' dice f'r th' dhrinks. He don't care whether we know what he's done or not. I'll bet ye, whin we come to find out about him, we'll hear he's ilicted himself king iv th' F'lipine Islands. Dooley th' Wanst. He'll be settin' up there undher a pa'm-three with naygurs fannin' him an' a dhrop iv licker in th' hollow iv his arm, an' hootchy-kootchy girls dancin' befure him, an' ivry tin or twinty minyits some wan bringin' a prisoner in. 'Who's this?' says King Dooley. 'A Spanish gin'ral,' says th' copper. 'Give him a typewriter an' set him to wurruk,' says th' king. 'On with th' dance,' he says. An' afther awhile, whin he gits tired iv th' game, he'll write home an' say he's got th' islands; an' he'll turn thim over to th' gover'mint an' go back to his ship, an' Mark Hanna'll organize th' F'lipine Islands Jute an' Cider Comp'ny, an' th' rivolutchinists'll wish they hadn't. That's what'll happen. Mark me wurrud."

This essay so suited the mood of the American public that it became a sensation, and within a few weeks Mr. Dooley was a national character. Reports came to Chicago that at a quarreling session of the Texas Bar Association the meeting had been restored to good humor by a member who read " On His Cousin George " to the assembly; that the famous Bohemian Club in San Francisco had been swept away by a recitation of the piece in excellent brogue, and, later, that Ambassador Choate had read it to a British audience. It was reprinted widely, members of the *Journal* staff counting a round hundred papers in which it had appeared. Moreover, every subsequent Dooley comment was reprinted widely until Turner and Dunne awakened to the possibilities of profit in the situation. In a short time, the *Journal* was copyrighting the pieces, and collecting for the privilege of reprinting them.

When the question was raised, as it immediately was, of the disposal of the Philippines, the Dooley essays took a position different from the editorial policy of the *Journal* and opposed retention. Not yet directly, perhaps, but by implication in the way in which the imperialist argument was satirized. Dunne had previously stripped British imperialism of its protective coloration of high moral purpose, and it would have been surprising had he seen American " expansion " in a different light. Then, too, he was undoubtedly encouraged to attack by the cant and hypocrisy in the arguments which the imperialists were using to support the plan — arguments which skipped blithely from religious duty and racial destiny to the enticing sound of the bell on the domestic cash register. He paraphrased Henry Cabot Lodge's slogans as: " Hands acrost th' sea an' into somewan's pocket," and " Take up th' white man's burden an' hand it to th' coons." But he summarized it all in one essay in January, 1899, which was republished widely as a factor in the controversy over ratifying the treaty with Spain, then before the United States Senate:

" Whin we plant what Hogan calls th' starry banner iv Freedom in th' Ph'lippeenes," said Mr. Dooley, " an' give th' sacred blessin' iv liberty to th' poor, downtrodden people iv thim unfortunate isles – dam thim – we'll larn thim a lesson."

" Sure," said Mr. Hennessy, sadly, " we have a thing or two to larn oursilves."

" But it isn't f'r thim to larn us," said Mr. Dooley. " 'Tis not f'r thim wretched an' degraded crathers, without a mind or a shirt iv their own, f'r to give lessons in politeness an' liberty to a nation that mannyfacthers more dhressed beef thin anny other imperyal nation in th' wurruld. We say to thim: ' Naygurs,' we say, ' poor, dissolute uncovered wretches,' says we, ' whin th' crool hand iv Spain forged man'cles f'r ye'er limbs, as Hogan says, who was it crossed th' say an' sthruck off th' come-alongs? We did, by dad, we did. An' now, ye miserable, childish-minded apes, we propose f'r to larn ye th' uses iv liberty. In ivry city in this unfair land we will erect schoolhouses an' packin' houses an' houses iv correction, an' we'll larn ye our language, because 'tis aisier to larn ye ours thin to larn oursilves ye'ers, an' we'll give ye clothes if ye pay f'r thim, an' if ye don't ye can go without, an' whin ye're hungry ye can go to th' morgue – we mane th' resth'rant – an' ate a good square meal iv army beef. An' we'll send th' great Gin'ral Eagan over f'r to larn ye etiket an' Andhrew Carnegie to larn ye pathreetism with blowholes into it, an' Gin'ral Alger to larn ye to hould onto a job, an' whin ye've become edycated an' have all th' blessin's iv civilization that we don't want, that'll count ye wan. We can't give ye anny votes because we haven't more thin enough to go around now, but we'll threat ye th' way a father shud threat his childher if we have to break ivry bone in ye'er bodies. So come to our arms,' says we."

Such essays endeared him to readers whose first knowledge of Mr. Dooley came from "On His Cousin George." With the war ended, William Jennings Bryan, recent Democratic presidential candidate, was left in Florida with his Nebraska regiment, and President McKinley came to Chicago for a speech and a great public reception. Mr. Dooley summarized his speech in a way that won the hearts of all but extreme partisans:

"Th' proceedin's was opened with a prayer that Providence might remain undher th' protection iv th' administhration. . . .

"'Again,' he says, 'we are a united union,' he says. 'No north,' he says, 'no south, no east,' he says, 'no west. No north east a point east,' he says. 'Th' inimies iv our counthry has been crushed,' he says, 'or is stuck down in Floridy with his rig-ment talkin',' he says, 'his hellish docthrines to th' allygatars,' he says. . . . 'We can not turn back,' he says, 'th' hands iv th' clock that, even as I speak,' he says, 'is rushin' through th' hearts iv men,' he says, 'dashin' its spray against th' star iv liberty an' hope, an' no north, no south, no east, no west, but a steady purpose to do th' best we can, considerin' all th' circumstances iv th' case,' he says. 'I hope I have made th' matther clear to ye,' he says, 'an', with these few remarks,' he says, 'I will turn th' job over to destiny,' he says, 'which is sure to lead us iver on an' on, an' back an' forth, a united an' happy people, livin',' he says, 'undher an administhration that, thanks to our worthy Prisidint an' his cap'ble an' earnest advisers, is second to none,' he says."

With the sudden burst of popular acclaim for Mr. Dooley, Dunne's friends renewed their arguments for putting a selection of the articles into a book. If he had had any doubts as to their appeal, they must have been removed by the requests that came with every mail for permission to reprint in newspapers and for similar but new copy for periodical publication. Turner had clipped the essays as they had been published in the *Journal*. From some other source Dunne secured a scattered group of clippings from the *Post* which went back as far as 1895. It was from these collections that the selection was made for the book. Dunne took them to Robert Hamill's home one evening, where he, Hamill, Mrs. Hamill, and Harrison Rhodes sat around the dining table, selecting and rejecting as they read. After this preliminary winnowing, Dunne arranged the essays in a particular sequence, revised some of them slightly, and wrote an introduction fondly descriptive of Archey Road. To these he added the new pieces which he had written for the *Journal* while the manuscript was in the process of being prepared and printed. The first half of the book grouped essays on the war, and was entitled "Mr. Dooley in War"; the second part, which was a varied selection of the essays, most of them older than those in the first part, was labeled " Mr. Dooley in Peace." With this division, *Mr. Dooley in Peace and in War* was a natural title. Dunne gave the manuscript to Small, Maynard & Co. of Boston for publication, and dedicated it to Turner. He subscribed his initials to his introduction, but refused to let his name go on the title page of the book. But when he went East to confer with the publishers, a group of former Chicago journalists in New York tendered him a dinner. This was publicized through the local papers until everyone who read New York papers might know that Peter Dunne was the author of Mr. Dooley.

The book appeared in November, with the peace negotiations under way. It was an instant and striking success. None but Chicago followers of Mr. Dooley had read all of the pieces, and consequently over half of them had all the appeal of being new. The reviewers who did not know who F.P.D. was soon learned, and before long he was a marked man in literary circles. The book was selling at a steady rate of ten thousand copies a month, and it remained on the best-seller lists for a year — remained there, in fact, until a second collection of the essays appeared to destroy the first's monopoly of the market for Mr. Dooley's remarks.

The reviews of the book were as flattering as the comments of Dunne's own friends. Frank A. Putnam hailed him as " the popular literary celebrity of the year "[8]; and *Current Literature* declared that " the

[8] *National Magazine*, X (June 1899), 207–10.

advent of Mr. Dooley marks a new era in American letters."[9] Best of all, the famous Harry Thurston Peck poured out his enthusiastic praise in *The Bookman*, ranking Dooley's author with "those humorists who have really made a genuine contribution to permanent literature. We have found nothing else this season which bears so unmistakably the marks of freshness, originality, and real genius."[10] Dunne was contrasted favorably with Artemus Ward, and Mr. Dooley was compared with Lowell's Hosea Biglow and Kipling's Mulvaney.

Too late Dunne and his publishers discovered that the book had a British market, for they had a copyright for only the United States. Three English publishers rushed editions to the market, one of them with paper binding that sold for a trifle. Soon all Britain too was laughing with Mr. Dooley — although much of the humor of highly specialized American incident must have been missed by non-American readers. The English reviews were as laudatory as the American, except a few that suggested that Dunne might have "shown a little more sympathy with the government."[11] Delightedly Small, Maynard & Co. used the English reviews in their advertising to keep sales booming in the United States.

Finley Peter Dunne at thirty-one was more than managing editor of the *Journal*. He was a literary celebrity of some eminence. He had invitations to write for most select periodicals; publishers were vy-

---

9 XXV (March 1899), 221–23.

10 VIII (February 1899), 574–6.

11 *The Spectator*, 82 (March 11, 1899), 344.

ing for his next book; and he now had a more direct influence on public affairs. As the newer Dooley essays were appearing in the papers, Secretary Gage was reading them at the meetings of the President's Cabinet. When he lost his copy of the January, 1899, essay on expansion, and appealed to Gilson Gardner, the *Journal's* Washington correspondent, for a copy, Gardner wrote to Dunne:

> As is known by most Washington correspondents, the celebrated Irishman's characteristic comments on public affairs and men have become a regular feature of the cabinet's Tuesday sessions. They are usually read by Secretary Gage at the close of routine business, and appear to afford great amusement to the President of the United States. It may not be saying too much to add that the philosopher of " Archey Road " is therefore in a position to exert as much influence on public affairs as any salaried member of the administration and doubtless much more than the vast unread editorial literature of the country.[12]

---

[12] No date (January 1899). Charlotte Dunne letters.

## A TRIP ABROAD AND ANOTHER BOOK

HAD Peter Dunne been of weaker fiber or of less intelligence, he might well have lost his head in the early months of 1899 as he read the laudatory reviews of his book, collected the royalties it earned, and received the large sums now coming to him from the syndication of the weekly Dooley essays. Wherever he went he was a marked man, and when an old Chicago friend induced him to come to Grand Rapids and talk to a small newspaper club, he found himself treated as a conquering hero rather than as the speaker of the evening.

He told his friends that he might as well capitalize upon his temporary popularity, and began to accept some of the offers that came to him for publishing and writing. In the spring he sold *Harper's Weekly* the right to reprint the Dooleys along with the newspaper syndicate; turned the syndication of the future essays over to Robert H. Russell, publisher of fine books, who was syndicating Ade's "Fables in Slang," and agreed to write far more than he was able: a dialect series for *The Ladies' Home Journal* centering about the character Molly Donahue, a series on Chicago for *The Saturday Evening Post*, and, eventually, a novel. When these plans were completed, he decided to go to England to try to come to some arrangement with the publishers there who were selling his book. Russell induced him to promise a series of Dooley pieces from abroad that would comment on Europeans and European affairs. These would be the basis of a new syndication arrangement and would later make a book entitled *Mr. Dooley Abroad.*

With all of these possibilities ahead of him, it was not hard for Dunne to decide to make the trip. He wanted to go anyway, and he needed time to write apart from his duties at the *Journal* if he were to produce all the copy he was promising. Before he left, however, he prepared the manuscript for the new volume of essays for fall publication, using many of those which he had written since the publication of *Mr. Dooley in Peace and in War*, but going back to the files of the *Post* for the greater number. To these were to be added a few which he would write from Europe.

He took leave from the *Journal* on May 1, and traveled to New York, where he was to transact considerable business with Russell and his publishers. Staying as usual with Charles Dillingham, he became the center of attention from the press and from friendly newspaper men. Now, as six months earlier, he was made the guest of honor at a dinner given by a group of journalists. This time some of the younger men, who had heard Chicago reporters boast of the sharpshooters of the Whitechapel Club, decided to test the wit of one of them. Sensing what was in the air, Dunne was on his guard, and his victim unfortunately turned out to be one who was to become an intimate and valued friend, Richard Harding Davis.

Dunne knew Davis slightly, having met him at the home of the Hamills when the novelist-war correspondent was in Chicago courting Cecil Clark, whom he later married. Davis's slightly theatrical manner, his extreme dress, his honest self-importance, had not left a favorable memory in Dunne's mind, and he had been satisfied to rank him as something of an effeminate dude and a poseur, as indeed was the general feeling among people who knew him slightly or merely by reputation. Davis knew of the plan to bait Dunne, and whether he wanted to get his digs in first, or whether he wanted to warm Dunne to his test, or whether, as is more likely, he was merely trying to make agreeable conversation, one cannot now know. Certainly Peter Dunne thought he was hearing the opening gun when Davis, in his rather superior manner, remarked: "Mr. Dunne, your appearance surprises most of us, because from your writings we assumed that we would see a tough old chap with red galloway whiskers, smoking a clay pipe." Dunne hesitated only a moment in the silence that followed, and then with brutal directness he answered: "Expectations are often deceptive, Mr. Davis. Now, I thought I would find you wearing a silk shirt-waist with lace sleeves." That ended all efforts at hazing that evening. The following day, as Dunne sailed for England, the *New York Journal* featured the dinner with

Opper's cartoons of Davis and Dunne as they had expected to see each other.[1] It is a tribute to the good sense and charity of both men that when during the next few months they were thrown together in Paris and London a warm and permanent friendship developed.

In London Dunne shared quarters " in what one of the papers sweetly calls an attic " with Harrison Rhodes and James H. Whigham, an Englishman who had been active in Chicago newspaper and golfing circles for the past few years. From here Dunne saw parts of England, made two and perhaps three trips to Paris, where Mary Abbott had taken her daughter Margaret to study art, and made arrangements with Grant Richards to designate his edition of *Mr. Dooley in Peace and in War* as authorized in return for a royalty. Russell, who was in London also, completed agreements for syndicating the new Dooley series in the British press. Since leaving Chicago, Dunne had not been supplying articles, and the new series was promised for late summer or early autumn.

Dunne was seeing a great deal of the theatrical group in London, many of whom were Americans he had met when they were playing in Chicago, as well as several of the English literary figures who frequented the same circle. Dillingham was there, Charles Frohman, Ethel Barrymore, Anthony Hope Hawkins, and James M. Barrie. Dunne found himself lionized only slightly less than in New York, as Mr. Dooley's fame was bright in both England and Ireland. Mark Twain was in London for a time, and at

[1] May 11, 1899.

one dinner Dunne found himself paired off with the great humorist. This was the first meeting of the two men, who were destined to see each other frequently in the next ten years. Dunne attended one of Henry Irving's big suppers at the Lyceum, and saw more of social life than he wished, certainly more than was conducive to his work. Perhaps one accident added to his distaste. He and Whigham canoed up the Thames to spend a holiday at Cookham with a group of friends. As they neared the destination they met their party in a large craft coming to meet them. Dunne, the perfect landsman, stood up to wave a greeting, and the canoe capsized, leaving the two men floundering in three feet of mud and water.

Most of the Americans in this crowd had left London by July 1, and Dunne tried to fulfill some of his contracts for writing. It was a new experience in that he had always done his essays as a by-product of a regular stint on a newspaper. Able to devote full time to them for the first time, he found he was unable to do much, if any, more than he had done when fully employed. This was clearly the result of the nature of his writing, which required not so much time for the writing itself as an opportunity for an inspiration to grow out of a deep knowledge of the situation, and a full appreciation of its incongruous elements. Only then could he develop adequately the elements of satire and humor. These inspirations were few in London, and Dunne found it laborious going. He read proof on his next book, and wrote several installments of the Molly Donahue series.

One of the most popular pieces in *Mr. Dooley in*

*Peace and in War* had been an essay on the Dreyfus case, which was still shaking French politics to its foundations. The best thing in this piece had been the inspired pun on Zola's *J'accuse!* which Mr. Dooley turned into "Jackuse," "which is a hell of a mane thing to say to anny man." Repeatedly during the trial, according to Mr. Dooley, Zola would appear in the courtroom and yell "Jackuse" at the court, and invariably "they thrun him out." This bit of high comedy seemed uproariously funny to most readers, and Russell thought its effect could be repeated if Dunne would attend the new court-martial of Dreyfus, now being held in the village of Rennes, and write a series on it for the syndicate. After considerable trouble, Russell secured a reservation for Dunne as a reporter of the trial. After Russell left, Dunne found it inconvenient to attend, or perhaps he had never had any intention of attending but allowed Russell to secure the reservation because he insisted on doing it. When Dunne wrote the series, as he did before he left England, he did it entirely from newspaper accounts of the trial. But in writing them he did a thing that he had not done before. He pictured Mr. Dooley as attending the trial and delivering a harangue in court — one of the very few essays, reprinted in book form, where Dunne let Dooley get out of character. This was in accord with the original idea of the new series, that it would take Mr. Dooley abroad to view foreign scenes for his comments.

A third of a century later Dunne would recall these London days with pleasure, but, at the time, he had a different feeling. "I have been very nicely received," he wrote his sister Amelia. "They really seem to think I am something of a man over here. They even go so far as to say I am a Great Humorist (which is itself a joke of no small dimensions) and if I listened to what I hear I might stay here forever." [2] To Robert Hamill he wrote in strong distaste:

> The place is a vile compound of all the slow poisons in the world – of dullness, of satiety, of headless self seeking & footless kindness, of bad bread and iceless drinks and empty wit. . . . If I were a grateful man – which God forbid! – I ought to feel well disposed toward London, for I have had a greeting that makes me doubt my real powers. But everything I see & hear makes me writhe. It is a den of horrors. . . . Paris is beautiful. I found Mrs. Abbott looking very well & Margaret – starry! [3]

To his youngest sister, pious Charlotte, he wrote of Paris:

> I need it [your prayer] because I have been in Paris which is a place Len ought not to visit. If he ever went there he would be lost to Chicago and to Heaven. I would like to see him pivoting at the Jardin de Paris with – but I will not continue. . . . I went to the Latin quarter to please Len & Bill [Hookway] & to the Church of the Madeleine to please you – a beautiful church with splendid singing and a man dressed up like a coachman passing the hat. (They don't forget that essential rite anywhere.) . . . The Church was full of American tourists who gaped around to see where the music came from, crossed themselves with their left hands and asked "Combien?" when the plate was passed. . . . I have never worked harder in my life than I have during this vacation. I wish I could also say I never worked better. But that would not be true.[4]

---

[2] June 8, 1899. Charlotte Dunne letters.

[3] June 16, 1899. Hamill letters.

[4] No date. Charlotte Dunne letters.

With his new Dreyfus articles mailed to Russell in New York, Dunne took a holiday by going to Ireland and traveling to Dublin, Cork, and the ancestral counties of his parents. His reputation had preceded him there, and at his hotel in Dublin reporters called to see Mr. Dooley. To one who asked how Mr. Dooley liked Ireland, Dunne replied: "You may say Mr. Dooley felt at home when he arrived in Dublin for the first time since he left Chicago."[5] He did not, apparently, visit Roscommon, the home of Mr. Dooley in West Ireland. Although Dunne seemed to have enjoyed this visit, he never repeated it.

When Dunne returned to New York in September, his arrival was considered as important news as his departure in the spring. The last week in the month found him in Chicago, and he resumed his work with the *Journal* on October 1. In the meantime, the Russell syndicate series had led off with the five Dreyfus articles, and after that Dunne kept it going by producing new ones according to schedule. The Molly Donahue series in *The Ladies' Home Journal* also began, but when Dunne returned he grew dissatisfied with it. It did not seem to him to be very good; as a matter of fact, it was simply different, as it attempted to picture the domestic life of Archey Road as seen in the parlor and kitchen of a home where the ambitious daughter was introducing the family to American middle-class culture. These essays were not easy for him to do, and after he returned Dunne was unable to add a single article to

---

[5] Reprinted from the *Irish Daily Independent* in the *Chicago Journal*, September 14, 1899.

the group he had written while abroad. He refused to continue, and the periodical simply had to announce that Dunne felt he was not doing his best work and wanted to end the series.

The new weekly Dooley stories attempted for a time to keep up the originally planned concept of Mr. Dooley abroad, and, like the Dreyfus group, assumed a trip by Dooley and Hennessy, in which various adventures were described and discussed. But this form quickly stopped, as its artificiality and departure from the character he had created became apparent. Dooley went back to his saloon on Archey Road, and Hennessy to the slag pile.

Then when William Waldorf Astor applied for British citizenship, or " renounced fealty to all foreign sovereigns, princes an' potentates an' especially Mack th' Wanst, or Twict, iv th' United States an' Sulu," Mr. Dooley could express Dunne's final reaction on his first foreign venture:

". . . An' when ye come down to it, I dinnaw as I blame Willum Waldorf Asthor f'r shiftin' his allegiance. Ivry wan to his taste as th' man said when he dhrank out iv th' fire extinguisher. It depinds on how ye feel. If ye are a tired lad an' wan without much fight in ye, livin' in this counthry is like thryin' to read th' lives iv th' Saints at a meetin' iv th' Clan-na-Gael. They'se no quiet f'r annybody. They'se a fight on ivry minyit iv th' time. Ye may say to ye'ersilf: ' I'll lave these lads roll each other as much as they plaze, but I'll set here in th' shade an' dhrink me milk punch,' but ye can't do it. Some wan'll say, ' Look at that gazabo settin' out there alone. He's too proud f'r to jine in our simple dimmycratic festivities. Lave us go over an' bate him on th' eye.' An' they do it. Now if ye have fightin' blood in ye'er veins ye hastily gulp down ye'er dhrink an' hand ye'er assailant wan that does him no kind iv good, an' th' first thing ye know ye're in th' thick iv it an' it's scrap, scrap, scrap till th' undhertaker calls f'r to measure ye. An' 'tis tin to wan they'se somethin' doin' at th' fun'ral that ye're sorry ye missed. That's life in America. . . .

"Now, if I'm tired I don't want to fight. A man bats me in th' eye an' I call f'r th' polis. They isn't a polisman in sight. I say to th' man that poked me: 'Sir, I fain wud sleep.' 'Get up,' he says, 'an' be doin',' he says. 'Life is rale, life is earnest,' he says, 'an' man was made to fight,' he says, fetchin' me a kick. An' if I'm tired I say, 'What's th' use? I've got plenty iv money in me inside pocket. I'll go where I can get something besides an argymint f'r me money an' where I won't have to rassle with th' man that bates me carpets, ayether,' I says, 'f'r fifty cints overcharge or good gover'mint,' I says. An' I pike off to what Hogan calls th' effete monarchies iv Europe an' no wan walks on me toes, an' ivry man I give a dollar to becomes an acrobat an' I live comfortably an' die a markess! Th' divvle I do! "

"That's what I was goin' to say," Mr. Hennessy remarked. "Ye wudden't live annywhere but here."

"No," said Mr. Dooley, "I wudden't. I'd rather be Dooley iv Chicago than th' Earl iv Peltville. It must be that I'm iv th' fightin' kind."

While Dunne was still in London, he had received disquieting news about the forthcoming book. In June a volume had appeared at various booksellers, entitled *What Dooley Says.*[6] As in *Mr. Dooley in Peace and in War*, no author was named, but in a snaky introduction the impression was definitely created that the real author would receive the royalties. Small, Maynard & Co. cabled Dunne, and with his permission brought suit to enjoin its sale.

---

[6] Chicago, 1899.

The publisher was the hitherto unheard of firm of Kazmar & Co. The essays in the book were all Dunne's, having been copied from the *Chicago Evening Post,* to which acknowledgment was made. Moreover, several of the essays were in the group which Dunne had selected for his second book. Kazmar had applied for copyrights both in Washington and London. The selection of essays was haphazard, as though an incomplete file of the *Post* had been used, and the transcription was exceedingly bad. The brogue spelling was difficult to see through the press under any circumstance, and little care had been exercised here. The suit was brought in Chicago, with Charles Hamill acting as Dunne's attorney. Before it came to trial, a compromise was arranged by which a small sum of money was paid to Kazmar for what remained of his supply of the books and for withdrawing his contest to the suit. Without his contest a favorable decision was handed down by the court, but nearly 15,000 copies had already been sold. It did not help the sale of either the first book or the second one announced for October.

The new book came from the press at the appointed time, with the title *Mr. Dooley in the Hearts of His Countrymen,* a natural sequel to *Mr. Dooley in Peace and in War.* Twenty-five thousand of the new volumes were ordered by booksellers before publication, and the book's sale, while never reaching the total of the first one, was large enough to place it on the best-seller lists immediately. With pleasure that was vengeful as well as fitting, Dunne had written the dedication after the failure of his efforts to secure some redress from the British publishers who had "pirated" his first book. It read:

To
Sir George Newnes, Bart.
Messrs. George Routledge & Sons
Limited
And other publishers, who, uninvited, presented
Mr. Dooley to a part of the British public.

The five new Dreyfus articles were included in the book. In his introduction Dunne begged indulgence for them as hardly suited to the title. "It is sincerely to be hoped that his [Dooley's] small contribution to the literature of the subject will at least open the eyes of France to the necessity of conducting her trials, parliamentary sessions, revolutions, and other debates in a language more generally understood in New York and London."

The critical reception of the new collection was even better than that of the first. Some of the comment on the first had implied that it was a rare gem that had been cast upon the shores of American literature by the war, and in all probability would have no satisfactory successor. Such implications were confounded by the book, and critic after critic expressed surprise that the stories held up as well as they did. What these commentators did not realize was that at least half of the essays in the new book had been written and published in the *Post* before any of those on the Spanish War which gave tone to *Mr. Dooley in Peace and in War*. In fact, many of the pieces in the new book were five years old. Consequently, unlike those syndicated during the year, they were new to the reviewers.

Because it represented a more nearly first choice from the files of the *Post* than did the earlier collection, the new book was the better one. Only the five hurried essays on the Dreyfus trial were inferior to those in the older volume. The new book had relatively few recently past public happenings; but its proportion of pathetic, tragic, and comic pictures of humanity on Archey Road was very high, and consequently its elements of permanence were of the best. It contained Dunne's finest tragic and didactic writing: "When the Trust is at Work," "A Brand from the Burning," "The Blue and the Gray," "The Idle Apprentice," "The Wanderers," "The Optimist," and "Shaughnessy." And along with these were the same high quality of satire and irony, gusty humor, and penetrating comment on public affairs as had characterized the better-known essays. Its failure to sell as well was in all probability caused by the fact that the newness of a popular fad was now over; there was no new emotional background for comment, such as the recent war, to stimulate sales; and, besides, Mr. Dooley was available to all every week in papers in every city in America, in *Harper's Weekly*, and in several British newspapers.

More public notice was taken of the second volume than of the first. Even the rural and religious press subjected it to comment that was uniformly favorable. The religious press acknowledged its didactic qualities, praised Dunne's "perpetual hunt for hypocrisy and meanness," and proclaimed that "he is a real reformer, gifted with virtues too rare in reformers, a sense of proportion and human charity." [7] On the more literary side, the praise was equally great of its other qualities. Only two exceptions can be found. One critic in *The Literary Review* damned the entire series for dealing in a friendly, humane way with saloon-keepers and " slum dwellers ":

> Their needs entitle them to great missionary efforts from all educators and philanthropists but not to apotheosis as " delightful " humorists or seers. . . . If Mr. Dunne will leave the environment of Archey Road, and write in decent English, he may yet deserve a wreath of unwithering smiles." [8]

The other reproof came from *The Dial*, high-brow literary review of Chicago, whose delicate editors kept their noses averted from such low-bred productions as those of Dunne and George Ade, which they classed together. The dedication was " in questionable taste." " But it is scarcely literature in any of the senses in which the ' Biglow Papers ' was. . . ." [9]

Almost typical of the majority was this, from *Time and the Hour:*

> There is nothing but exquisite humor, tender pathos and keen wit . . . and under it all Mr. Dunne has shown a perhaps unintentional seriousness of purpose, a comprehension of " life as she is lived," which qualifies him to take rank as a highly dramatic writer. Only the reading public will never accept him as anything but a humorist. *Vide* the unhappy fate of Mark Twain. The utmost justice which Mr. Dunne

[7] *Unity*, November 2, 1899.

[8] December, 1899.

[9] November 16, 1899.

will ever receive from the general reader will be to be linked with Artemus Ward and "Hosea Biglow." [10]

The British reviews were more numerous and more favorable than they had been the year before. This was natural in that the latest collection of essays contained fewer pieces that depended upon local atmosphere and incident for appreciation. Small, Maynard reprinted *The Spectator's* comment as a folder, and circulated it in the book trade.

None of the critics who reviewed either of the books had been familiar enough with the individual essays as they had appeared in newspapers originally to note the important revisions that Dunne had made before presenting them in book form. One of these was to eliminate the essays which had Mr. Dooley out of character to any degree. The five Dreyfus articles were an exception, added after the book had been planned and the manuscript prepared. There were not many of these in the newspapers, and they were not reprinted. Still more important was the strong tendency for Dunne to eliminate anything of a personal nature that would deeply wound some individual. A few of these he eliminated because he considered them unfair and, on further consideration, below his standard as an observer of life. Others were deserved but unkind, and he failed to give them permanent form. Not one of the vigorous attacks on Powers, Pullman, or Yerkes, for instance, quoted earlier, was ever published in one of his books, not because any of them were untrue, but simply because his kindliness forbade it. An example of an unfair

[10] October 14, 1899.

statement he had made in an original essay was a reflection on President McKinley's indebtedness, which wealthy friends had paid off prior to his becoming a candidate for president. As originally published in the *Journal*, the essay on Fitzhugh Lee had ended with the cracker:

"Why wudden't he make a good prisident?" said Mr. Hennessy.

"Sh-h!" said Mr. Dooley. "He don't owe enough."[11]

When the essay was reprinted this was eliminated, and it appeared without the typical ending.

But the fame of Mr. Dooley was spread far more by the newspaper syndication than by the books, and everywhere Mr. Dooley was a synonym for wisdom, humor, wit, and ready sympathy for those who deserved it. He was the Paul Bunyan and John Henry of all the cracker-box philosophers of the American tradition. Three months after the publication of *Mr. Dooley in the Hearts of His Countrymen*, Professor J. W. White of the University of Pennsylvania suggested in *The Bookman* an all-American football team from American literature, designating for the coach the well-known philosopher from Archey Road with another observant character named David Harum as his assistant.[12]

---

[11] April 9, 1898.

[12] X (February 1900), 525–26.

# FAREWELL TO CHICAGO

In the new series of weekly essays which appeared after Dunne returned from England, certain important changes are notable. Some of these were necessary for national and even international syndication. No longer could Dunne utilize purely or primarily Chicago affairs for his comments, nor could he exploit local characters. He kept the already-used names, such as Father Kelly, but these meant no more to the wide circle of readers than would have any other Irish names. It should be kept in mind that in using such names Dunne was not sketching the actual character of the person who bore the name in real life. He had started the practice to lend reality and interest to his articles, and simply continued it. Hennessy, the embodiment of general human ignorance, and Hogan, " who's full iv larnin', an' th' ignorance that so often goes with it," were rounded out in more complete fashion. But the Archey Road character went out of the articles in the sense that there were now few essays descriptive of the life of that community.

Its place was taken in the new series by a high percentage of articles on national and international public affairs. These could be appreciated by Californian and Rhode Islander, by Canadian and Englishman, and they, together with comments on general topics, such as St. Patrick's Day, Christmas, fame, and golf, made up the great majority of essays after systematic syndication began. There is no doubt that comment on public affairs was the most popular type of essay, proved not only by " On His Cousin George," but also by all subsequent tests of popularity.

On this type of subject Dunne's vision widened, and his ability to express himself increased as his experience deepened. Nothing he afterwards wrote of tragic or pathetic nature equaled his already-published sketches, but the comment on world and national affairs continued to show a steady growth in perspective and insight. Even an elderly and dyspeptic intellectual like Henry Adams found it worthy of recommending to English friends.

One of Dunne's first essays after his return from abroad was a comment on war-makers in terms of the current Boer War and the attempt of the United States to crush the Filipino forces of Aguinaldo. " I wisht it cud be fixed up so's th' men that starts th' wars cud do th' fightin'," Mr. Dooley declared, and then reduced it to Archey Road terms of a conflict between himself and his competitor, Schwartzmeister:

" Now he [Chamberlain] don't go over as I wud an' say, 'Here Schwartzmeister (or Kruger as th' case may be) I don't like ye'er appearance, ye made a monkey iv me in argymint befure th' neighborhood an' if ye continyue in business ye'll hurt me thrade, so here goes to move ye into th' sthreet! ' Not that lad. He gets a crowd around him an' says he: ' Kruger (or Schwartzmeister as th' case may be) is no good. To begin with he's a Dutchman. If that ain't enough he's a cantin', hymn singin' murdhrous wretch that wudden't lave wan iv our counthrymen ate a square meal if he had his way. I'll give ye all two dollars a week if ye'll go over an' desthroy him.' An' th' other lad, what does he do? He calls in th' neighbors an' says he: ' Dooley is sendin' down a gang iv savages to murdher me. Do ye lave ye'er wurruk an' ye'er families an' rally around me an' where ye see me plug hat wave do ye go in th' other direction,' he says, ' an' slay th' brutal inimy,' he says. An' off goes th' sojers an' they meet a lot iv lads that looks like thimsilves an' makes sounds that's more or less human an' ates out iv plates an' they swap smokin' tobacco an' sings songs together an' th' next day they're up early jabbin' holes in each other with baynits. An' whin it's all over they'se me an' Chamberlain at home victoryous an' Kruger an' Schwartzmeister at home akelly victoryous. An' they make me prime minister or aldherman but whin I want a man to put in me coal I don't take wan with a wooden leg.

". . . If Chamberlain likes war so much 'tis him that ought to be down there in South Africa peltin' over th' road with ol' Kruger chasin' him with a hoe. Th' man that likes fightin' ought to be willin' to turn in an' spell his fellow-counthrymen himsilf. An' I'd even go this far an' say that if Mack wants to subjoo th' dam Ph'lippeens — "

" Ye're a thraitor," said Mr. Hennessy.

" I know it," said Mr. Dooley, complacently.

" Ye're an anti-expansionist."

" If ye say that again," cried Mr. Dooley, angrily, " I'll smash in ye'er head."

That last exchange is, apart from the immediate humor involved, Dunne's method of keeping Dooley in character. He fully realized that the value of the editorial material he could put in Dooley's mouth would be ruined the moment he made him a platonic philosopher. Always there had to be something to keep him the Irish saloon-keeper of Archey Road, intensely human, and true to his natural limitations. There was no secret of Dunne's great success more important than this.

The imperialistic division of China among the great Powers had been the subject of Mr. Dooley's comments before. Now invasion of that country and the capture of Peking by the allied forces, together with the rapacious action of the German contingent of the allied troops, called forth several comments which represented Dunne's indignation at the needless massacres and his repugnance toward the Hitler-like bombast then being proclaimed by Emperor Wilhelm II.

"He's th' boy f'r me money. Whin th' German throops takes their part in th' desthruction iv Peking they'll be none iv th' allied forces'll stick deeper or throw th' backbone iv th' impress' ol' father higher thin th' lads fr'm th' home iv th' sausage. I hope th' cillybration'll occur on Chris'mas day. I'd like to hear th' sojers singin' 'Gawd rest ye, merry Chinnymen' as they punchered thim with a baynit."

"'Twill be a good thing," said Mr. Hennessy.

"It will that," said Mr. Dooley.

"'Twill civilize th' Chinnymen," said Mr. Hennessy.

"'Twill civilize thim stiff," said Mr. Dooley. "An' it may not be a bad thing f'r th' rest iv th' wurruld. Perhaps contack with th' Chinee may civilize th' Germans."

Dunne's intense sympathy for an abused individual was capable of being aroused, even when the subject was not an obscure "Connock man" from back of the tracks. Admiral Dewey, after returning to as tumultuous a welcome as ever a conquering hero saw, and being presented with a house paid for by popular subscription, made the error of deeding the gift to his newly acquired wife, who, it happened, was a member of the Catholic Church. This turned him from a great hero to the butt of press and orator. Dunne came warmly to his rescue.

"This man Dewey — " began Mr. Dooley.

"I thought he was ye'er cousin George," Mr. Hennessy interrupted.

"I thought he was," said Mr. Dooley, "but on lookin' closer at his features an' readin' what th' papers says about him, I am convinced that I was wrong. Oh, he may be a sicond cousin iv me Aunt Judy. I'll not say he ain't. There was a poor lot, all iv thim. . . . As long as George was a lithograph iv himsilf in a saloon window he was all right. Whin people saw he cud set in a city hall hack without flowers growin' in it an' they cud look at him without smoked glasses they begin to weaken in their devotion. 'Twud've been th' same, almost, if he'd marrid a Presbyteeryan an' hadn't deeded his house to his wife. 'Dewey don't look much like a hero,' says wan man. 'I shud say not,' says another. 'He looks like annybody else.' . . .

"Well," Mr. Dooley continued, "I was on'y goin' to say, Hinnissy, that in spite iv me hathred iv George as a man — a marrid man — an' me contimpt f'r his qualities as a fighter, in spite iv th' chickens he has stole an' th' notes he has forged an' th' homes he has rooned, if he was to come runnin' up Archey road, as he might, pursooed by ladies an' gintlemen an' ol' cats, I'd open th' dure f'r him, an' whin he come in I'd put me fut behind it an' I'd say to th' grateful people: 'Fellow-citizens,' I'd say, 'lave us,' I'd say. 'They'se another hero down in Halstead Sthreet that's been marrid. Go down an' shivaree him. An' ye, me thrusted collagues iv th' press, disperse to ye'er homes,' I'd say. 'Th' keyholes is closed f'r th' night,' I'd say. An' thin I'd bolt th' dure an' I'd say, 'George, take off ye'er coat an' pull up to th' fire. Here's a noggin' iv whisky near ye'er thumb an' a good seegar f'r ye to smoke. I'm no hero-worshiper. I'm too old. But I know a man whin I see wan, an' though we cudden't come out an' help ye whin th' subscription list wint wild, be sure we think as much iv ye as we did whin ye'er name was first mintioned be th' stanch an' faithful press. Set here, ol' lad, an' warrum ye'er toes be th' fire. Set here an' rest fr'm th' gratichood iv ye'er fellow-counthrymen, that, as Shakespere says, biteth like an asp an' stingeth like an adder. Rest here as ye might rest at th' hearth iv millyons iv people that cud give ye no house but their own! "

"I dinnaw about that," said Mr. Hennessy. "I like Dewey, but I think he oughtn't to've give away th' gift iv th' nation."

"Well," said Mr. Dooley, "if 'twas a crime f'r an American citizen to have his property in his wife's name they'd be close quarthers in th' pinitinchry."

The Admiral, hurt beyond understanding by the outcry he had raised, read the piece and wrote Dunne a stiff letter of thanks.

Just the week before his defense of Dewey, Dunne had published what was to be perhaps the most famous of all Dooley articles. The last week in November the essay appeared which reviewed Theodore Roosevelt's book, *The Rough Riders*, on the exploits of his regiment. Dooley had commented upon "Rosenfelt" before, usually with admiration for his impetuosity and frank honesty, and in agreement with his political ideas. Dunne picked up the book one morning when he was not in his usual kindly temper. As he read, the realization grew upon him that it was made for Mr. Dooley; for the young Governor of New York, with the naïve egotism that was his weakness and his most attractive quality, had told his story from a purely personal standpoint.

"'Tis 'Th' Biography iv a Hero be Wan who Knows.' 'Tis 'Th' Darin' Exploits iv a Brave Man be an Actual Eye Witness.' 'Tis 'Th' Account iv th' Desthruction iv Spanish Power in th' Ant Hills,' as it fell fr'm th' lips iv Tiddy Rosenfelt an' was took down be his own hands."

And Mr. Dooley offered a parody of the book that played up its egotistical elements in hilarious satire.

"I think Tiddy Rosenfelt is all right an' if he wants to blow his horn lave him do it," said Mr. Hennessy.

"Thrue f'r ye," said Mr. Dooley, "an' if his valliant deeds didn't get into this book 'twud be a long time befure they appeared in Shafter's [the commanding general whom Roosevelt had publicly criticized] histhry iv th' war. No man that bears a gredge again himsilf'll iver be governor iv a state. An' if Tiddy done it all he ought to say so an' relieve th' suspinse. But if I was him I'd call th' book 'Alone in Cubia.'"

The essay started the entire country laughing in good-natured amusement, and to Dunne's surprise and gratification the victim, however much he may have felt the sting, took it like a good loser and sent Dunne this letter:

I regret to state that my family and intimate friends are delighted with your review of my book. Now I think you owe me one; and I shall exact that when you next come east you pay me a visit. I have long wanted the chance of making your acquaintance.[1]

---

[1] November 28, 1899. F. P. Dunne letters.

Dunne answered:

. . . the way you took Mr. Dooley is a little discouraging. The number of persons who are worth firing at is so small that as a matter of business I must regret the loss of one of them. Still, if in losing a target I have, perhaps, gained a friend I am in after all.[2]

Some months later, during the presidential campaign, Dunne met the candidate for Vice President and Mrs. Roosevelt on the train. They were returning from a large political rally. As Dunne remembered it, this was the conversation:

"Tell him what happened," said Mrs. Roosevelt, with the angelic smile of a loving wife who has a joke on her husband.

"Well, I oughtn't to," said the Colonel. "But I will. At a reception I was introduced to a very pretty young lady. She said, 'Oh, Governor, I've read everything you ever wrote.' 'Really! What book did you like best?' 'Why that one, you know, *Alone in Cuba*.' "[3]

But long before this meeting, Roosevelt had acknowledged Dunne's rather tardy reply with a more specific invitation to visit him.

I was very much pleased at getting your note of the 10th. Now I want to say that it seems to me certain of your articles – those for instance on the Dreyfus case, on the Transvaal war at its opening, and I am sorry to say, on some of our politics, are not only as humorous bits of reading as I have ever read, but are also full of a very profound philosophy – which I suppose is always a mark of the real master of humor whose works are more than evanescent.

I am obliged to recognize this even on some of the points where I disagree with you. As you know, I am an Expan-

[2] January 10, 1900. Roosevelt mss.

[3] Recollections of Peter Dunne.

FINLEY PETER DUNNE
*about 1900*

sionist, but your delicious phrase about " take up the white man's burden and put it on the coons," exactly hit off the weak spot in my own theory; though, mind you, I am by no means willing to give up the theory yet.

However, all of this and much more I shall talk over with you when you come to spend a night or two with me at our house on your next visit east.[4]

But Dunne was not yet ready to accept that hospitality.

The remarkable series of essays which Dunne produced after his return from Europe was continued through the early months of 1900, with only an occasional lapse. His work with the *Journal* went on as usual, his presence always being evidenced by a very superior editorial page. In March and April he took a vacation, and with John Grier went to the Pacific Coast, stopping at Boise, Portland, San Francisco, and Los Angeles. Here as in New York he was a celebrity; his arrival was hailed by the press, and invitations were showered on him for luncheons and banquets, as were vain requests for speeches. He returned to Chicago in time to prepare for the big political news of the national conventions and presidential campaign.

As usual, Dunne covered the national conventions, writing now, in addition to his news reports, a daily Dooley observation on the convention proceedings for his syndicate. That was no easy task in the bustle of such a gathering, but it was done, and although these essays were never reprinted, they read very well today.

Dunne's first Dooley piece on the Republican con-

[4] June 16, 1900. F. P. Dunne letters.

vention at Philadelphia had made sport of the attempts to coerce Governor Roosevelt into taking the vice presidential nomination. When Herbert L. Jones, also representing the *Journal*, saw Roosevelt afterwards, the latter insisted that Jones bring Dunne around to meet him. But Dunne dodged the meeting, fearing that a friendship which went beyond the letter-writing stage might destroy his effectiveness as a satirist by the elimination of one of the best subjects in America. Finally Roosevelt sent Senator Thomas Carter of Montana to find Dunne. Carter succeeded in bringing back his quarry, and as a reward for coming, Roosevelt confided to Dunne the news that he had decided that he would accept the vice presidential nomination, and permitted Dunne to wire the news back to the *Journal* before the announcement was made to the press as a whole.

The position of the essays on the campaign, now that they had an international circulation, was almost exactly the same as that which they had taken in the *Post* during the campaign of 1896: they satirized both campaigns, and pricked such bubbles as both campaign committees were trying to disguise as arguments. Underneath them ran the healthful stream of mockery at pretentious nonsense and at silly attempts to create panic.

"Be hivins, Hinnissy, I want me advice up-to-date, an' whin Mack an' Willum Jennings tells me what George Wash'n'ton an' Thomas Jefferson said, I says to thim: 'Gintlemen, they larned their trade befure th' days iv open plumbin',' I says. 'Tell us what is wanted be ye'ersilf or call in a journeyman who's wurrkin' card is dated this cinchry.'

. . . An' did ye iver notice how much th' candidates looks alike, an' how much both iv thim looks like Lydia Pinkham? Thim wondherful boardin'-house smiles that our gifted leaders wears, did ye iver see annythin' so entrancin'? Whin th' las' photygrapher has packed his arms homeward I can see th' great men retirin' to their rooms an' lettin' their faces down f'r a few minyits befure puttin' thim up in curl-papers f'r th' nex' day's display. Glory be, what a relief 'twill be f'r wan iv thim to raysume permanently th' savage or fam'ly breakfast face th' mornin' afther iliction! "

The piece on " Troubles of a Candidate " is the most delightful satire on the political roorback that has ever been written.

" 'Twas on'y th' other day me frind Tiddy Rosenfelt opened th' battle mildly be insinuatin' that all dimmycrats was liars, horse thieves an' arnychists. 'Tis true he apologized f'r that be explainin' that he didn't mean all dimmycrats but on'y those that wudden't vote f'r Mack but I think he'll take th' copper off befure manny weeks. . . ."

Before the campaign was over Dunne had left Chicago and the *Journal*. On his return from Europe the year before, he had found irksome the necessary delay in New York in connection with proofs of his book. He was then genuinely anxious to get back to Chicago. To his sisters, brother Leonard, and future brother-in-law William Hookway, he had written a joint letter:

Here I am again like the clown in the circus — horribly tired, not quite strong in the stomach, but oh! so glad to be back and to have nothing more difficult than American wheat-fields between me and my dear ones. I expected to go west with little delay but I find I have work enough to keep me here — and busy — for at least another week. . . . I ought to be in Chicago and in the hearts of my countrymen some time next week.[5]

After another year in Chicago he was not so sure that he wanted to stay there. In every other city he was a celebrated figure, and little as he cared for the gaudier aspects of fame, it must have been a noticeable change to return home to Chicago, where everyone took him for granted — the Dooley stories were eight years old to Chicagoans. Then there was a young man's natural desire to escape from the scenes of his boyhood and youth, where large numbers of people who " had known him when " took an egotistic pleasure in addressing him as " Pete," which he disliked, and made bores of themselves by using up valuable time with dull conversation. Dunne, whose loyalty and kindliness would not permit him to drive away the bores, would have been only human had he developed a desire to escape the source of such embarrassments. Most important of all, he no longer needed the salary from a paper, as his books and syndicate were bringing in more than he needed, and they promised to bring in even more. Why should he not devote all his time to his specialized kind of writing? Seemingly he gave up, at least temporarily, his ambitions to become a publisher. He decided that the critical reception of his second book and the increasing popularity of his syndicated articles were proof that his future as a writer was assured, and that he should devote his entire time to it. He had given in, too, to the urgings of some of his theatrical friends, and had agreed to put Mr. Dooley in a play. E. W. Townsend, the author

[5] No date (October 1899). Charlotte Dunne letters.

of the "Chimmie Fadden" stories, had successfully put that character on the stage, and Dunne had become associated with Townsend in order to present Mr. Dooley in a similar manner. There was still a vague plan for a novel in a medium aside from Irish brogue. And all of these, if they were carried out, would take time. New York seemed clearly a better place of residence for a writer than Chicago; for the publishers of books and periodicals, the newspaper syndicates and theatrical interests were centered in the larger city. There is no evidence that Dunne ever regretted the change. Two years later he was to write John T. McCutcheon:

> I think you will make a great mistake in not coming to New York. I think there is twice as much money here for you, as there is in Chicago, and I say this with due allowance for my wish to have you here, where I might see you occasionally.[6]

A minor factor may have been that the *Journal* was not turning out very well. Its political orientation began to fluctuate, with its outside ownership interfering from time to time. The rapidly increasing circulation during the Spanish War had not been maintained, and whether or not due to Dunne's irregular work after that, it was now clear that no great journalistic achievement was probable there.

Dunne left Chicago for New York in time to see his third volume of Dooley essays through the press. In accordance with what seemed good publishing strategy, another book had been planned for the

---

[6] February 13, 1903. McCutcheon letters.

Christmas season, this one to be published by Russell. The day it appeared, October 23, Dunne wrote Amelia, in the reaction to the work and worry of seeing it completed:

> Today I am in a state of nervous prostration. I fear the new book, know the critics will roast it, and the public won't buy it. I have had signs already of a frosty reception. The play is horribly bad but I hope to pull it up a little before it goes on the stage to be damned – be damned to it.[7]

The new book, *Mr. Dooley's Philosophy*, was made up of nearly two-thirds of the articles written and published during the past year, and naturally the review of Roosevelt's *Rough Riders* was the opening essay. Russell had included illustrations by E. W. Kemble, William Nicholson, and F. B. Opper, and these, with more expensive printing and binding, gave the book a much better appearance than the earlier volumes. It was dedicated "To the Hennessys of the World Who Suffer and Are Silent."

The critical reception was favorable, but the interest was not so widespread as that aroused by the two former books. When Mr. Dooley spoke every Saturday or Sunday to millions of readers, there was not much news value in a selection from the essays of the past year. The critics were inclined to rate the new book as "just a little bit below" the first two books.[8] An exception proclaimed: "It is wonderful how well the author keeps up his standard of wit and humour in spite of his great productivity. No doubt there will be a falling-off presently, but we detect no signs of it

[7] October 23, 1900. Charlotte Dunne letters.

[8] *The Bookman*, XII (December 1900), 322.

yet."[9] Few American reviewers distinguished between the book as a book and the weekly syndicated articles, and, beginning in 1899, more and more comment tended to center upon the political and social implications of Dunne's writings. "It is easier to change prejudices with laughter than with preaching. And that is Dooley's way," commented *Life*.[10] And *The Nation* had called attention to the wide influence of the Dooley articles on political thinking:

> What Mr. Dooley has to say of the careers of sundry local politicians is more instructive than the disquisitions of most writers on political science. To the people of "Archey Road," the issues decided at elections are not related to abstract principles of legislation, but are intensely local and personal. . . . He "shoots folly as she flies," and allows no humbug to remain unexposed, no cant to pass for genuine feeling.[11]

Referring to those essays during the excitement of the recent election, the unsigned review in *The Bookman* noted: "There is something in his sanity and cynicism that tends to keep the balance in such times of turmoil."[12]

One amusing comment came from the London *Spectator*, which took Dunne to task for presenting Roosevelt as "a vulgar braggart" and especially for spelling his name "Rosenfelt," thereby making public his Jewish background.[13] Actually Dunne's only reason for that spelling was that it seemed to him the

[9] *Literature*, VIII (January 12, 1901), 35.
[10] November 2, 1899.
[11] Vol. 69 (December 21, 1899), 476.
[12] XII (December 1900), 321.
[13] Vol. 86 (March 16, 1901), 389–90.

way Mr. Dooley would pronounce the name. Dunne showed the review to Roosevelt, and was told by him that as far as he knew he was pure Dutch and Irish. "I wish I had a little Jew in me." [14]

The book was listed but once on a best-seller list. While its sales were at least forty thousand copies, its returns were far short of the revenues from the syndicate or from the previous books. Dunne had walked on the heights of acclaim too steadily the past three years to endure complacent acceptance happily. It was the beginning of a bleak winter. After failing to get the play in a shape where he would let it be presented, he washed his hands of that and went back to Chicago to spend the Christmas holidays with his family. He arrived seriously ill with typhoid fever. His recovery was slow, and it was two months before he was able to return to New York. His spirits continued low, and he found writing most difficult. In this mood of depression he seized an opportunity to visit the Mediterranean, and let pleasure and travel renew his good spirits. To Amelia he wrote:

Dearest, dearest E. E. — I am scheduled to schedaddle on the Bismarck tomorrow and this is by way of waving you au revoir. The ship goes straight to Naples, touching at Gibraltar, where I will curse Bill's gory flag [Hookway was a Canadian]. I don't expect to be gone more than three weeks — long enough perhaps to induce my heart to behave itself. It has an unpleasant habit of trying to keep time with the ticking of my watch. The doctor says it will be all right after awhile. But Lottie must keep on praying — adding a line or two for those who go down into the sea in boats. You know one of the ancient philosophers said there were

[14] Recollections of Peter Dunne.

two kinds of dead men – those in their graves and those who travel by water. But the F. B. is a stout ship and ordinarily the southern crossing is easy. From Napoli I may go to Roma – you see I speak Italian already, spaghetto meo. (That is as we should say, " My darling.") And I may go to Cannes, to Nice, to Monte Carlo, to Palermo, to the Divvle – but wherever I go – even to the last named – I shall think of you with deep love. If there is anything Lot would care to have me say to the P-pe she has but to write it care P. J. Rampolla, Cardinal. Otherwise letters addressed to Russell, 3 W. 29, may be forwarded – or not.

God bless you all

Peter.[15]

[15] February 13, 1901. Charlotte Dunne letters.

CHAPTER
X

## THE NATIONAL WIT AND CENSOR

DUNNE'S trip abroad cured him of his fit of depression, and restored him to good health after the ravages of typhoid. He had written nothing since the appearance of *Mr. Dooley's Philosophy*. Back in New York in the late spring, he revived the weekly syndicated essays for *Harper's Weekly* and the newspapers, and wrote some special articles for other periodicals. He and Robert Russell had taken a small cottage in rural Long Island, and there, with " a horse and a parrot and mosquitoes almost as big as either," [1] he lived out the summer, writing, swimming, playing tennis, and seldom going into the city. With satisfactory articles going out in regular sequence, the pessimism of the preceding winter seemed very remote. " I feel there is prosperity and happiness ahead for all our little clan," he wrote Amelia. " Don't think . . . because I have cut loose from some of my old moorings and have made a venture of new fortunes that I have any other home port than the old friendly one

[1] Peter to Charlotte Dunne, July 13, 1901. Charlotte Dunne letters.

of your respect and affection. . . . I am by no means rich but I have to some extent recovered what my illness cost me."[2]

As usual, after a vacation from writing, Dunne's first essays of the new series were exceptionally fine, as if he had in the interval stored up a reservoir of wit and wisdom that he could now tap at will. The striking news events of the summer of 1901, the Northern Pacific panic, Carnegie's gift to the Scottish universities, the yacht races, and the Sampson-Schley controversy, were all celebrated in proper style. Revenge for the inconveniences which Dunne had suffered in re-entering the United States was taken in an article on the Custom House. His experience in his rural retreat gave him ideas for a satire on life in the country, which he wrote under the title: "The City as a Summer Resort." His illness of the past winter was exploited in an essay on "The Practice of Medicine," which ended with the oft-quoted opinion: "I think that if th' Christyan Scientists had some science an' th' doctors had more Christyanity, it wudden't make anny diff'rence which ye called in — if ye had a good nurse."

The great financial mergers, such as Morgan's erection of the United States Steel Corporation, and the boom and panic surrounding the Morgan-Harriman fight for control of the Northern Pacific, gave Dunne excellent opportunities to comment on Wall Street. "Glory be," Mr. Dooley greeted the Northern Pacific fight, "whin business gets above sellin' ten pinny nails in a brown paper cornucopy, 'tis hard to tell it

[2] June 11, 1901. Charlotte Dunne letters.

fr'm murther." The struggle itself he compared to a fight between two local bruisers in his own saloon.

"Well, th' big lads is sthrong an' knows how to guard, an' whin they're spread out, small harm has come to thim. But th' little dhrunk financeers that're not used to th' flowin' dividend an' th' quick profit that biteth like a wasp an' stingeth like an adder, th' little lads that are carryin' more thin they can hold an' walk, are picked up in pieces. An' as f'r me, th' innocint man that let th' two burlies into me place to riot, I've got to make a call on th' furniture dealers in th' mornin'. That's what Hogan calls, Oh, Finance. Oh, Finance, as Shakespeare says, how many crimes are committed in thy name!"

For the rapid disappearance of the apparent profits of the preceding boom Mr. Dooley had an apt description:

"Th' effect iv th' boom on th' necessities iv life, like champagne an' race horses an' chorus girls, common an' preferred, was threemenjous. It looked f'r a while as though most iv th' meenyal wurruk iv th' counthry would have to be done be old-line millyionaires who'd made their money sellin' four cints worth if stove polish f'r a nickel. But it's all past now. Th' waiter has returned to his mutton an' th' barber to his plowshare. Th' chorus girl has raysumed th' position f'r which nature intinded her, an' th' usual yachtin' will be done on th' cable cars at eight a.m. an' six p.m. as befure. Th' jag is over. Manny a man that looked like a powdher pigeon a month ago looks like a hunchback to-day."

In a manner much like his defense of Dewey, Dunne now defended Admiral Schley against the attacks of his enemies. He also had a warm reply ready for those who declared that Theodore Roosevelt, skyrocketed into the presidency by the assassination of

McKinley, was too young for the responsibilities of that office:

"So whin I come to think it over, I agree with th' papers. Prisidint Tiddy is too young f'r th' office. What is needed is a man iv — well, a man iv my age. . . ."

"Go on with ye," said Mr. Hennessy. "Whin do ye think a man is old enough?"

"Well," said Mr. Dooley, "a man is old enough to vote whin he can vote, he's old enough to wurruk whin he can wurruk. An' he's old enough to be prisident whin he becomes prisidint. If he ain't, it'll age him."

The principal event during the year which enlisted Dunne's strong sympathies was the controversy stirred up when Booker T. Washington was Roosevelt's luncheon guest at the White House:

"Well, annyhow," said Mr. Dooley, "it's goin' to be th' roonation iv Prisidint Tiddy's chances in th' South. Thousan's iv men who wudden't have voted f'r him undher anny circumstances has declared that undher no circumstances wud they now vote f'r him."

There was some delicious satire on both Roosevelt and Washington:

"They'd been talkin' over th' race problem an' th' Cubian war, an' th' prospects iv th' race an' th' Cubian war, an' th' future iv th' naygro an' th' Cubian war, an' findin' Booker T. was inthrested in important public subjects like th' Cubian war, th' prisidint ast him to come up to th' White House an' ate dinner an' have a good long talk about th' Cubian war. . . . An' Booker wint. So wud I. So wud annywan. I'd go if I had to black up."

Then followed a realistic and meaningful discussion of the Negro in America, ending with the statement that there was only one right the Negro needed. " What's that? " " Th' right to live," said Mr. Dooley. " If he cud start with that he might make something iv himsilf."

Roosevelt well remembered this piece, and when he invited Dunne to the White House, he added that they would not talk of the Cuban War and " you need not black your face."[3] Dunne replied:

> Your stipulations are gracious but unnecessary. A Chicago man is always " blacked up " even after a year in the East. As for the Cubian War it would be rank ingratitude on my part to forget the obligations I am under to that episode. I ought to divide my royalties with the survivors, but I hope I won't.[4]

The best known Dooley essay of this series was that on the decision of the Supreme Court on the Insular Cases. The total effect of the Court's action was to approve expansion by making it legally feasible; in the popular phrase it decided that the Constitution did not follow the flag. Dunne had made Mr. Dooley satirize courts and legal proceedings before. In commenting on the speed with which the Puerto Ricans had become pro-American after the arrival of the army in 1898, Dooley had observed that " a proud people that can switch as quick as thim lads have nawthin' to larn in th' way iv what Hogan calls th' signs iv gover'mint, even fr'm th' Supreme Court." The essay was important for its picture of the workings of the Court,

[3] November 11, 1901. Quoted in Henry F. Pringle: *Theodore Roosevelt* (New York, 1931), p. 249.

[4] November 12, 1901. Roosevelt mss.

for Dunne did not use the opportunity to consider the problem of expansion itself. The doctrine of the Court's infallibility was accepted everywhere in conservative circles as the respectable doctrine. The Supreme Court was the one sacred institution of property interests in the United States, and to speak against this concept was the worst of all political crimes. It was this atmosphere to which the essay addressed itself, attempting to bring the sunlight of common sense to bear upon the Court as upon other institutions. Mr. Dooley described the action of the Court on the case in this manner:

"F'r awhile ivrybody watched to see what th' Supreme Court wud do. I knew mesilf I felt I cudden't make another move in th' game till I heerd fr'm thim. Buildin' op'rations was suspinded an' we sthud wringin' our hands outside th' dure waitin' f'r information fr'm th' bedside. 'What're they doin' now?' 'They just put th' argymints iv larned counsel in th' ice box an' th' chief justice is in a corner writin' a pome. Brown J. an' Harlan J. is discussin' th' condition iv th' Roman Empire befure th' fire. Th' rest iv th' Court is considherin' th' question iv whether they ought or ought not to wear ruchin' on their skirts an' hopin' crinoline won't come in again. No decision to-day.' . . . Expansionists contracted an' anti-expansionists blew up an' little childher was born into th' wurruld an' grew to manhood an' niver heerd iv Porther Ricky except whin some wan got a job there. . . . I woke up wan mornin' an' see be th' paper that th' Supreme Court had warned th' constitution to lave th' flag alone an' tind to its own business.

"That's what th' paper says, but I've read over th' decision an' I don't see annything iv th' kind there. They'se not a wurrud about th' flag an' not enough to tire ye about th' constitution."

The lack of agreement with the Court's opinion was presented in this manner:

"Says Brown J.: 'Th' question here is wan iv such great importance that we've been sthrugglin' over it iver since ye see us las' an' on'y come to a decision (Fuller C. J., Gray J., Harlan J., Shiras J., McKenna J., White J., Brewer J., an' Peckham J. dissentin' fr'm me an' each other).' . . .

"An' there ye have th' decision, Hinnissy, that's shaken th' intellicts iv th' nation to their very foundations, or will if they thry to read it. 'Tis all right. Look it over some time. 'Tis fine spoort if ye don't care f'r checkers. Some say it laves th' flag up in th' air an' some say that's where it laves th' constitution. Annyhow, something's in th' air. But there's wan thing I'm sure about."

"What's that?" asked Mr. Hennessy.

"That is," said Mr. Dooley, "no matther whether th' constitution follows th' flag or not, th' Supreme Court follows th' iliction returns."

This last phrase was a capital hit, and translated into non-dialect it became the most quoted and most influential line in all of Dunne's writing. The plain implication was that the Supreme Court was not some institution of supernatural infallibility. Supporting this view was not only a very confusing decision and a badly divided Court, but also the great authority of the popular oracle, Mr. Dooley, who was even less fallible than the Court. The expression became part of the American language of political discussion the truth of which was not to be denied. It was quoted years later by persons who had never heard of Mr. Dooley, and even the upholders of a sacred character for the courts would not go so far as to deny its essential truth. The probability of making the Court a symbol too sacred to be the subject of discussion or of change went out with the acceptance of that concept. No idea contributed more toward rationalizing the discussion of the place of courts in American politics than this almost accidental phrase of Dunne's.

Although Dunne had written less during the past year than any year since he had created Mr. Dooley, he put the essays together into a new book, *Mr. Dooley's Opinions*. After seeing it through the press, he and John Grier accompanied Henry White Cannon, president of the Chase National Bank, on a long railroad journey to the Pacific Coast and Mexico. They spent nearly six weeks on the trip, Dunne visiting for a short time in Chicago on the way. By the first of the year Dunne and Grier were back in New York. Cannon was going to Florence, where he had remodeled an old monastery into a luxurious dwelling. Before he left he invited Dunne and Grier to visit him there. Dillingham and Charles Frohman were going to London, and Frohman was still talking with Dunne about a Dooley play. Dunne needed little urging; he and Grier went to London with the producers. From there Dunne went to Paris, and then with the Abbotts to Florence to visit Cannon. The week after Easter he was in Rome, and he was invited to an audience with Pope Leo XIII, whom Dunne had seen the year before.

Dunne was impressed deeply by these two visits to Rome. Although not a pious person, he found the reality of the Catholic Church's power impressive, and the sincere piety of the aged Pope near overwhelming. After the public audience on his first visit, he and Laurence Hamill, who was with him, were invited to a private audience with a small group of men. Afterwards Dunne comforted his sister Charlotte with the opinion: "I don't understand how anyone can be a Protestant after a visit to Rome."[5] His impression of the second visit was recorded in some detail to this same sister:

> It was at a public audience given to the Piedmontese pilgrims and the huge Sala Rejia was crowded with persons of high and low degree from cardinals to peasants. You never heard such a roar of "Viva Il Papa Re!" as went up when the Holy Father was carried in, high on the shoulders of the Swiss Guard. . . . He rose as the crowd cheered and smiled and bowed repeatedly and blessed us but he looked, oh, so old – a thousand years older than when I saw him last year. He delivered an allocation from the throne, which I could hear but not in the least understand. Dear soul, he can hardly last much longer. Yet when one of the foreign cardinals said to him: "May your Holiness live to be a hundred," he said, with a smile, "Why put a limit on the goodness of Almighty God?" Isn't it beautiful. I send you some beads blessed by him.[6]

A favorite story of Peter Dunne's to illustrate the transition from the sublime to the ordinary came from the first of these audiences with the Pope. As he liked to tell it, he was in an antechamber awaiting the appointed moment and vastly moved by the solemnity and dignity of the occasion. When the feeling of religious emotion was heaviest upon him, a most unprepossessing minor cleric sidled up to him and said: "You're Dunne from Chicago aren't you? How's

[5] In "Ag. Jno." to "Elizabeth Eliza," March 6, 1901. Charlotte Dunne letters.

[6] June 7, 1902. Charlotte Dunne letters.

young Carter Harrison making out as mayor, any-how?"

Back in Florence again at Cannon's beautiful and comfortable palace, Dunne relaxed in the warm Italian sun. The tourist colony, which included many literary people, made a pleasurable setting. To Amelia he related these things:

> Gabriele D'Annunzio the great Italian poet lives a few miles from where I was. I met Villari the Italian historian, whom a good many people consider the greatest of living Italians. I don't. My money goes on Duse, the actress. But tastes differ. At all events he was clever and agreeable. Also came one Alfred Austin, Pote Laureate, a really nice little man, about as tall as Stubby's boy. He also was disposed to be friendly but his wife spoke of the immortal hero of modern humor as Mr. "Tim" Dooley. Ignorance. Some day they will speak of Shakespere as "Clarence" Shakespere or William Hookway as "Gus."[7]

After a restful and pleasant time Dunne returned to New York by way of London. Before he left Paris, he had proposed to Margaret Abbott, and a marriage date was set for the following winter. Dunne would be thirty-five years of age in July. Margaret Abbott had been a mere school girl when he had first known her in the nineties, and was much younger than Peter Dunne. But friends recalled that he had greatly admired her beauty back in the Chicago days before 1898, and that admiration had not lessened with her growing maturity, as he had seen her on his three trips abroad. She was an athletic girl, with a substantial education in art and music, abilities and interests which were the converse of Peter Dunne's.

[7] June 7, 1902. Charlotte Dunne letters.

Dunne did not plan to tell his friends of his engagement until shortly before the wedding. He returned to New York, and plunged back into the task of writing, now having an office in the city, where he boasted that he worked from "early morn till Dooley eve."[8] He took on the added work of supplying *Collier's Weekly* with editorials. Most of the summer and autumn he spent in the company of Charles Dana Gibson, the illustrator. Dunne had become an intimate of the Gibsons the year before, and when Mrs. Gibson, the former Irene Langhorne, decided to spend the summer at her parental home in Greenwood, Virginia, Dunne and Gibson joined forces for meals and recreation for Gibson's period of temporary bachelorhood. Although Dunne did more and better work during this summer than he had done during either of the two previous years, his routine must have presented a contrast to that of the hard-working Dana Gibson. One of his duties, perhaps his sole one as the illustrator's companion, was to keep Mrs. Gibson informed of her husband's health, work, and recreation, and of the news of New York City. This he did in a series of mock-romantic letters that were as entertaining as the letters of a humorist should be. A fairly typical report on the news from the city in this collection of nonsense, the blanks being, of course, Dunne's own:

Very little news in your set. I see John D. Rockefeller in the Journal every day. Morgan has gone abroad. George M. Pullman is dead. So is poor, dear Mr. Armour. John W. Gates is disconsolate without you and Russell Sage says he

[8] Peter to Charlotte Dunne, October 7, 1902. Charlotte Dunne letters.

would give thirty cents to see you & he would kill a man for twenty-five. The stock market is dull but there is a movement in corn on foot and lard is firm in spite of the weather. That is all I know that would interest you now. There was a time when you cared for other things but it has passed. I might tell you that Mrs. Dodge ——— ——— and that Tommy Hastings ——— ——— and that Ethel ——— ——— and that Tom McIlvaine — but what's the good? It would only bore you. I saw ——— at Sherry's last night. She said that little ——— ——— denies it and has threatened to sue any one who repeats the story but ——— swears he saw them — *in a cab!* He says it was the funniest thing he ever saw, ——— had just ———. But why go on. Did you get the cards for ——— ———? But I forgot. They are no longer friends of yours. It was very pretty or would have been but for the scandalous behaviour of ———. I never could bear that woman! The idea that she should come to the altar in tights! Bourke Cockran was furious. He told Smalley and Smalley wrote a little song about it. He and Bourke are singing it this week at Hammerstein's. It goes like this ——— ———. But never mind. . . .[9]

Dunne accompanied Gibson to Greenwood in September, where he spent a very pleasurable week with the Langhorne family — the father, " the Chauncey Depew of the South " as Dunne called him; the mother; their daughter Nancy, who was soon to become Lady Astor; Dana and Mrs. Gibson — and several other friends. Shortly after he returned to New York, Dunne received a letter from Mrs. Gibson, written in verse, and he replied in what was an imitation or forerunner of Walt Mason's rippling rhymes. " Our Bob " was the publisher Russell, whose laugh was one of the toasts of New York publishing circles.

[9] June 1, 1902. Mrs. Charles Dana Gibson letters.

The " Lennoxes " were the Lord and Lady Algernon Gordon-Lennox.

I never knew, Irene my dear, that you could versify. Although it really should be clear to me, at least, you needn't fear to fail at anything you try. The Sapphic fragment from your pen is worthy of a loftier theme. To ask Apollo's helping when you write inflammable men, does not a generous heart beseem. I'm really crushed enough, God knows, at thinking I must stay in town. I hardly could resist your prose and now you try to rhyme me down. The Lennoxes, avant-hier,* were at the Albemarle hotel. I felt that Dana should be near to valet Algy but I fear he acted, in a word, like Hell. He never once went near the pair till half past ten o'clock or more; meanwhile " our Bob " had set a snare and lured them to his lodgings where he loosed his fearsome sea-lion roar. It must be fine for those who come across the sea to pleasure quaff to land at Bobby's princely home and hear the steady roar and rumble of that ingrowing laugh. But so they did & now they're off to where my lady Irene reigns. How grand it is to be a toff, do nothing else but laugh and chaff and go to any place one fains (obsolete). I wish I were of noble birth; I wish I wore a coronet. I'd travel all around the earth, I'd fill the world with endless mirth, I'd surely whoop it up, you bet. But now I think of it, I'd not. I never would to Shivaz go or Timbuctoo or Tommyrot. For me there's but one garden spot. It's Greenwood on the C & O. And there I'd thrive, mild and serene, consume the Colonel's mountain grog, play sqush and drive with dear Irene, hold hands with Nanny, fair if lean; and kick the moist and faithful dog. But here I sit to toil condemned, beside the many voic-ed sea; in sheets of Irish dialect hemmed, my temper sadly sawed and phlegmed (new word), my brow with perspiration gemmed, my chin unshaved my hair unkemmed, my hatred of the world unstemmed; by doubt distraught, by fear o'erwhe'med. Oh, this demnition grind be demn'd!

Come back, Irene, come back to me. From Algy Gordon-Lennox flee; from Fleming and from Fitzhugh Lee. Come back, Irene, to

F.P.D.[10]

* Pronounced properly for rhythm; improperly, or not at all, for rhyme.

Through the year of 1902, Dunne was producing a steady stream of Dooley essays, most of which went to his syndicate, but a few to periodicals. Many of the important events of the year were discussed in his happiest style. Perhaps none of his single essays was as good as that on the Supreme Court's decision of the year before, but the general level was higher and his productivity was much greater. His readers laughed at the pretentiousness of Newport society, the Sherlock Holmes stories, the visit of Prince Henry of Germany to the United States, the controversy over imported and native art, the reading of books, the movement to restrict immigration (or at least the arguments used to support it), King Edward's coronation, Arctic exploration, and the home life of literary geniuses. By far the greatest number of essays were upon American politics, and these included most of the better ones.

Although Dunne was becoming a regular visitor at the White House, there was no indication of any tendency on his part to change the tenor of his writing because of it. During 1902 he vigorously satirized many things connected with the Administration. He was especially prone to ridicule the President's habit

[10] October 7, 1902. Mrs. Charles Dana Gibson letters.

of speech when he was dealing with any economic issue. This was Dooley's play upon Roosevelt's statements on the trust problem:

"'Th' thrusts are heejous monsthers built up be th' inlightened intherprise iv th' men that have done so much to advance progress in our beloved counthry,' he says. 'On wan hand I wud stamp thim undher fut; on th' other hand not so fast. What I want more thin th' bustin' iv th' thrusts is to see me fellow counthrymen happy an' continted. I wudden't have thim hate th' thrusts. Th' haggard face, th' droopin' eye, th' pallid complexion that marks th' inimy iv thrusts is not to me taste. Lave us be merry about it an' jovial an' affectionate. Lave us laugh an' sing th' octopus out iv existence. Betther blue but smilin' lips anny time thin a full coal scuttle an' a sour heart.'"

Toward the end of 1901, General Nelson A. Miles received a rebuke from the President for publicly criticizing the decision of the Naval Court of Inquiry in the Schley-Sampson controversy. Of course, Roosevelt had been known to criticize his military superiors in the "round-robin" of 1898. With two such figures as Roosevelt and Miles, it was a natural for a Dooley essay.

"Man an' boy Hinnissy, I've taken manny a chanst on me life, but I'd as lave think iv declarin' th' sentimints iv me heart in an Orange meetin' as dhroppin' in f'r a socyal call at what Hogan calls th' ixicutive mansion. . . . There was me frind Gin'ral Miles. No more gallant sojer iver dhrew his soord to cut out a patthern f'r a coat thin Gin'ral Miles. He's hunted th' Apachy, th' Sioux, th' Arapahoo, th' Comanchee, th' Congressman an' other savages iv th' plain; he's faced death an' promotion in ivry form, an' no harm come to him till he wint up th' White House stairs or maybe 'twas till he come down. . . . 'I've come,' says Gin'ral Miles, 'to pay me rayspicts to th' head iv th' nation.' 'Thank ye,' says th' prisidint, 'I'll do th' same f'r th' head iv th' army,' he says, bouncin' a coal scuttle on th' vethran's helmet. 'Gin'ral, I don't like ye'er recent conduct,' he says, sindin' th' right to th' pint iv th' jaw. 'Ye've been in th' army forty years,' he says pushin' his head into th' grate, 'an' ye shud know that an officer who criticizes his fellow officers, save in th' reg'lar way, that is to say in a round robin, is guilty iv I dinnaw what,' he says, feedin' him his soord. . . ."

Sardonic Henry Adams chortled when he read this. "The round-robin was neat. . . . I am curious to know how Theodore took it. Poor Miles never had the faculty of taking a joke. . . ."[11]

There was, moreover, one subject on which Dunne laid into the President and his administration with vigor and frequency. That was his militaristic-imperialistic habits of thinking. A friend of Dunne's once asked him how such an inveterate enemy of poseurs was able to enjoy the President's company, and Dunne replied that he enjoyed every minute of it, with the exception of those times when Roosevelt began to glorify war as a good in itself. Then he had to leave. This theme of criticism runs through the Dooley essays of these years, whether Dunne was sniping at Roosevelt in an entirely humorous way about appointing gunmen to offices in the territories, or less jocularly about his attacks on anti-imperialists at home. When General Funston took it upon himself to damn and threaten all anti-imperialists, Mr. Dooley satirized Roosevelt's gentle rebuke:

---

[11] Adams to Elizabeth Cameron, January 12, 1902. In *Letters of Henry Adams, 1892–1918*, edited by W. C. Ford (Boston and New York, 1938), p. 366.

" 'Dear Fred: Me attention has been called to ye'er pathriotic utthrances in favor iv fryin' Edward Atkinson on his own cuk stove. . . . So I am compilled be th' reg'lations iv war to give ye a good slap. How are ye, ol' commerade-in-arms? Ye ought to've seen me on th' top iv San Joon hill. Oh, that was th' day! Iver, me dear Fred, reprovingly but lovingly, T. Roosevelt.' "

Then followed this representation of the career of a general, presumably Funston himself:

" Now suppose Gilligan's father whin he was young had looked him over an' said: 'Agathy, Michael's head is perfectly round. It's like a base-ball. 'Tis so pecoolyar. An' he has a fightin' face. 'Tis no good thryin' to tache him a thrade. Let's make a sojer iv him.' An' he wint into th' army. . . . 'Tis Gin'ral Gilligan he'd be be this time – Gin'ral Mike Gilligan suspindin' th' haveas corpus in th' Ph'lippeens an' th' anti-imperialists at home; . . . Gin'ral Mike Gilligan abolishin' th' third reader; Gin'ral Mike Gilligan discoorsin' to th' public on 'Books I have niver read: Series wan, th' Histhry iv th' United States.' "

As for William Howard Taft's report on the Philippines, of which he was now governor, Dunne did not spare the administration, for the reports of atrocities by American forces attempting to subdue the insurgents had sickened Dunne more than ever of imperialism. Mr. Dooley paraphrased Taft's report:

" 'All th' riches iv Cathay, all th' wealth iv Ind, as Hogan says, wud look like a second morgedge on an Apache wickeyup compared with th' untold an' almost unmentionable products iv that gloryous domain. Me business kept me in Manila or I wud tell ye what they are. Besides some iv our lile subjects is gettin' to be good shots an' I didn't go down there f'r that purpose. . . . Ivry wanst in a while whin I think iv it, an iliction is held. Unforchnitly it usually happens that those ilicted have not yet surrindhered. . . . It is not always nicessary to kill a Filipino American right away. . . . We are givin' hundherds iv these pore benighted haythen th' well-known, ol'-fashioned American wather cure. Iv coorse ye know how 'tis done. . . . He is thin placed upon th' grass an' given a dhrink, a baynit bein' fixed in his mouth so he cannot rejict th' hospitality. Undher th' infloonce iv th' hose that cheers but does not inebriate, he soon warrums or perhaps I might say swells up to a ralization iv th' granjoor iv his adoptive counthry. One gallon makes him give three groans f'r th' constitchoochion. At four gallons, he will ask to be wrapped in th' flag. At th' dew point he sings Yankee Doodle. . . . I have not considhered it advisable to inthrajooce anny fads like thrile be jury iv ye'er peers into me administration. . . . Ivrywhere happiness, contint, love iv th' shtep-mother counthry, excipt in places where there are people.' "

No issue since 1900, not even the cruelties practised on weaker peoples by the imperialistic Powers, had roused Dunne's indignation as did the blind and selfish attitude of the owners of the anthracite coal mines in the fall of 1902. Subject to a strike by the United Mine Workers, the management refused all proposals for compromise or arbitration, and insisted that if people suffered from a coal shortage with winter near, it was the fault of the Union, and the management had no responsibility in the matter. In fact, George F. Baer, President of the Philadelphia & Reading Railroad, who was the leader of the operators, issued public statements in which he upheld the sacred right of ownership to do as it pleased regardless of public interest. These revolution-stimulating statements of ownership were capped by a letter in which Baer declared: " The rights and interests of the laboring man will be protected and cared for — not by the labor agitators, but by the Christian men to whom God in His infinite wisdom has given the control of the property interests of the country. . . ."

" It'll be a hard winther if we don't get coal," said Mr. Hennessy.

" What d'ye want with coal? " said Mr. Dooley. " Ye'er a most unraisonable man. D'ye think ye can have all th' comforts iv life an' that ye mus' make no sacryfice to uphold th' rights iv property? Ivrybody will have plinty iv fuel this winther. Th' rich can burn with indignation, thinkin' iv th' wrongs inflicted on capital, th' middle or middlin' class will be marchin' with th' milishy, an' th' poor can fight among thimsilves an' burn th' babies. I niver thought iv babies befure as combustible, but they are. At wan stroke ye can keep th' baby warrum an' th' rest iv th' fam'ly comfortable. Befure th' winther is over I expict to hear ye callin': ' Packy, go out to th' woodshed an' bring in a scuttleful iv little Robert Immitt. Th' fire is burnin' low.' They'll be nawthin' else to burn. . . .

" List, will ye, to what Baer, th' great Baer, Ursa Major as Hogan calls him, has to say iv th' histhry iv th' wurruld an' th' ways iv Providence as revealed to him wan day as he was readin' th' Scriptures on th' ticker:

" ' Years ago,' says Baer, ' Nature decided that some day, afther she'd had a long peeryod iv practice an' got her hand in be makin' th' stars, th' moon, th' sun, th' stock exchange an' other divine wurruks, she'd compose me,' he says. ' It was no aisy task, an' she had to make a lot iv preparations f'r me arrival. . . . An' she piled mud an' rock on th' timbers an' washed thim with th' floods an' cuked thim with fire an' left thim to cool, an' through long cinchries she wint fr'm time to time an' patted thim an' said: " Afther a while a man with whiskers will come along an' claim ye. Don't laugh at him. That'll be Baer."

" 'Thin she mannyfacthered a lot iv dilicate people that had to keep warrum or die, an' she taught thim how to burn hard coal, an' thin I come. I call it Nature,' he says, 'but ye know who I mean. I am th' agent iv Divine Providence in this matther. All this coal was enthrusted to me be Hiven to look afther. Some say 'twas Morgan, but I know betther. I'm th' agent iv Providence – Providence Coal Comp'ny, Limited; George Baer agent. It's thrue I haven't made anny accountin' to me principal, but that'll come later. In th' manetime I stand as th' riprisintative iv visted inthrests, th' champeen iv ordher an' th' frind iv th' rights iv property. Great inthrests are at stake, as th' Southern lyncher said at th' burnin'. I'm a wondherful man. An' funny, too,' he says.

"So what are ye goin' to do about it? If thim lads on'y got to own th' coal be th' same way that I own th' part iv this house that ain't got a morgedge on it, an' ye own ye'er hat an' shoes – because a lot iv fellows come together in th' ligislachoor an' decided 'twas a good thing that a man who had shoes an' a hat shud keep thim – 'twud be diff'rent. But seein' that th' Lord fixed it, there's nawthin' f'r us to do but pray. . . .

"But I'm with th' rights iv property, d'ye mind. Th' sacred rights an' th' divine rights. A man is lucky to have five dollars; if it is ten, it is his jooty to keep it if he can; if it's a hundherd, his right to it is th' right iv silf-dayfinse; if it's a millyon, it's a divine right; if it's more thin that, it becomes ridickilous. In anny case it mus' be proticted. Nobody mus' intherfere with it or down comes th' constichoochion, th' army, a letther fr'm Baer an' th' wrath iv Hivin.

"If I own a house I can do what I plaze with it. I can set fire to it anny time I want, can't I? Ye may have foolish sintimints about it. Ye may say: 'If ye set fire to ye'er house ye'll burn mine.' But that don't mine anny coal with me. 'Tis my house, give me in thrust be th' Lord, an' here goes f'r a bonefire. What's that fireman comin' down th' sthreet f'r? How dare he squirt wather on me property? Down with th' fire departmint! I've some gun powdher in me cellar. I'll touch a match to it. I'm uncomfortable in summer. I'll take me clothes off an' go f'r a walk. Th' sign above th' dure belongs to me. I'll loosen it so it will fall down on th' top iv ye'er head. Ye want to go to sleep at night. I'm goin' to have a brass band sur'nade me. I own a gun. I think I'll shoot me property into ye. Get out iv th' way, f'r here comes property, dhrunk an' raisin' Cain. . . ." [12]

On another essay of about the same time, Dunne tied a better-humored tag that was perhaps as effective as his denunciation:

"What d'ye think iv th' man down in Pinnsylvanya who says th' Lord an' him is partners in a coal mine? "

"Has he divided th' profits? " asked Mr. Dooley.

But the coal strike and the attitude of the owners had not been a thing that was humorous to Dunne, and he had not found it easy to write lightly about it. To Roosevelt, he confided: "The strike situation must have been funny to one on the inside, but to those of us who saw only the ignorance and selfishness and blank stupidity of the operators, it was a tragedy. I confess that I made several attempts to deal with it as comedy but I had to give it up." [13] There is no doubt that Dunne would have agreed with the many who felt that Roosevelt's dealing with the situation was the most masterly feat of his entire career.

For the fifth consecutive year, Dunne planned a volume of his essays, which Russell published in November of 1902 under the title, *Observations of Mr. Dooley*. As he had been more industrious during the

---

[12] *New York Journal*, October 12, 1902.

[13] October 23, 1902. Roosevelt mss.

past year than the one before, he had more essays from which to choose. The book was published on schedule, and was reviewed freely. The comment on both the *Observations* and the *Opinions* of the previous year was laudatory. None contrasted the books unfavorably with the first two, although they were not quite as good. A selection from the two would have been, but each one alone included too many of the poorer pieces to maintain that standard. Rather, the comment was more likely to be amazement that they held up so well, and that in their peculiar form Dunne succeeded in treating so many aspects of American life. Many of the reviews were merely a choice selection of quotations, always good copy for a newspaper or periodical. But the accepted literary critics of America paid unanimous tribute. W. P. Trent, in an essay on the older humor of America, remarked that the school of political humor had culminated in the *Biglow Papers*, " but has surely suffered no grievous decline in the hands of Mr. Dooley." [14] William Dean Howells, in *The North American Review*, commented upon the entire series: " It is upon a review of the whole course of Mr. Dooley's musings on men and things that we recognize Mr. Dunne as of the line of great humorists. . . . To have one's heart in the right place is much; it is in fact, rather indispensable; but to have one's head in the right place, also, adds immeasurably to the other advantage." [15] And H. W.

---

14 " A Retrospect of American Humor," *Century*, vol. 63 (November 1901), 46.

15 Vol. 176 (May 1903), 745.

Boynton wrote in *The Atlantic:* " I do not think anything like justice has been done to the literary merit of the Dooley books." [16]

The English reviewers were equally friendly. *The Spectator*, always laudatory, was now unrestrainedly so:

> And what an example of Irish improvidence we have in Mr. Dunne, – pouring out these amazing improvisations week after week, each of them containing enough wit and sense to set up an ordinary journalist for life, carefully husbanded as they probably would be. . . . It is time to take seriously a man who can so discriminate – time to recognize that Mr. Dunne is a profound and farsighted critic. No man who cannot write good sense can ever get a reputation as a humourist, and it is not until he writes inspired sense that he is considered a great one. Mr. Dunne is a great humourist; his books are packed with true words spoken in jest. And he has the great humourist's instinct for what is universal, elemental. Whatever his subject, he strikes his fingers on its essentials. . . . He misses nothing. The whole pot of civilization, so to speak, boils in his pages all the time. . . .[17]

The only criticism was the comment that Dunne seemed, in the words of a reviewer in *The Nation*, to lack " fundamental political conviction. . . . To him Imperialist and Anti-Imperialist, Republican and Democrat . . . are equally ridiculous. . . . He belongs to the great class of those who live to make us laugh at ourselves in all our aspects." [18] This point was

---

[16] Vol. 90 (September 1902), 414.

[17] Vol. 90 (February 14, 1903), 258–59.

[18] Vol. 75 (December 25, 1902), 501. Only a blind partisan, as the anti-imperialist *Nation* then was, could have failed to see clearly Dunne's partisanship on the question of expansion. Dunne did satirize the organized anti-imperialist movement, and that is why *The Nation*

certainly not true of " fundamental political conviction," for the Dooley essays were mere entertainment apart from their consistent attack upon humbug, pretentiousness, and cruelty. But, of course, it was true — although no reviewer pointed it out — that Dunne did pull his punches a little when he put the essays into books. He did not reprint, for instance, the essay on the coal strike, although he did the one on Taft's report on the Philippines. But Dunne's basis of judgment was, at least in part, that the former was not great humor, while the latter was. That he was not partisan as between Democrat and Republican was true. But it is also true that the differences between the two parties in 1902 were nothing that would appeal to Dunne as fundamental; certainly not nearly so significant as the hollow pretensions in both organizations.

On December 9, Peter Dunne and Margaret Abbott were married quietly in an apartment which Mrs. Abbott had taken in New York. The prominent Jesuit, Father William Pardow, performed the ceremony, and Ethel Barrymore and John Grier were the attendants. After a brief trip south, the couple returned to New York for the winter. The press, which had discovered the plans for the marriage a few weeks before, generally covered it by quoting Mr. Dooley on the subject of marriage, not an entirely happy choice for the bridegroom's peace of mind. It would seem that Dunne had expected it, and his last essay before his marriage was a delightful piece in which

could say he found the anti-imperialist ridiculous. But " equally " it certainly was not.

Mr. Dooley speculated on the nature of women, and admitted his ignorance.[19] But too often before had Dooley made good copy by boasting of his bachelorhood. And this had been the one and only point on which the quiet Mr. Hennessy had always been permitted to score:

"But th' childher? " asked Mr. Hennessy slyly.

"Childher! " said Mr. Dooley. "Sure I have th' finest fam'ly in th' city. Without scandal I'm th' father iv ivry child in Archey road fr'm end to end."

"An' none iv ye'er own," said Mr. Hennessy.

"I wish to hell, Hinnissy," said Mr. Dooley savagely, "ye'd not lean against that mirror. I don't want to have to tell ye again."

It would be over twenty years before Mr. Dooley would hazard the opinion that "th' on'y good husbands stay bachelors. They're too considerate to get marrid."

---

[19] "Mr. Dooley Guesses About Women," *Collier's Weekly*, December 6, 1902.

# IN THE HEARTS OF HIS COUNTRYMEN

AT the time of Dunne's marriage in 1902, he had been writing weekly dialect essays for ten years; during the last four of those years these had been syndicated so widely that newspaper readers in every city in the country had them at their command regularly. Moreover, *Harper's Weekly* had also published them, with illustrations drawn by William Rogers, and later *Collier's* had taken them over, and now and then one was published in such magazines as the *Century*, *Cosmopolitan*, *Ladies' Home Journal*, or reprinted from the newspapers by *The Literary Digest*. Everywhere Mr. Dooley was recognized as the synonym for delicious humor, penetrating common sense, and a highly American, close-to-the-soil point of view. Such nativistic sentiment as existed in the country was never directed against Mr. Dooley's Irish brogue, and the only Prohibitionist objections as yet raised to the fact that he was a saloon-keeper came from a literary review. Readers recognized him as a fine product of the American tradition in popular literature. He was quoted widely, both in brogue and out of it; not in printed sources so much as in ordinary conversation. " Mr. Dooley says " was an introduction to a bit of borrowed wit or wisdom that had become a common feature of American conversation. So popular were the Dooley essays that Dunne's publishers were continually on the lookout to keep advertisers from reprinting them, or from printing parodies that pretended to be real products of the Dooley authorship.

One amusing aspect of Mr. Dooley's vast popularity was that the only real objection to him came from a small contingent of Irish. The stock figure of the ignorant Irishman on the American stage had aroused the natural opposition of many of that descent, and it was not lessened by the baboon-like caricatures of Irishmen which American comic artists took over from the English humorous weeklies. Pat and Mike jokes, with their " beggorah " and " bejabers," had as a rule only one point, the supreme ignorance of one or both of the pair. A well-organized movement was on foot by 1900 to drive this concept off the stage and out of the press, and a few of its supporters for reasons of their own included Mr. Dooley in their denunciations. This attack received little attention and, such was the standing of Mr. Dooley, it appears in the extant record only because of demands that it be answered. To the editor of *The Papyrus*, Michael Monahan, who wanted to flay the authors of the suggestion, Dunne wrote:

> I have got over caring about the few stupid attacks on " Dooley " by men who call themselves Irishmen, but have none of the intelligence or humor which we are proud to

Steele's *Dooley without bottles or bar, a concession to prohibitionists*

F. B. Opper's *Happy Hooliganish Mr Dooley for a Hearst Series in 1902*

*A* W. A. Rogers *illustration for the 1899 articles in "Harper's Weekly"*

GORDON ROSS *made a conservative of Mr. Dooley for a N. Y. "Times" series*

*A* JAMES MONTGOMERY FLAGG *version for the "American Magazine," October, 1909*

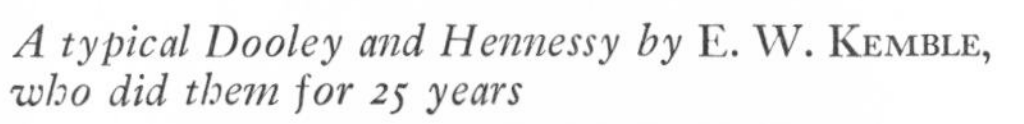

*A typical Dooley and Hennessy by* E. W. KEMBLE, *who did them for 25 years*

attribute to our race. The Chicago interviews mean nothing at all, but are the natural result of the publication of the report that I am getting a very large sum of money for my work. I know the men very well. They don't quarrel with "Dooley" but with the reported success of the author of "Dooley." They hate me because I am both Irish, and, as they think, prosperous. . . . That will do for these people. I have never seen a baboon-faced Irishman, but our race, like all others, has to suffer for the occasional appearance of the baboon-minded person, whom the newspapers always put forward with malice as a representative of the Irish race. I hope you will not bother your head or disturb the symmetry of your paper by attempting a defense of me against these bootblacks. Let them howl.[1]

Dunne could well afford to despise such attacks, as Mr. Dooley was treasured above all literary characters by the public. Symbolic of this was a "Mr. Dooley March" published in 1901, and the following year the reputation and fame of the great philosopher was used as the basis for a popular song, "Mister Dooley." It was one of the featured songs of the musical comedy *The Chinese Honeymoon.* Dunne was first made aware of it when W. C. Whitney insisted that he attend the opening of the comedy with him. Dunne went, occupied Whitney's box with the older man, and when a popular singer came upon the stage and sang the song in Dunne's direction, with the spotlight turned upon Whitney's box, the creator of Mr. Dooley derived such embarrassment and satisfaction as that type of public attention would inspire in a modest author.

---

[1] May 2, 1903. Monahan letters.

There is a man that's known to all, a man of great renown
A man who's name is on the lips of everyone in town
You read about him every day, you've heard his name no doubt
And if he even sneezes they will get an extra out.

Chorus:

For Mister Dooley, for Mister Dooley
The greatest man the country ever knew
Quite diplomatic and democratic
Is Mister Dooley-ooley-ooley-oo.

Then followed nine additional stanzas, each relating some achievement in history or recent news event, and each of which was followed in turn with the credit line of the chorus: " 'Twas Mister Dooley . . ."

The song was a hit. Surely no prophet could be more solidly intrenched in the hearts of his countrymen than was Mr. Dooley's creator. However momentarily disconcerting it may have been to Dunne to have his creation's praises sung at him in the presence of a theater full of people, its effect in the long run must have been thoroughly satisfying.

If Dunne needed assurances of his standing in circles not influenced by a musical comedy, he had only to look at his own correspondence to be aware that his writing was being subjected to discussion in newspapers as foreign to his intended audience as those in Russia, and that both statesmen and college presidents were requesting the sources of previous essays so that they might locate favorite quotations to be used in speeches. These and the strong competitive demands for his essays from syndicates, newspapers, magazines, and book publishers were guarantee enough to satisfy anyone that he was read and appreciated.

Dunne had not found that his desertion of journalism in 1900 placed him in an entirely happy situation. His Dooley essays did not keep him busy, for difficult as he found them to do, the actual writing was not time-consuming. Among the many friends he was making in New York were many in journalism, in book publishing, and many of great wealth. His association with Robert Russell brought him into contact with many of the latter, as Russell, in addition to being a publisher, was somewhat of a social climber. Dunne's response to a question regarding Russell's whereabouts, that he was "warming his feet at the Social Register," is declared to be the origin of that now shopworn pun. But principally these acquaintances were the natural outgrowth of his established reputation and his personal qualities. William C. Whitney, wealthy traction magnate and former political manager for the Cleveland Democracy, was now one of the most intimate of these. Whitney had been intellectually the most gifted of the important political bosses of the past generation, and had never lost his interest in all aspects of public life. It was natural that he should find Peter Dunne a congenial companion, but, according to the traditional story, Whitney first sought out the humorist because of a debt of gratitude which he owed him. Whitney's young wife had been a bedridden invalid for some time before her death, and her chief pleasure in that unfortunate condition was to have her husband read Dooley essays to her. However, the acquaintance developed into a great friendship between the political satirist and the retired politician, for the men had in common wit, a taste for sumptuous living, and an intense fascination with the great game of American politics.

Another of Dunne's new friends was young Robert Collier, whose personal qualities were exceedingly attractive and whose enthusiasms were easily shared by Peter Dunne. Collier had taken over *Collier's Weekly* from his father, and was making it a real force in American periodical journalism. Backed by the resources of his father's profitable publishing business, he was paying unusual prices for the best in fiction, feature articles, and popular art. The magazine's editorial page had been undistinguished, and it was logical for him to seek out Dunne to contribute to it.

Dunne had accepted, and during the six months before his marriage he was doing this weekly task, with considerably greater ease than he was turning out his Dooley pieces. The editorials which he wrote were of the type he had supplied to the *Chicago Post* eight years before, and were admirably suited to weekly journalism. Collier was greatly pleased, and many of Dunne's friends thought that this was an ideal place for the humorist, as it would extend his influence beyond his Dooley essays. But Dunne soon tired of it. Perhaps his disinclination grew out of the fact that he frequently detected himself using the same ideas for both editorials and essays. Hardly a dialect essay which he wrote during the six months was not paralleled by a short editorial on the same subject and from a similar viewpoint. An editorial on alcohol ended with: "The best opinion is that alcohol sustains life only for saloon keepers."[2] And in the cracker of the Dooley essay published not long afterwards, Mr. Hennessy asked: "Do ye think ye'ersilf it sustains life?" "It has sustained mine f'r many years," said the saloon-keeper.

The editorials were like the Dooley essays in another way: they did not assume any sharply pointed direction on public affairs. While liberal, reformistic, and pro-Roosevelt, they were not so in a partisan sense. Collier thought highly of them, and used Dunne's name in his advertising, proudly proclaiming him as the author of the page and promising his readers to double the space given to that feature. But Dunne asked Collier to relieve him of the work at about the time of his marriage. Very reluctantly Collier did so, and asked Dunne for help in finding a suitable successor. Dunne named Norman Hapgood, who was an occasional contributor to *Collier's*. Hapgood had been active in New York journalism since he had left Chicago, specializing in the theater. He had also written several superficial biographies of American political leaders, and perhaps few would have thought of him as a possible editorial writer. But Collier offered him the place, and he accepted. Dunne was free of that connection, although the weekly continued to publish such Dooley essays as Dunne gave it from time to time.

Not long after this, Dunne took on another journalistic task. W. C. Whitney had acquired title to the *New York Morning Telegraph*, and he urged Dunne

[2] November 1, 1902.

to become its editor, making a generous offer both in salary and in a third interest in the paper. It may be that Dunne had broken off his connection with *Collier's* to be free to accept this. The *Telegraph* had a checkered history, but was now definitely a theatrical and sporting newspaper with few interests outside of New York City. Part of the inducement that had led Dunne to accept the editorship was an understanding between himself and Whitney that they would build a different kind of newspaper on this foundation. Their idea was that it would be remade on the model of the Paris *Figaro*, continuing its peculiar New York character, but broadening its scope to include not only news of entertainment, but of everything of value in the metropolis. Coming out shortly after midnight, it would become, it was hoped, the breakfast or late supper reading of the intelligentsia of the city. Here was unquestionably a revival of Dunne's old dream of becoming a great editor and publisher, and wielding a pervasive influence on American life by directing the policies of a great newspaper.

As for actual performance during the months when Dunne had control, little can be said. Dunne and Whitney met at lunch nearly every day to talk over the paper. Some persons liked to say that the arrangement was merely Whitney's expensive way of insuring that he would have the daily pleasure of Dunne's company. Their table talk was more often on American history and politics than on the *Telegraph*. During the season they attended the races together to watch Whitney's horses run, and not infrequently there was a dinner party which included Mrs. Dunne. It seems clear that Dunne was not very active in the management of the paper and that the staff seldom saw him. But that was part of his understanding with Whitney. Except for deciding general policies and selecting the staff, he seems to have been content to let it run itself. William E. Lewis, an old Whitechapel friend, was placed in immediate charge as managing editor; Bert Leston Taylor was brought from Chicago; Hutchins Hapgood was added to the staff of reporters; and Laurence Hamill, just returned from four years in Paris, was employed to translate dramatic and literary items from Europe. Whatever plans Dunne had for the paper were shattered by Whitney's sudden death in February of 1904, for the paper went to his estate, which meant to one of his sons, Harry Payne Whitney. There was some disagreement between young Whitney and Dunne, and, in the end, Dunne accepted thirty thousand dollars for his interest and retired from the paper. It was his last connection with a daily paper.

The failure of the plans for the *Telegraph*, whether or not they had promised any real addition to Dunne's own career, left him depressed and disappointed. In the meantime, he was writing his Dooley essays with at least average success as far as quality was concerned. More and more he was having difficulty in meeting the deadline, and commitments to both syndicates and periodicals were not infrequently unfulfilled. It was these failures which were the cause of such fits of depression as he suffered from time to time. He tried a variety of methods to bring on a will to write when it was not present, but these were of little use, and he continued to run into difficulty. The distribution of the Dooley essays after 1904 was in the hands of the McClure Syndicate, and, in contrast to the *Chicago Post's* weekly ten dollars for each essay, it began by paying a round one thousand and later still more. McClure found newspaper publishers easily angered by the failure of an essay to appear on time or at all. Dunne refused, positively, to concede anything, or even to promise to deliver every week. His position was stated in a letter to an official of the syndicate:

I have intended to call on you before this but a great press of business has prevented. I thoroughly agree with you as to the advisability of getting out early copy but I can give no assurance beyond promising to do the best I can. Of course, I thoroughly appreciate the troubles of the newspapers. I have been through them myself. In the case of the Boston Globe I would be very glad for many personal reasons to get the copy in ten or twelve days in advance of publication. But I have my own limitations and there are weeks when it is an absolute impossibility to finish the article before Saturday, Sunday or Monday. If the Dooley articles are to be worth the price paid for them, they must represent my best effort, and if the article is not ready on Friday or does not seem good enough to send out, I cannot let it go. . . . The price paid for these articles entitles the papers to great consideration but I would rather accept a much smaller sum and do the work to my own satisfaction. In a word, I cannot give any guarantee that the articles will be finished on any particular day.

To-day I was told that Mr. Harry McClure had left word that if the article did not arrive to-day, the papers should be notified that there would be none. I don't wish to be unpleasant, and I thoroughly appreciate the work that has been done by Mr. McClure in distributing the articles, but I must insist that I am the only person that shall say whether an article shall be sent out or not. If this is not your understanding of our arrangement, we must make a new contract. I am very much surprised that Mr. McClure should take this action without consulting me and solely on his own responsibility.[3]

This was the beginning of several years of intermittent production in which syndication would begin, Dunne would produce his essays regularly for a few months, then a few would be omitted, and finally they would stop entirely. When he failed to keep his series coming regularly in 1907, the *New York Times* filled his space with parodies written by T. R. Ybarra, in which Mr. Hennessey became the talkative philosopher. One can easily imagine that this did not add to Dunne's pleasure in his creation, nor did it stimulate him to more regular production.

The real explanation of all this was not Dunne's laziness and not entirely his need of the spur of financial necessity, but simply that the great critical approval of the essays had led him to set a high standard for them; and rather than write one that was not up to that standard he would await a better inspiration. Each essay was concentrated humor, as many intelligent critics had pointed out. John Kendrick Bangs, no mean humorist himself, had written in 1900:

If Mr. Dunne were our sole refuge [from the charge of having no great humor] there would still be little reason for despondency, for his humor is a precipitate; it is humor boiled down until that which remains is the pure, undiluted essence of humor; it becomes a mass of scintillating crystals in so

[3] Letter to H. N. Phillips, November 5, 1904. Copy in F. P. Dunne letters.

small a compass and so bewilderingly many that each new reading of the resulting books reveals mirth-provoking qualities not previously discovered.[4]

The very "Irish improvidence" with which Dunne loaded his essays, and that *The Spectator* had pointed out, was his own undoing. The pace which Dunne thus set for himself was too fast to maintain after ten years of weekly essays. Either he caught himself re-using old situations for his effects, or actually repeating himself. By 1903, for instance, he had celebrated Christmas, St. Patrick's Day, football, golf, and other general topics of this kind at least seven or eight times. To do a new essay on one of them was virtually impossible in his dialect form without actual or near repetition. This he would not do. His only new source of topics was the stream of current affairs, and most of such topics fell into types of subjects which he had discussed over and over again. He had found from his editorials for *Collier's* that even in pure English he repeated essential elements of his dialect pieces, and that was far from comforting as far as the future was concerned. He let the fall of 1903 go by without producing a book, the first omission in six years. He had had a bad summer. He and Mrs. Dunne spent most of it at Cornish, New Hampshire, with the Augustus Saint-Gaudenses, Norman Hapgoods, and a number of other congenial friends. But Mrs. Abbott's serious illness in New York brought them back to the city early. A serious operation gave Mary Abbott a short extension of her lease on life, and she

[4] "A Word Concerning American Humor," *Book Buyer*, XX (April 1900), 206–7.

did not die until the next year. To Peter Dunne her suffering through the illness was a great emotional shock such as he had not experienced since his own mother's death. After the operation, and when he thought that she was on the way to recovery, Dunne wrote to a friend:

> By the mercy of God Mrs. Abbott has been called back to life and I took her to the country Saturday in a car which Mr. Whitney was kind enough to lend me. I cannot tell you, Michael, how I have suffered while my dearest friend and comrade lay struggling with death but I hope it has made me a better man and one more sympathetic with the sufferings of poor humanity.[5]

After one more trip abroad the Dunnes settled down to a routine of living which consisted of maintaining a permanent home in New York City and spending the summers at some coastal resort. They fitted easily into the social life of New York. Both of them had a wide circle of friends, and they were able to select their own society. A definite home life modified Peter Dunne's established habits. Club evenings were replaced to some extent by entertaining groups of friends at home. Receptions, large dinners, musicales, parties, and all the usual affairs of New York society became a part of the Dunnes' life. Few things where Peter Dunne was concerned failed to turn out to be pleasurable and gay, and his home life was of this character. He chose company for the pleasure it gave him, and at home he was the same witty leader of the conversation that he was in his clubs. Margaret Dunne's interests in art and music led

[5] Letter to Michael Monahan, August 23, 1903. Monahan letters.

her into activities in which her husband was uninterested, but the Dunnes found many intimates among the artists and musicians. The Walter Damrosches and the Benjamin Guinnesses were among the most important, possibly with the single exception of the Dana Gibsons, whose friendship was older. Perhaps the most intimate friends of the Dunnes immediately after their marriage were Robert and Sally Collier, who had been married at about the same time. But the extent of these friendships was wide and the types were extremely varied. At all times, they included some notable political and financial leaders, and many of these who were not family friends were close associates at clubs where Peter Dunne spent a large part of his time. There were fewer professional writers among these intimates than might have been expected. John Fox, Jr., Richard Harding Davis, and Thomas Nelson Page were the exceptions, and at the Dunnes' favorite summer resort, York Harbor, Maine, William Dean Howells proved to be another delightful associate.

But the most important of all of Dunne's friendships with other writers was with Mark Twain. He and Collier were frequent guests of the great man, and Dunne helped Collier plan his celebrated hoax of the gift of an elephant to Twain — it turned out to be a stuffed one. Dunne became a favorite billiards opponent of the elderly humorist. Out of these games came several stories, one of them about Twain's betting Dunne that he could not make fifty successive caroms, which brought on a series of contests that extended over several afternoons. Another concerned

FINLEY PETER DUNNE
*with Richard Harding Davis and John Fox, Jr.*

Twain's trick of introducing one white billiard ball that was not quite round, and watching the consternation of his opponent as he tried to use it as his cue ball. But Dunne was either forewarned or quick to detect the imperfection; for he ignored it until Twain's back was turned, and then he reversed the white balls and the shoe was on the other foot. It was an enviable friendship that developed between the two humorists whose philosophies had so much in common. Dunne later recalled one incident that must be recorded:

In New York after the death of that lovely creature Jean, Mark Twain tried to brighten his life a little by going to theatres, having friends come to his house and making new friends among the younger generation. I was lucky enough to be among this group. He always treated me as if I were still in my adolescence although when I first met him I had been a hard boiled newspaper man for at least 17 years, had written four or five books and edited or published about that many newspapers and magazines. He would say " I like you young fellows. I like to have you around me. But you mustn't expect me to listen to your opinions. They are too immature. Wait till you and Collier have made a reputation. Then you can talk to me and I will stay awake." I think that one day I squared accounts with him for this and similar admonitions. In his last years, he, who had once been rather shy, took very kindly to the publicity that was poured on him. He liked attention; he even demanded it. In the streets of New York he was a more marked figure than Theodore Roosevelt or J. P. Morgan. His noble countenance, his splendid head would distinguish him in any crowd however great but when he took to wearing white clothes — a sensible thing to do, but conspicuous — no one who had ever seen a picture of him in the paper could miss him. One bright spring afternoon I met him at the crowded corner of

Fifth Avenue and 42nd St. As usual we stopped to exchange our customary banter about the ignorance of youth and the impotence of age. Thousands and thousands of men, women and children passed us and every mother's son and daughter turned his or her head to look at the picturesque figure. Some of them stopped and listened. At one time there must have been fifteen or twenty typical New York rufuses gawking at him. Mark loved it. His face was aflame. His eyes shone. He talked better and louder than I had ever heard him. Finally I said, "Let's get out of here and go over to the Century and have a drink."

"I'm not a member of the Century. What's the matter with staying here."

"But aren't you embarrassed standing here in these crowds, talking to a celebrity," I said.

He answered like a man coming out of a trance. His eyes were wide open and staring. He stammered: "Wh—wh—why, do *you* think these people are looking at *you?* Why, you conceited fellow, they're looking at *me!*" Then the fact dawned on him that youth had at last rebelled. His face broke into a great grin. "Oh, come on over to the Century and have a drink."

"But you just said you weren't a member."

"I'm not. That makes my hospitality all the more remarkable. What could be finer than to entertain a friend at a club where you're not a member."

"But I'm a member."

"I knew that or I wouldn't have invited you." [6]

Something of the quality of Dunne's genius for friendship is apparent in a letter which Dunne wrote to Twain a few years later. At this time Dunne was on the staff of *The American Magazine*, and he was asking Twain to write a brief sketch of Henry M.

[6] Recollections of Peter Dunne.

Alden, the elderly and somewhat puritanical editor of *Harper's Magazine*.

My dear and respected Subordinate in the G. D. Human Race Association:

The enterprising gentlemen who are associated with me in this philanthropic undertaking have secured by unparalleled enterprise and prodigious expense, a photograph hitherto unpublished of the new comet in the literary sky, Mr. Henry M. Alden. I am opposed to publishing it. I believe that they should not be carried away by Mr. Alden's momentary popularity. I want them to wait until the patient judgment of the world has been delivered on works that have merit, but seem to me to be a little too flashy for permanence. Besides, I am opposed to the fleshly school in literature. You and I, my dear friend, have tried to keep our art pure. Mr. Alden ought to prove himself before he can be considered worthy of a place in our gallery of distinguished artists, including in the past such names as James J. Jeffries, Captain Chance, Kyrle Bellew and others who shall be nameless (or should be). Still they think in this office that a picture of Mr. Alden would help our circulation in the Tenderloin, and they have had the cheek to ask me, to have the cheek to ask you to write an "appreciation" of this best seller — four hundred words they crave to go with the photograph. I am told Mr. Alden is prepared for the blow. I don't want you to do it unless you can't find any reason, personal, commercial, artistic or other for not doing it — unless indeed you are urged to do it by strong reasons of your own. I realize that it is too much for the magazine to ask, and not enough for me to ask, when I consider the obligations you are under to me for not calling the attention of the police to your nefarious billiard game while you are rioting in Capuan luxury on money wrung from a guileless friend.

Rob Collier and I have been planning to descend on you, but Rob has had his brains addled by having an intoxicated horse fall under him while hunting, and my liver has been so disturbed by constant meditation, that I have had to take a cure at French Lick Springs. But you may expect us soon, if the invitation has not been withdrawn and we are still welcome. Is there any possibility that you will be in New York this autumn, so that the three of us can have a mild spree, if only to lunch together?

Please present my regards to Miss Clemens, and think of me, in spite of this request for copy, as

Affectionately yours,[7]

Dunne continued the club life to which he had become habituated. In part it was a pleasant method of picking up hints for his essays, and in part it was merely his way of enjoying life. Heywood Broun, who recalled that Dunne got him his first newspaper job, also credited Dunne's record in one club with inducing Broun's father to turn Heywood toward writing as an occupation. " My father was in business and sometimes he worked until 6 and 7, and occasionally he would get off early in the afternoon. But no matter how early my father got to the club he always found Finley Peter Dunne sitting there, having a drink or playing backgammon or having a good time in one way or another. And he always seemed to be in funds. My father got the idea that writing must be the easiest job in the world, and when I was 9 he nominated me for the craft."[8]

Among a wide circle of friends and acquaintances in New York, Dunne had attained the position of an oracle on public affairs. He usually lunched at the

---

[7] November 26, 1909. S. L. Clemens papers. Secured through the courtesy of Mr. Bernard De Voto.

[8] *New York World-Telegram*, April 26, 1936.

Holland House, and there until about two-thirty in the afternoon he would be found in the center of a discussion group. After that, if not being pressed for his copy, he would be in one of the clubs, similarly engaged until time to leave for a late dinner at home. Always near the center of this circle, he was drawn out on the day's news, some of his friends insisting that a large proportion of the city's editorial writers frequented the circle in order to get ideas for use on their own pages; indeed, Norman Hapgood is accused of openly taking notes on Dunne's comments and using them in his pages in *Collier's*. Whether this is true or not, there is no question that these informal gatherings that occurred at the various restaurants and clubs were notable chiefly for Dunne's comments on the day's news, his estimates of political trends, and his evaluation of political leaders. Perhaps a great deal of wisdom and wit was used here that could have made copy for Mr. Dooley, but the compensations of the admiring circle and the give-and-take of questioning and discussion were immense in personal satisfaction. To those who repeatedly listened to the steady flow of witty philosophical comment, the idea that Peter Dunne could produce Dooley essays by the hour, if he wished, was permanently established. There seemed no human limit to the wisdom and wit, and any failure to write must arise from some Achilles heel of perverseness or sheer laziness.

This regular routine was varied by special luncheons or dinners for some visiting writer or scholar. Dunne was a prize guest whom visitors wanted to meet, and whose witty and interesting talk made any affair memorable. He and Mrs. Dunne were almost invariably present when Clemens or Collier or Hapgood entertained a notable friend. Edith Wharton recalls her efforts to bring Dunne and Henry James together on the novelist's visit to the United States in 1907:

> Once when I had arranged a meeting between him and the great Mr. Dooley, whose comments on the world's ways he greatly enjoyed, I perceived, as I watched them after dinner, that Peter Dunne was floundering helplessly in the heavy seas of James' parentheses; and the next time we met, after speaking of his delight in having at last seen James, he added mournfully: "What a pity it takes him so long to say anything! Everything he said was so splendid – but I felt like telling him all the time: 'Just 'pit it right up into Popper's hand.'"[9]

Dunne was still the omnivorous reader that he had been as a young reporter. It was his habit to take a half dozen books with him when he retired at night and to read himself to sleep. These books might vary from standard classics to a recent mystery story. Some of his more literary interests are implied in a letter to Michael Monahan:

> Many thanks for the Heine – at all events for the spirit that prompted the gift. I won't look a gift horse in the mouth but the edition is something to weep over. Leland is a bastard if ever there was one. A specially hot vile hell is heating for bad editors and Leland deserves a seat – near the fire – with the Hazlitt who edited the old one's works and Wm Rossetti who fouled his own brother and Byron with his abominable prefaces and footnotes. There are other can-

[9] *A Backward Glance* (New York, 1934), p. 178. Quoted by permission of D. Appleton-Century Co.

didates for this immortality. Have you seen the posthumous Froude pamphlet published last summer, in which Froude defends himself against the charge that he was unfair to Carlyle by declaring that Carlyle was impotent? If not I will send it to you. It will make copy if you can read it without going wild. Froude is the vilest dog that ever learned to write English and that is going far. . . .[10]

Dunne had discovered Montaigne, and the French philosopher had touched a responsive chord in Dunne's mind and had become his favorite reading. But Montaigne and the other great literary figures of the past were merely a leisure-time matter with Dunne. Newspapers were his meat and drink. Habitually he read most of the papers in the city, seldom letting anything keep him from devouring the new editions soon after they came out, expertly estimating and allowing for newspaper bias and reportorial inefficiency, to come to an intelligent approximation of what was under way. He would read anywhere and everywhere, scanning and devouring the small parts that had real meaning. His very success with the Dooley essay was basically this vast understanding of public affairs, and it was maintained now largely by the press and to a less extent by personal observation. Then in his role as an oracle Dunne was being cast into a character such as he had created for Mr. Dooley, only instead of the humble Archey Road saloon, its center was the best clubs of New York City or the private circle of intimate friends like Robert Collier. It was the logical development of the talk fests of the Whitechapel Club, of Mary Abbott's gatherings, or

[10] December 19, 1903. Monahan letters.

the small groups at Robert Hamill's in Chicago. And to those who were a part of it, it seemed more important than anything which Dunne was writing. There can be no doubt that it was also significantly important to Peter Dunne.

All this is implied in Michael Monahan's excellent poetical tribute to Dunne in 1908, where it is not alone the role of the public censor, the symbol in the hearts of his countrymen, which is celebrated, but equally the friend and companion:

To Finley Peter Dunne (" Mr. Dooley ")

The only art I boast is this –
  I too have laughed with all the crowd,
When the rich wonder of your wit
  Challenged their plaudits loud;

And then, the jester's role aside,
  A finer spirit have I known,
A man with sorrow, too, acquaint,
  A brother – yes, mine own.

A look into the merry eyes –
  Lo! here are tears unshed
That do not ask a kindred soul
  To leave their fountain head.

For you have more than Falstaff's mirth,
  Nor less than Hamlet's teen;
" Wilt weep for Hecuba " – and then
  With laughter shake the scene.

One of God's players playing out
  With zest a weary part;
Teaching the sad world how to smile
  With strokes of genial art;

Launching the scorn that blasts the knave,
The jest that flays the fool,
And by the right divine of wit
Giving a nation rule.

Laugh on, laugh on, dear Wit and Sage,
The roaring crowds above;
Yet keep for your own chosen few
The Poet of their love.[11]

---

[11] *The Papyrus* (February 1908), p. 22.

# ROOSEVELT AND THE MUCKRAKERS

Of all Dunne's friendships after leaving Chicago, none was as important to him as that of the President of the United States. Some of Theodore Roosevelt's enemies liked to say that the President cultivated Dunne because he feared that scourge of princes, Mr. Dooley. It seems that Dunne himself suspected this at first, which accounts for his reluctance to accept Roosevelt's friendship. Surely no factor was more important in removing this suspicion than the good temper with which Roosevelt, from " Alone in Cubia " on, accepted Dooley's satire of the Governor and President. For Dunne, with his own suspicions and his integrity as a journalist constantly before him, never pulled his punches on a single one of the President's policies. From the beginning Dooley had taken the popular attitude of prideful tolerance of Roosevelt, personally, and this became more marked as Dunne knew the President better. Mr. Dooley would and could give many reasons why " a lot iv us likes Tiddy Rosenfelt that wudden't iver be sispicted iv votin' f'r him." More typical were hilarious exaggerations of Roosevelt's doings, such as the account of the reprimand to General Miles. Mr. Dooley would say of Roosevelt's campaign methods: "An' whin Thaydore Rosenfelt kisses a baby thousands iv mothers in all corners iv th' land hear th' report an' th' baby knows its been kissed an' bears th' hon'rable scar through life. Twinty years fr'm now th' counthry will be full iv young fellows lookin' as though they'd grajated fr'm a German college." [1]

One of the most interesting exchanges between Dunne and Roosevelt was over the American-Irish. Peter Dunne was his father's son, with no sentimental love for the English. This sentiment was not blind; for Dunne in his Chicago days had enjoyed satirizing the professional Irish. John F. Finerty, editor of *The Citizen* and sometime Congressman, who was always making capital of the Irish cause, appeared in the Dooley stories in a friendly but still critical light. Especially Dunne liked to make fun of the manner in which Finerty conceived of his duties as Congressman as centering upon promoting the Irish Independence cause. "Well, glory be, th' times has changed since me friend Jawn Finerty come out iv th' House iv Riprisintatives; an' whin some wan ast him what was goin' on, he says, 'Oh, nawthin' at all but some damned American business.'" The talk that began with the Spanish War about the Anglo-Saxon allegiance was a regular object of Dunne's derision. The subservience of the Anglo-Americans, especially the many he found in financial and academic circles,

1 *Chicago Record-Herald*, October 20, 1907.

roused his Irish nationality, and no notable manifestation of the trend developed without a satirical Dooley essay following to laugh it out of countenance.

One instance was the use of the idea as expressing the meaning of the Republican victory in the presidential campaign of 1904. Mr. Dooley appeared with comment on "The 'Anglo-Saxon' Triumph." Joseph Choate, American Ambassador to Great Britain, was frequently satirized by Dunne for his Anglophilism, and here Dooley remarked: ". . . th' king sint f'r Ambassadure Choate, who came as fast as his hands an' knees wud carry him." Then Dooley described a typical American political campaign in which the Irish did all the work in electing a Silas Higgins president, and, after his election, Higgins proceeded to give all the offices and honors to men of like background, leaving out the Irish politicians who did the actual work of electing him. Then Dooley switched to a Harvard and Yale football game with teams made up of boys of Irish descent, "an' that night Prisidint Hadley or Prisidint Eliot makes an addhress at th' king's birthday dinner, an' rejoices in our interest in Anglo-Saxon spoorts, an' congratylates th' wurruld that hereafter if England has a war we will have a chance to do most iv th' fightin' an' pay half th' money." After reading it, Roosevelt, who knew it was directed in part at him, wrote to Dunne in self-defense. For himself he denied any such discrimination in politics, and any pro-English feeling.[2] Dunne's reply is revealing as to his own thought on the sub-

[2] This letter has been published in Joseph Bucklin Bishop: *Theodore Roosevelt and His Time*, I (New York, 1920), 346–48.

ject, and like everything else on which there is an adequate check, it squares precisely with what he was writing in dialect.

. . . I cannot wait until I see you to make some reply to the kind but firm whaling you administered to Mr. Dooley. In the first place, let me disavow at once the slightest purpose to create bad feeling between the Hogans and Rafferties and the Saltonstalls and Witherspoons. It would be useless to attempt it. The ideal of the young Irishman of this country is the straight American character. This is perhaps no more than to say that one good American likes another good American, but in the case of men of Irish descent this attachment is much more marked than among Germans or Englishmen or people of other nationalities. You may be sure that straight Irishmen (I mean by that, of course, Americans with Irish blood) will never quarrel with straight Americans. But it is straight Americans that they like, not dilute Englishmen — the dudes around New York and the enfeebled literary men around Cambridge and New Haven. I ought to be the last man to be accused of disliking the descendants of that enormous shipload that landed at Plymouth Rock. I am ascended from them myself through my son. . . .

I suppose my joking was rather heavy. I never suspected that there was personal or social discrimination against Irishmen in the universities. I know better. But I would like to teach the young Irishmen of this country that they owe much to Ireland and that it is no part of their duty to accept without protest the social and political campaign in the Eastern states among university professors and associations of wholesale pawnbrokers to create an "Anglo Saxon alliance." I am not an Anglophobiac. I hope I am not a "phobiac" on any subject, but I resent the present tendency: first, because I think it is very dangerous for this country; and secondly, because I believe it has created a general impression in England and Ireland that the century-old sympathy of this country for Ireland has disappeared. You say, my dear Mr. Roosevelt, that you feel a sincere friendliness for England. That must mean the English government, and I hope you will forgive me for saying that I do not see how you can hold such a sentiment. If in the individual, in such men as you mention in your postscript, you hate and despise crookedness and cowardice and injustice and insincerity and inefficiency how can you like a government that has shown all these things in its dealings with other governments and especially in its dealings with us? I cannot. I dislike and distrust the English government and the classes that control it because I am of Irish blood, because I have suffered in my own family from their cruelty, and especially because I believe they are as much the enemies of this country to-day as they were one hundred years ago, forty years ago or ten years ago. Whatever I can do to prevent the progress of this foolish partnership, I will do with all my heart. Probably it will not be much, but I take consolation in the fact that some pretty big follies have been laughed away in their time.

As for the point about Irishmen holding office, I simply wanted to emphasize the fact that Irishmen are the most unsuccessful politicians in the country. Although they are about all there is to politics in the North between elections, there is not, with one exception, a single representative Irish man in any important cabinet, diplomatic, judicial or administrative office that I know about. I am not sorry for this. I think they are better off without office. I would not want an appointive office myself, but appointment to office is one of the recognized ways of demonstrating political friendship. In this respect every administration has managed to dissemble its love even if it has not actually kicked us downstairs.[3]

But this was the only exchange on the subject, and it seldom appears in Dunne's writing except in his frequent satires on the Anglo-Saxon allegiance. More important to both Dunne and Roosevelt was the central problem of domestic politics.

[3] December 1, 1904. Roosevelt mss.

As part of the cutting edge of the reform movement during the first decade of the century, the public was treated to a great campaign of exposure of corruption in public life. The leaders in the movement proudly accepted the title of muckrakers, after Roosevelt had applied John Bunyan's concept in *The Pilgrim's Progress* to the more spectacular and less objective of the critics. There had been, of course, muckraking before, and some would have classified a few of the early Dooley essays as of this type. Certainly F. U. Adams's periodical in Chicago in the late nineties was of this character. But the new movement was a journalistic response to a widespread public demand for the exposure of fraud. *McClure's Magazine* was the first to see its commercial possibilities, and with Lincoln Steffens, Ida Tarbell, and Ray Stannard Baker as its stars, it took the lead with rigidly factual research studies on governmental and business corruption. As a natural sequel to the much more sharply pointed editorial policy that Norman Hapgood had brought to *Collier's*, that periodical soon followed the lead of *McClure's*. Samuel Hopkins Adams's exposures of fraud in proprietary medicines and the food industries was its first contribution. Soon Mark Sullivan's exposures of the interests' power in Congress made *Collier's* the leader in the field of national politics. In addition to these, there was a host of minor writers and publications, whose work varied exceedingly in its accuracy and balance.

Dunne had close relations to the movement which were both personal and professional. Moreover, his relations to many of the individuals who were engaged in the work was close, for the group included not only Collier and Hapgood, but also such old Chicago friends as Brand Whitlock, who, as an active reform politician, was pointing out the better way in his work in Toledo. Perhaps Dunne's principal relation to the movement was one that neither he nor his friends recognized, which was that his Dooley articles had helped to create a reading public which was ready for realistic writing of the muckraking type; writing that was less genial and tolerant than Mr. Dooley, and more directly pointed toward specific evils and policies.

Beyond this Dunne's relation to the movement is peculiar, because he had gone through the intellectual development of many of the agents of exposure six or seven years earlier, and none of them, not even the most philosophical, Steffens, would ever go much further in his analysis of the causes of political corruption than Dunne had gone in his *Chicago Post* articles of 1897. Consequently, it is not surprising that Dunne failed to share the astonishment and horror that gave the necessary emotion-arousing undertone to the work of most of the muckrakers.

There were some exceptions to Dunne's usual geniality. One was his treatment of the corrupt management of the life-insurance companies that Charles Evans Hughes was exposing in 1905. Mr. Dooley satirized the testimony of the officials of these companies under Hughes's cross-examination in a way that was far from humorous; it was a biting, cutting attack, without a real smile in the long essay, which did not spare even such a figure as J. P. Morgan. But there were things in the general work of the muckrake group that he did not like. The most prominent of these was the anti-democratic assumption made by some of the writers, especially editorial writers commenting on the political corruption brought to light, that political officials were naturally corrupt, and what was needed was more businessmen and business methods in politics. He attacked this silly assumption a month after his blistering of the insurance companies, again in *Collier's*.

"Ivry year, whin th' public conscience is aroused as it niver was befure, me frinds on th' palajeems iv our liberties an' records iv our crimes calls f'r business men to swab out our governmint with business methods. . . . We must injooce th' active, conscientious young usurers fr'm Wall Sthreet to take an inthrest in public affairs. Th' poolrooms is open. To thim gilded haunts iv vice th' poor wurrukin' man carries his weekly wage, an' thries to increase it enough so that he can give it to his wife without blushin'. Down with th' poolrooms, says I. But how? says ye. Who betther, says I, thin th' prisidint iv th' Westhren Union Tillygraft Comp'ny, who knows where th' poolrooms are. . . .

"Yes, Hinnissy, me ideel iv a great statesman is a grocer with elastic bands on his shirt-sleeves, ladlin' public policies out iv a bar'l with a wooden scoop. How much betther wud Wash'nton an' Lincoln have been if they'd known enough to inthrajooce business methods into pollyticks. George was a good man, but he niver thought iv settlin' th' trouble be compromisin' on a job as colonyal governor. . . . 'Tis sthrange people can't see it th' way I do. There's John Cassidy. Ye know him. He's a pollytician or grafter. Th' same thing. His graft is to walk downtown to th' City Hall at eight o'clock ivry mornin' an' set on a high stool ontil five in th' afthernoon addin' up figures. Ivry week twinty dollars iv th' taxpayers' money, twinty dollars wrung fr'm ye an' me, Hinnissy, is handed to this boodler. He used to get twinty-five in a clothin'-store but he is a romantic young fellow, an' he thought 'twud be a fine thing to be a statesman. . . ."

And after this satire of the usual argument against politicians, Cassidy is quoted:

"We may be a tough gang over at th' City Hall. A foreign name always looks tough whin it's printed in a reform iditoryal. But, thank th' Lord, no man iver accused us iv bein' life-insurance prisidints. . . . Th' pollytician grafts on th' public an' his enemies. It don't seem anny worse to him thin winnin' money on a horse-race. He doesn't see th' writin' iv th' man he takes th' coin fr'm. But these here high financiers grafts on th' public an' their inimies, but principally on their frinds. Dump ye'er pardner is th' quickest way to th' money. Mulcahy [the political boss] wud rather die thin skin a frind that had strung a bet with him. But if Mulcahy was a railroad boss instead iv a pollytical boss he wud first wurruk up th' confidence iv his frinds in him, thin he wud sell thim his stock, thin he wud tell thim th' road was goin' to th' dogs, an' make thim give it back to him f'r nawthin'; thin he wud get out a fav'rable report, an' sell th' stock to thim again. An' he'd go on doin' this till he'd made enough to be ilicted prisidint iv a good government club. . . . In time I hope to see th' same honesty, good faith, an' efficiency in th' Life Insurance Comp'nies an' th' Thrusts that we see now in th' administration iv Tammany Hall."

There were other things about the muckrakers that Dunne did not like. He obviously did not like the seeming blackmail which marked the writing of the speculator Thomas W. Lawson in *Everybody's*. When Lawson was in the midst of his attacks upon his recent friend, high finance, Mark Twain sent for Dunne, and in the profanity to which he would resort when angered he asked: "Can't you write a Dooley about that —— Lawson and the —— publisher of that —— magazine? I have tried to flatten out these ——s. I have written thousands of words but I am always just cussing. If I could keep my faculty for humor uppermost I'd laugh the dogs out of the country. But I can't. I get too mad."[4] He went on to tell Dunne that most of the attack was directed against Henry H. Rogers, who had taken over Twain's finances when Twain was bankrupt and had put the author beyond the need of financial worries by his good management; and now, when Rogers was under an unfair attack, Twain would like to help him. Dunne answered that while he did not know Rogers, he could not bring himself to defend any of the Standard Oil crowd; and he tried to mollify Twain by the argument that Rogers would prefer not to be defended publicly.

Dunne was not disturbed by the fact that Lawson was telling tales about the methods he and his former associates had used; but he was disturbed by the constant assumption of many of the writers that these evil conditions were characteristic only of democratic government in the United States. In a Dooley article on the muckrakers themselves, he satirized the excited element in a tolerant way, not even sparing *Collier's*, in which the article was published, and made fun of the tendency to despair of democracy. The reference to "Th' use iv Burglars as Burglar Alarums" is a reference to Lawson which should not be overlooked, and perhaps "Graft be an old Grafter" is

[4] Recollections of Peter Dunne.

meant to apply to him also. " Idarem " is, of course, Ida M. Tarbell.

" It looks to me," said Mr. Hennessy, " as though this counthry was goin' to th' divvle."

" Put down that magazine," said Mr. Dooley. " Now d'ye feel betther? I thought so. . . . Here ye are. Last edition. Just out. Full account iv th' Crimes iv Incalculated. Did ye read Larsen last month on ' Th' use iv Burglars as Burglar Alarums '? Good, was it? . . . Read Idarem on Jawn D.; she's a lady, but she's got th' punch. Graft ivrywhere. ' Graft in Congress,' ' Graft in th' Supreme Court,' ' Graft be an old Grafter,' ' Graft in Its Relations to th' Higher Life,' be Dock Eliot; ' Th' Homeeric Legend an' Graft; Its Cause an' Effect; Are They th' Same? Yes an' No,' be Norman Slapgood.

" An' so it goes, Hinnissy, till I'm that blue, discouraged, an' broken-hearted I cud go to th' edge iv th' wurruld an' jump off. . . .

" Do I think it's all as bad as that? Well, Hinnissy, now that ye ask me, an' seein' that Chris'mas is comin' on, I've got to tell ye that this counthry, while wan iv th' worst in th' wurruld, is about as good as th' next if it ain't a shade betther. But we're wan iv th' greatest people in th' wurruld to clean house, an' th' way we like best to clean th' house is to burn it down. We come home at night an' find that th' dure has been left open an' a few mosquitoes or life-insurance prisidints have got in, an' we say: ' This is turr'ble. We must get rid iv these here pests.' An' we take an axe to thim. We desthroy a lot iv furniture an' kill th' canary bird, th' cat, th' cuckoo clock, an' a lot iv other harmless insects, but we'll fin'lly land th' mosquitoes. If an Englishman found mosquitoes in his house he'd first thry to kill thim, an' whin he didn't succeed he'd say: ' What pleasant little humming-burrds they are. Life wud be very lonesome without thim,' an' he'd domesticate thim, larn thim to sing ' Gawd Save th' King,' an' call his house Mosquito Lodge. . . .

"Th' noise ye hear is not th' first gun iv a rivolution. It's on'y th' people iv th' United States batin' a carpet. Ye object to th' smell? That's nawthin'. We use sthrong disinfectants here. A Frinchman or an Englishman cleans house be sprinklin' th' walls with cologne; we chop a hole in th' flure an' pour in a kag iv chloride iv lime. Both are good ways. It depinds on how long ye intind to live in th' house. What were those shots? That's th' housekeeper killin' a couple iv cockroaches with a Hotchkiss gun. Who is that yellin'? That's our ol' frind High Finance bein' compelled to take his annual bath. Th' housecleanin' season is in full swing, an' there's a good deal iv dust in th' air; but I want to say to thim neighbors iv ours, who're peekin' in an' makin' remarks about th' amount iv rubbish, that over in our part iv th' wurruld we don't sweep things undher th' sofa."

President Roosevelt wrote Dunne in enthusiastic praise of this article as well as of the one on the life-insurance scandals. Dunne replied with an exact statement of his own attitude:

I have just come back from Chicago to find your very kind letter. I need not tell you how gratified I am to know that you liked the articles. Perhaps the insurance one was too bitter — but I felt bitterly about these people. I can sympathize with a fellow who breaks a statute and takes his chances of jail, but these smug operators who keep inside the law and deliberately violate their implied trusteeship oughtn't to expect much mercy here or hereafter. They accept a confidence that springs from a well-advertised reputation for uprightness and then lightly violate the obligation at the expense of a lot of poor devils. The job is one for a hangman, not a humorist. I liked the other article better. I am so tired of the perpetual scolding in the newspapers and magazines. Our public men and even our business men compare very favorably with those of any other country. Steffens and the rest of our friends in the literature of exposure seem to forget that it is the greater facility of investigation and not the greater amount of crime in this country that makes us appear so bad in comparison with England and France. Besides, as I said, one of the greatest troubles of the world is that it is infested with human beings for whom we ought to feel a little reflected self pity. Whenever I see the worst of these rascals marching through McClure's or Collier's, I feel like saying, " But for the grace of God, there goes John Bunyan." When I wrote the article I had particularly in mind the unpunished scandals in England and France — the cases of Hooley, the Guinea Pigs, the Army Remounts, the South African forage and Lord Dufferin's connection with the Whittaker Wright case in England; and, among others, the Wilson-Grevy case in France — but all this is too much like preaching. William Allen White has promised to take up the " merry sunshine " work in a more serious and effective fashion, and I look to him to save our countrymen from the suicide which is the logical consequence of believing all we read now-a-days.

I would also respectfully suggest that you give the Nelson Miles reprimand with a coal scuttle to that military genius who has been telling the world that an army can only be managed by an autocracy. It might be a good plan to have Fortescue pound him over the head with a singlestick while you read him the history of the Russian army.[5]

Dunne reviewed the most effective of all pieces of muckrake literature, Upton Sinclair's novel *The Jungle*, with its revoltingly realistic picture of the meat-packing industry in Chicago. Although the essay contained a derisive account of the plot of the novel, its main substance was a hilarious comedy which rang the changes on the packer's sins. Lorimer was a senator from Illinois and leader in the fight

[5] December 28, 1905. Roosevelt mss.

against a better meat-inspection law, all in the name of the farmer, of course. As for the packers, before *The Jungle* came along:

"If they had a blind man in th' Health Departmint, a few competint frinds on th' Fedhral bench, an' Farmer Bill Lorimer to protect th' cattle inthrests iv th' Great West, they cared not who made th' novels iv our counthry."

Dunne ended the essay:

"They ought to make thim ate their own meat," said Mr. Hennessy, warmly.

"I suggisted that," said Mr. Dooley, "but Hogan says they'd fall back on th' Constitution. He says th' Constitution f'rbids crool an' unusual punishmints."

Mr. Dooley's description of the effect of the book on President Roosevelt is one of Dunne's most effective burlesques.

"Tiddy was toying with a light breakfast an' idly turnin' over th' pages iv th' new book with both hands. Suddenly he rose fr'm th' table, an' cryin': 'I'm pizened,' begun throwin' sausages out iv th' window. Th' ninth wan sthruck Sinitor Biv'ridge on th' head an' made him a blond. It bounced off, exploded, an' blew a leg off a secret-service agent, an' th' scatthred fragmints desthroyed a handsome row iv ol' oak trees. Sinitor Biv'ridge rushed in thinkin' that th' Prisidint was bein' assassynated be his devoted followers in th' Sinit, an' discovered Tiddy engaged in a hand-to-hand conflict with a potted ham. Th' Sinitor fr'm Injyanny, with a few well-directed wurruds, put out th' fuse an' rendered th' missile harmless. Since thin th' Prisidint, like th' rest iv us, has become a viggytaryan, an' th' diet has so changed his disposition that he is writin' a book called *Suffer in Silence*, didycated to Sinitor Aldrich."

Some months later, Dunne had Mr. Dooley discussing the President in his usual affectionate fun-making vein:

"He's not doin' much. Ye seldom hear iv him. Whether 'tis old-age creepin' on – he must be all iv twenty-four – or th' responsibilities iv th' office I don't know, but he's kind iv quieted down. Now ye take last week. With th' exception iv bouncin' a few indispinsible cabinet officers, invintin' a battleship, writin' an article on th' sports iv th' ancient Greeks, lecturin' th' Presbyterryan Church on infant damnation, refereein' a poker bet between wan iv his old companyons in arrums an' th' estate iv another, describin' th' delights iv ocean travel to th' navy, passin' out a bunch iv legal tips to th' Supreme Court, divisin' a tackles back play f'r football, an' sindin' a recipe f'r preparin' pie plant f'r th' table to th' Ladies Cookin' Club in Omaha, ye might say he hardly done annythin' last week." [6]

Mr. Dooley's readers enjoyed such fooling, and Dunne thought correctly that Roosevelt did. Certainly Roosevelt was being most generous in his invitations to the White House and in praise of Dunne's writing. Perhaps because of a steady tone of derision at Roosevelt's military policy, the President had the Dunnes with a small group of personal guests at the review of the Atlantic Fleet in September, 1906. When Mr. Hennessy had asked Mr. Dooley: "D'ye think a foreign fleet cud capture this counthry?" the philosopher had answered: "Not unless it was operated be a throlley. Supposin' ye an' I had throuble, Hinnissy, an' both iv us was armed with bricks an' ye was on roller skates an' I was on th' top iv a house, how much chance wud ye have again me? Ships is good

[6] *New York Times*, December 16, 1906.

to fight other ships. That's all. I'd sooner be behind a bank iv mud thin in th' finest ship in th' wurruld."

At one of his luncheons with the President, Dunne was responsible for what became for a time his most widely quoted bit of wit. Vice-President Fairbanks was not the type of public leader for whom Dunne would feel much sympathy, and through Mr. Dooley he had satirized his unctuous political qualities on several occasions. At the luncheon in question, Roosevelt was expressing his desire to take a trip in one of the Navy's new submarines, and several guests remonstrated that these were too dangerous for the President to assume such a needless risk. Finally Roosevelt appealed to Dunne for support in his plan, asking if Dunne did not think it were safe for the President to go. Dunne, as we are assured, replied: "Well, you really shouldn't do it — unless you take Fairbanks with you."

Because of some approval of Mr. Dooley's comments on the President in the wrong quarters, Dunne raised the question directly with Roosevelt:

Now that I am at my desk, I want to express the hope that you have not been displeased by my recent unmannerly jibes and jeers. You have always been so good-natured about Dooley that it never occurred to me that he might carry a joke too far until recently when I was congratulated by some people who are as objectionable to me as they are to you. Now, I am very strongly of the opinion that the character of a man's work is accurately reflected by the character of its admirers, and I am disturbed by the congratulations of Wall Street. I hope I am wrong, for, as I have often told you, you are my most valuable asset. Without you, the roof falls in, the mortgage is foreclosed on the old homestead, and I see my seed begging bread. In making up my inventory I list my possessions this way: —

| | |
|---|---|
| Roosevelt | 75% |
| Root | 8% |
| Taft | 6½% |
| German Emperor | 3% |
| Current Topics | 5% |
| Beveridge | ½% |
| The Senate | ¼% |
| Foraker | ⅛% |

But to speak seriously, and not to magnify my office, if I thought my feeble fun was in any way harmful to the present undertakings of your administration I would sacrifice my necessities. But I cannot think it is — or I could not until I found the enemy so cheerful about it. . . .[7]

Dunne endeavored to keep Roosevelt on good terms with his friends Collier and Hapgood. "I have a sincere regard for Norman Hapgood," he wrote, "and am sorry you do not like him. I suppose he has given you a good reason. As for Robert Collier, he has done more than any other person I know to promote the purposes of clean and honest journalism, and that it seems to me is one of the greatest necessities of the hour."[8] Roosevelt was especially angered at some of Hapgood's editorials, and Dunne went to some lengths to make the editor's faults seem of less magnitude to the President. He induced Roosevelt to invite Collier to the White House, and tried to bring the two men together intellectually. He had great faith in the social qualities of Collier, and felt confident that acquaintance would be followed by friendship.

[7] January 7, 1907. Roosevelt mss.

[8] September 11, 1906. Roosevelt mss.

And he had a similar feeling about Roosevelt. When the President invited Miss Tarbell to meet him and discuss certain political matters, Dunne is said to have remarked: "If the President can't convince the lady, he'll vamp her." [9]

More and more Dunne was being caught up by the better part of the muckrake movement. He helped to promote a luncheon in New York to raise money to aid Brand Whitlock in his campaign for the mayoralty of Toledo, and contributed generously himself. Whitlock's success must have brought back to Dunne memories of some of the old nights in the Whitechapel Club, and the political and literary discussions which were their most serious feature. If not, Whitlock's note, after his election was assured, would have recalled these memories: "Yesterday I had a telegram from Tom Powers asking me to appoint him Water Commissioner, you Police Commissioner, and Griz [Adams] Street Commissioner. You may have anything you want and whenever you all or any of you can come here I am ready with the keys to the city and willing to take off the lid." [10] And Whitlock went on for six years of brilliant administration as mayor of a fortunate city.

The next year, 1906, the *McClure's* group of muckrakers withdrew from that publication, and, with its managing editor, John S. Phillips, took over *The American Magazine*, recently created out of the older *Leslie's*. Ida Tarbell, Ray Stannard Baker, and Steffens asked Dunne and William Allen White to go in

---

[9] Cale Young Rice: *Bridging the Years* (New York, 1939), p. 186.
[10] November 18, 1905.

with them, as editors and owners of the periodical. The two outsiders accepted, although White remained in Kansas. Dunne discontinued his irregular contributions to *Collier's*, revived once more his newspaper syndicate of Dooley articles, and prepared to assist actively in editing the monthly periodical. He conceived of his place in the galaxy of stars as somewhat of a brake upon the greater enthusiasm and energy of his colleagues for reform.

As if to celebrate the new work or to end fittingly a period of low productivity, he permitted Harper's to bring out a new selection of the dialect pieces written since 1902 under the title *Dissertations by Mr. Dooley*. Moreover, Harper's took over the plates of the five older books and republished them all in a uniform binding.

Dunne's increased productivity in 1905 had provoked applause from many sources. F. A. James had entitled a laudatory article about him, "The Laugh-Maker of the Century."[11] The reviews of the new book were uniformly congratulatory, but, generally, it was taken as a matter of course. Most reviewers contented themselves by quoting some of its best lines. Mr. Dooley had reached the stage where he was accepted as an institution, not quite as productive as he should be perhaps, but still everyman's philosopher without rival.

[11] *The Republic,* May 13, 1905.

CHAPTER XIII

## IN THE INTERPRETER'S HOUSE

THERE were several incentives behind Dunne's joining the group of associates on *The American Magazine*. Perhaps the main one was a partly unconscious search for some medium of expression other than dialect. The editorial writing for *Collier's* and the editorship of the *Telegraph* were early responses to this search, and they are evidence of the damning up to some degree of the springs which supplied Mr. Dooley. Dunne had written to Roosevelt in 1905: "Two or three times I have been tempted to stop writing because I felt I had taken out of my head all that the good God had put in it, when along came a pleasant letter from you to cheer me up and hurry me on."[1]

Then there was a strong implication in some of the critical comment that Mr. Dooley was, after all, journalistic in character, and from an author of Dunne's demonstrated powers something of a more permanent nature should be expected. In 1903 Howells had

[1] December 28. Roosevelt mss.

raised the question of "how long he expects to keep on the mask of Mr. Dooley, and why he does not come into the open with a bold, vigorous and incisive satire of our politicians and their methods." [2] When this was added to the doubts which Dunne himself had expressed about Mr. Dooley, it was natural that he should want to try writing in a different form; success here might be a more permanent achievement, and at least it would prove that Mr. Dooley was not the limit of Dunne's literary powers.

But Dunne had not sought to associate himself with the group; the solicitation had come from the other side, and it began at the very time when he had satirized the muckrakers in *Collier's*. Ray Baker was an old friend from Chicago journalism, but not a very close friend. There is no evidence that Dunne and Steffens were ever very friendly. John S. Phillips and Albert Boyden, the managing editor and his assistant, were much closer to him. William Allen White and Dunne had a mutual admiration for each other's work, but saw little of each other at any time. Miss Tarbell was closer to Dunne than any of the group, perhaps, and she cultivated him in a forthright way from the beginning.

There was not much difference in fundamental political philosophy within the group. Like Dunne, Miss Tarbell, Phillips, Baker, and White were not promoters of any program for changing society. They believed in democracy, individual economic enterprise, and liberal ideals. Even Steffens's thinking

[2] "Certain of the Chicago School of Fiction," *North American Review*, vol. 176 (May 1903), 746.

could be included in these categories at this time, although the signs of change were clearer in his writing than in that of the others. None of them had Dunne's fatalistic tendency and his lack of any substantial optimism about the improvement of society; but they could all agree upon a program of telling the truth about American life and letting democratic processes make adjustments in the light of that truth, told honestly and unsensationally.

Dunne's own work on the publication was not very definitely settled except that he was to write Dooley essays for it, apart from his newspaper syndicate, and contribute to the editorial section. Miss Tarbell had assured him before he joined: "I know you would be of great use to us editorially. What I don't see is just how to work the thing out to your advantage. I think the relation would have to grow; we fumble a lot here in our efforts to keep straight. We are pretty brutal and skeptical with one another but you know us well enough to know that all this is perhaps the unavoidable pain of producing a thing which will really be sane and worth while, and the disillusion resulting from nothing ever coming up to our hopes. I believe if we could get down to some kind of a working basis that you would like us and believe in us just as we do in you."[3]

In addition to the dialect essays and editorials, Dunne shared the general editorial burdens of policy decisions and the search for talent. The names of some of his old Chicago friends appeared in the magazine during the next six years. Horace Taylor and John

[3] January 19, 1906. F. P. Dunne letters.

McCutcheon illustrated his Dooley stories; F. U. Adams contributed fiction; and Henry Ten Eyck White supplied an interesting feature on horse racing. Beyond these, Dunne worked to induce his literary friends to contribute articles; his wealthy friends to invest money; and his journalistic friends to help with technical advice on circulation methods.

As for the general policies, Dunne's ideas were already well known and for the most part they were agreed to by other members of the staff. Only one inter-staff controversy was important enough to leave a record, and that was between Steffens and Dunne over an article on Hearst. Dunne knew Hearst slightly, and knew his right-hand man in New York, Arthur Brisbane, very well. Dunne felt no antagonism towards Hearst's stylistic innovations in journalism. He had used many of them in Chicago, and defended their usage. Moreover, Hearst had outbid competitors in New York for the Dooley stories for several years, and had contributed heavily to Dunne's income. But Dunne distrusted Hearst completely. Steffens presented for his first article in the *American* one on the publisher. When he read it, Dunne saw that the fine public-relations-counsel hand of Brisbane was in every line, and knew at once that Steffens had let himself be duped into a defense of Hearst. Dunne's anger and disgust were thorough-going, and in an editorial conference he opposed printing the article, at least in its present form. Most of the editors were with him, and when Miss Tarbell thought to calm the seething waters with the oil of a changed subject, she asked: " What shall we call the article? "

"Oh," said Phillips, "we'll take a simple title, say, 'William Randolph Hearst, by Lincoln Steffens.'"

"Out of Arthur Brisbane," amended Dunne.

Though the article was published, it was changed so that it bore a closer relation to the discriminating intelligence that was supposed to mark the work of the editors.

For his own department, Dunne had already declared himself on such questions. He had written to William Kent:

One thing I am certain about and that is that the editorials will not be permitted to sink to the level of mere newspaper roastings, simply because we have the ability to roast and the means of doing it, while the victims have neither the means nor the ability to reply. I don't believe in libeling a man merely because he is afraid to begin a libel suit. If I have anything to say about it, our editorial department will continue to discuss all sides of every important question with kindest tolerance and good nature as well as candor.[4]

"Kindest tolerance" was to be Dunne's special contribution to the *American.* For the third issue of the magazine, the Christmas number, he wrote a concluding section for the editorials which illustrates that aspect of his thinking, and the basis of his objection to much in reform movements:

It seems to me — said the Poet — that we are serving up a savory Christmas number — a lament for Jerome, an advertisement for an esteemed contemporary, and an anecdote on lynching in the South. That would be a nice present to be found in the bottom of a stocking. Oh, I know what you think of me. Serious questions are before the people. The

---

[4] November 23, 1906. Copy in F. P. Dunne letters.

final test of civilization is at hand. There must be no laggards. Christmas comes but once a year, and the reformer is sorry it comes so often, because it breaks up with a little twenty-four hours of sunshine the melancholy work of making the world better. I know what my friend, the Enthusiast over there, is saying to himself. He is lamenting the fact that I permit the frivolity of a Christian (or would he say Pagan?) festival to divert me for a day from the cares and anxieties of the Responsible Person. Is there no political meeting in Hoboken or Coharies that I can attend on the night of December 25th, when by the Grace of God I hope to be whittling a turkey? Why should I be beaming down on my well-fed (or soon to be well-fed) children, cracking old jokes, slashing at the savory white meat and probing for the stuffing, when I might be addressing a meeting of the down-trodden in some center of freedom and tyranny? A few enlightened words from me might spur an indignant citizenship to the last superb effort that will land Hans Machsnixaus as coroner, and thus at once abolish poverty, crime, suffering, boodle, graft, disease, Jerome, the *Atlantic Monthly*, and lynching in the South. But I refuse to permit the Christmas feeling that mounts within me to be put aside by any other feeling, human or political. If there is one man at that reform meeting on Christmas night, I say disenfranchise him — strike him from the rolls, deprive him of speech, reform *him* into the shape of a donkey! Nay, if the great Hans Machsnixaus is there himself, if he is anywhere but beside his own Christmas-tree with a fur cap on his head and false white whiskers on his chin, then may he never achieve his crown. May he never hold inquest on me or mine. I agree with you, this is no time for laggards. We must hasten to the toy shops. . . .

Who wants to change this spirit for any other? Who fails to see in it the beginning of all good work in the world? *The spirit of Christmas, the unselfish selfishness of giving happiness and taking it, the desire to do good if it is only for one day, and only toward one's own and the beggar at one's gate, this is the true source of all right improvement. You cannot go to the Patent Office in Washington and take out a patent that will transform men into angels. The way upward, long and tedious as it is, lies through the hearts of men. It has been so since the Founding of the Feast. And nothing has been proved more clearly in the political history of the race than this, that good will to men has done more to improve government than laws and wars.* Let us close down our desks for the year. If you want to find me for another week, I will be in the wonderful little toy shop around the corner.[5]

The editorial work of which Dunne was to have charge was in a section of the magazine which the managing editor, Phillips, had aptly named "In the Interpreter's House," carrying out the Rooseveltian analogy from *The Pilgrim's Progress.* The original plan had been that all associates, and even outsiders, would contribute to this section, and then Dunne would fit and dovetail the contributions into something that would have continuity and coherence. After a few months, it worked out that Dunne was writing most of it; in fact a few years later the periodical announced that he had written more than three-fourths of the material that had gone into the section. The literary form was that of a round table, as that lent itself to contributions from many hands because of the variety of viewpoints presented. In a typical section, the symbolical characters, the Poet, the Philosopher, the Cynic, the Reporter, and the Observer would present different aspects of the same general problem. Whatever the original purpose, there is no evidence that these characters represented different

[5] *The American Magazine,* December 1906.

individuals among the associates, except, perhaps, that Dunne used the Responsible Editor to give the point of view of Phillips. Miss Tarbell recalls that she seldom made the section, Dunne telling her that "you sputter like a woman," [6] but the evidence seems clear from other sources that during the life of the section, she wrote more for it than anyone else except Dunne.

To Peter Dunne, "In the Interpreter's House" was a great opportunity. It was his chance to escape Irish dialect as a medium of expression, to put his thoughts before readers in as pure English as he could write and still not be hampered by the demands of daily journalism. The only restrictions on his writing were such as he made himself.

It matters little who wrote the portions of the "Interpreter's House" that Dunne did not produce himself, for they all presented Dunne's philosophy as already expounded by Mr. Dooley. That did not change, and, if he could duplicate in straight English a fair measure of his literary and popular success with dialect, it would give him an influence that few writers had on public life. But after the first joys of new creation were over, Dunne found it nearly as difficult to write "In the Interpreter's House" as Dooley essays. Miss Tarbell recalls that his labor affected the entire office — "sympathy with what he was going through, fear that his copy would not be on time, eagerness to see it when it came, to know if it was 'one of his best.' But Peter's work was never what he thought it ought to be, and he sought forget-

[6] Ida M. Tarbell: *All in the Day's Work, an Autobiography* (New York, 1939), p. 260.

fulness."[7] And Steffens recalls that although Dunne provided most of the entertainment about the office, "he could not make himself write. I never knew a writer who made such a labor of writing; he seemed to hate it; he certainly ran away from it whenever he could."[8]

There was no laziness in Dunne's failure to write more — about that his colleagues on *The American* were agreed. It was compounded of two things, a perfectionism that went beyond all usual limits, and a psychosis about the deadline, which made it nearly impossible for him to write according to a schedule. It was not so much the work of writing once it was under way, as it was the labor of getting started satisfactorily. Phillips or Baker would go into Dunne's office at the editorial rooms near lunch time and find the floor covered with sheets of paper, each of which had a few sentences written on it, each an unsatisfactory start of an article. If he succeeded in completing the first page before discarding it, he usually finished with fair rapidity. In one of the early "Interpreter's House" essays, in which Dunne discussed the nature of literary inspiration, he quoted and paraphrased the explanations of great artists to develop an interpretation which was, in essence, his own experience. The key to literary inspiration was the power of improvisation. The degree "to which the act of improvising brings out of the storeroom of the brain the best that has been hidden there, the degree of lightness and certainty with which it can penetrate the most remote and se-

[7] *All in the Day's Work*, p. 261.

[8] *The Autobiography of Lincoln Steffens* (New York, 1937), p. 537.

cret caverns of the mind and produce the long-buried and half-forgotten treasure is the final measure of genius." "The fact . . . is that the actual writing is not hard but the beginning is painful to the point of tragedy — the attempt to produce the state in which work of an imaginative nature can be done, that terrible dislocation of mind in which he is capable of receiving what is called 'inspiration.'" This apparently outside force is not his to command at will, and there is always the terrifying fear that it will fail him. "He knows how small is the part that really represents him. His learning, his ordinary imagination, the disciplined forces that he can pleasurably summon to his aid, may construct a clumsy cargo boat useful in navigating the slow canals of contemporary literature, but it is not until the wind blows off the mountain of the gods that he is carried far into the unknown sea." [9]

Still, with all this trouble, Dunne turned out a reasonably large amount of copy during these years. There was the "Interpreter's House" each month for *The American*, as well as a Dooley article for many issues of the magazine. In addition there was a newspaper syndicate receiving weekly Dooley articles during substantial portions of the years from 1906 to 1914. These were not maintained with great regularity, but the quality was high. Indeed, some of his finest dialect essays were written while he was with *The American Magazine*.

There were traces of Dooley expressions in the nondialect essays, which were all characterized by Dooley wisdom. But the differences go far to show what a

[9] May 1907.

struggle it had been to express the breadth of wisdom which Dunne possessed through means afforded by Mr. Dooley. To keep Dooley in character, Dunne had to attribute any superior knowledge to the bookish Hogan, or the spiritual as well as learned Father Kelly, and this was, to say the least, awkward. These restrictions were only slightly less in the brief editorial paragraphs he had written for *Collier's* in 1902. But the "Interpreter's House" was a good basis for a broad humanistic philosophy, and Dunne used it effectively.

The essays ordinarily concerned either public affairs or political theory, and much less often literary matters. Without exception they were marked not only by great learning, but also by the penetrating wisdom that had made Mr. Dooley famous. Dunne never attempted to be humorous here, but now and then a Dooley-like line would creep in, as when he described a part of New York society as "scions of old nobility dating from the first Cleveland administration."[10] A comparison of an essay on socialism which he wrote within a few months of a Dooley essay on the same subject indicates clearly some of the advantages of the new form; for it penetrated the heart of the matter more deeply, and it was even fairer to opposing points of view — a thing that Mr. Dooley in his true character could hardly be. But it also had the weakness of the more formal essays as compared with the dialogues of the famous saloon-keeper. It was too learned for popular reading, and did not possess that type of wit which made Mr. Dooley the favorite of

[10] May 1907.

millions. More clearly than in the Dooley essay, he could set up the strength and weaknesses of socialism as compared with that of the society he knew and approved. Its strength was that it had a remedy. " The old practitioner has shaken his head and said: ' No, it is incurable; poverty, like cancer, defies human remedies; the best we can do is to make the sufferer as comfortable as possible. . . . No wonder the patient turns with joyful expectancy to the new and irregular physician. He may be a quack . . . but he says he has a remedy and it is a remedy, not a lecture on the impossibilities, that people are always demanding in politics." Socialism's weakness, Dunne held, was that it demanded the surrender of thrift, one of the oldest and most fundamental virtues. " But," he warned, " because thrift is a virtue, it does not justify men in exalting greed. The great trouble with the man who has annihilated Socialism is that he believes he has justified piracy. And because we have proved the divine use of thrift in the scheme of life furnishes no reason why society may not regulate the trough of trade so that the hog cannot get all four feet into it." [11]

For the most part, however, the " Interpreter's House " commented on public affairs of the day. Dunne covered the conventions and campaigns with Mr. Dooley, and also commented upon them in the " Interpreter's House." When Roosevelt left the Presidency in March, 1909, Dunne spent some time with him in talking over his administration, and then summarized it in his section of *The American*. He did not overstate the case, but his tribute to Roosevelt's

---

[11] June 1907.

statesmanship was high. He was an example Dunne used to defend the politician as a type. " Every politician is not a good administrator, but every good administrator is a politician." The article ended with the admonition that may have only referred to Roosevelt's trip to Africa or it may have had deeper implications. " Good-by, Teddy, take kerr of yourself." [12] A year before Dunne had taken a hand in the discussion of what the President should do to occupy himself after he retired, and had Mr. Hennessy ask Mr. Dooley: " What wud ye do if ye were an ex-Prisident? " " Well," said Mr. Dooley, " if I wanted something rale hard to do, something that wud keep me busy an' take up all me time to th' end iv me days, I'd thry to be Prisident again." [13]

The editorial associates considered the " Interpreter's House " and Dunne's Dooley articles in *The American* as being among its strongest features. One or the other was occasionally made the leading article in the magazine, when it had something of special importance. When Dunne sent in from his summer vacation a Dooley story on " Uplifting the Farmer," Phillips gave it a big play, calling attention to it by declaring that " never, at least in our time, has the philosophy of happiness and unhappiness been so perfectly stated." [14]

The most notable development in the " Interpreter's House " was the creation of a modern counterpart for the Worldly Wiseman of *The Pilgrim's*

---

[12] March 1909.

[13] *New York Times,* June 23, 1907.

[14] November 1908.

*Progress*. Dunne made him a full-fledged character drawn from his wide acquaintance among leaders in business and finance. He appeared as a member of the round table to damn himself and his fellows by making his system of belief clear. Dunne was careful not to overdo it; his Mr. Worldly Wiseman was wise and sharp and not ungenerous in a paternal sort of way. "Please don't think of Mr. Worldly Wiseman as the pursy city man of Dickens tales, brought up in a counting-house and gorging himself on turtle fat at the Lord Mayor's banquets. He can show you a degree from Harvard." Physically, and mentally too, he is a superior specimen. "Don't underestimate him. That is the greatest of mistakes." [15]

What Dunne did with the character was to make him convict himself of as unqualified a belief in a system of aristocracy as if he had been a German Junker or a British Tory of the eighteenth century, albeit through the superficial forms of democracy. "They [the people] want to be jollied," Mr. Worldly Wiseman declared in his forthright manner. "They expect to be told every month that they are the finest things ever created, that the Lord made them masters of the world, the equal of kings, and that they are the controlling spirits in governing the country. I don't mind the politicians preaching that kind of nonsense. It keeps the menagerie quiet. So long as able men like Uncle Joe Cannon can hypnotize farmers and mechanics by flattering their stupid egotism, we will have no real trouble in the country. They will vote as he

---

[15] February 1910.

suggests and he will vote as I direct. But if they knew the truth they might be ugly. It might be necessary to sit on them hard. . . . People are poor and laborious because the chance of birth and Nature itself have conspired to make and keep them poor and laborious. . . . It seems to me that inadequacy must be punished and efficiency rewarded the same in the human world as in the forest. . . . They are just as selfish as I am, only they haven't the ability to turn their selfishness to the best account." One law for the rich and a different one for the poor was just and sensible. "In nearly every case so-called financial crimes are not crimes against property but crimes to protect property." Popular education was condemned severely as tending to make people dissatisfied with a stratified society. And in probing deeper as to the nature of this select group and its composition, Mr. Worldly Wiseman was asked if it should include Harvard's President Eliot. "Why he's broke!" he answered, in what was a complete revelation of his basic assumption.

The satirical figure of Mr. Worldly Wiseman attracted considerable attention and high praise from the press and from readers. Dunne continued to introduce him to make the "Interpreter's House" a real forum, as well as to make clear the basic assumptions of many people in dominant places in American life. For a brief time, this character seemed to promise to repeat on a smaller scale the success of Mr. Dooley, but his strictly limited possibilities as popular literature soon destroyed that illusion. Still Mr. Worldly Wiseman was extremely useful in making clear what type of political action such a philosophy led to in contemporary politics. It may be that this was Dunne's chief purpose in introducing him, for he was in most respects the exact counterpart of Mr. Dooley.

The " Interpreter's House " essay which attracted the most praise was one which Dunne wrote when he was deeply moved over the sinking of the *Titanic*, and horror-struck by the way in which the American press had treated the tragedy. Unlike the other essays, he did not resort to the round-table form in this instance. He began with the examination of the nature of courage. The ideas expressed about this subject paralleled exactly a Dooley piece on the same subject. " Happy is the man who in Death loses only his life. . . . It is no discredit to the human race to say that cowardice is a gift of the devil which has been impartially distributed among mankind. Every man who thinks at all is afraid of death. He may be more afraid of something else, of loss of honor, health or money, of going to a dentist, or, like the man in Pickwick, of life without buttered muffins, but he chooses death only as a bad alternative for a worse. If he is not afraid of one thing you may be sure he is afraid of another." [16]

But the thing that had really stirred Dunne was the manner in which many American newspapers and people had manufactured wild rumors out of the first news of the tragedy. Unconscious of the way they were revealing their class and racial prejudices, they had concocted horrible tales on the one hand of rioting by the steerage passengers in an attempt to get posses-

[16] July 1914.

sion of the lifeboats, and, on the other hand, great sob-stories of the superiority of " Anglo-Saxon courage " over any other, especially that of the Latin nationalities. Mr. Worldly Wiseman, he pointed out, readily accepted as probable that a person who paid thirty instead of a thousand dollars for a ticket would act like a beast in the presence of danger. With an accurate story now being told, Dunne sketched the actions and feelings of the peasant immigrants in the steerage with an indignation and sympathy that did the subject justice. For the racial superiority implied in the comment, Dunne had no patience whatever. " Cowardly Portuguese," he pointed out, was becoming a stock phrase of American journalism and fiction. Actually Portuguese sailors were as brave as those of any other nation. " Meanwhile, we thank God that it has pleased Him that the nations should speak different languages, for if others knew what we say about them wars against us would never cease."

The " Interpreter's House " contributions were notable for the very things the Dooley essays were: highly intelligent discussion of either current affairs or of permanent American problems. Those which are not dated by the peculiar contemporary events discussed are as readable and valuable today as when they were published; for like most good writing, it was timeless. Dunne ended a discussion of a quarrel among students and faculty at Harvard in 1912 with a proposed statement of the purpose of a university which could hardly be improved upon. " Whatever ideas may be brought to us from whatever source, we will hear them; if they are false we will explode them;

if partly true we will sift them; if wholly true we will accept them, — but always provisionally, always pressing onward and seeking something better." [17]

Occasionally, too, as in the dialect articles, he would use an essay to right an individual wrong, or to call attention to one. Such a case was the requested resignation of Charles R. Crane from his post as envoy to China before he had time to leave the United States. Philander Knox, Taft's Secretary of State, was the culprit, and Dunne blasted him in that article in a way that reminded those who knew the inside history of the case of some avenging angel of justice. "It is very powerfully done," Mark Sullivan wrote to Dunne. "Of course the deed is in proportion to the need — only the fact that Crane had been subjected to such brutality would have stimulated you to write with so much feeling; and probably finding out that his friends feel this way about him is adequate compensation for what he endured." [18]

Dunne remained a member of the associates of *The American* from 1906 until the spring of 1913. Before he broke his official connection, he was separated in part by another effort to find a different medium of expression. His friend H. J. Whigham, who in 1906 had been writing to Dunne from London about the possibility of establishing a labor paper in New York, was now in charge of *The Metropolitan Magazine*, owned by Harry Payne Whitney as part of the property he had inherited along with the *Telegraph*. Whigham was making the magazine a right-wing socialist periodical, without any objection from its

[17] October 1912.

[18] No date. F. P. Dunne letters.

owner. For Whigham, Dunne started a series of monthly articles in 1911, entitled " From the Bleachers." These were neither dialect nor round table in form, but straightforward essays. In them Dunne discussed the class nature of American society, the uses of oratory, realism in literature, peace and war, the presidential possibilities, and the ways of democracy. Unhampered by any special form, or the necessity of being brief that governed newspaper writing, Dunne expressed his own beliefs here more clearly than anywhere else save in his personal correspondence. The essays were as carefully polished and as well thought out as anything he had written. But they attracted little attention. They were conservative, compared with the general trend of material in *The Metropolitan*, and among its readers few showed any real enthusiasm for them. After six months Dunne dropped them to resume a Dooley series for a newspaper syndicate.

He did not drop the " Interpreter's House " when he left *The American* in 1913, but kept it going with a few breaks until shortly before the Crowell Publishing Co. took over the magazine in 1915. But by that time Dunne had completely severed all connection with *The American*, and was no longer contributing to *The Metropolitan*. Moreover, the Dooley articles for the newspaper syndicate had virtually ceased. Dunne was nearing the end of his career as a writer. The degree of success with the " Interpreter's House," compared with the popular acclaim of Mr. Dooley ten years before, had been slight indeed. But Dunne knew his writing here was every bit as good;

the wisdom and comment was as penetrating, and the ends sought were as far-reaching in importance. But it was not humorous, and, compared with the millions who read Mr. Dooley, its audience was highly restricted. On the dialect essay, alone, Dunne now realized, would depend his reputation as a writer.

## *COLLIER'S WEEKLY*

AFTER Dunne began his work on *The American Magazine* he continued to produce the Dooley essays in reduced numbers. These included several brief runs published in a group of newspapers headed by the *New York Times,* as well as those in *The American* itself. There was little change in these essays over the earlier ones, except a tendency to make them longer, a result of the needs of magazine publication, and of a failure to secure his effects in as brief a space as formerly.

Although Mr. Dooley's denunciation of the life-insurance scandals attracted more attention than any other dialect article after 1905, there were many other notable essays and many frequently quoted lines. Dunne's balancing of his "assets" in his letter to Roosevelt had been unfair, for Andrew Carnegie should have been allotted a place close to the then President. Unlike Roosevelt, Carnegie was not treated with admiring consideration, for Mr. Dooley made fun of nearly every public act of his life, playing up his weaknesses and making sport of his idiosyncrasies. Not that there was any denunciation such as had formerly been aimed at Pullman and the life-insurance presidents; it was much more effective ridicule that had the attractiveness of great humor. "There's a man ye'd think ought to enjye life. He has ivrything that ought to make a man happy. He has money, he has fame, he has Andhrew Carnaygie, and he's a little deaf."

John D. Rockefeller was not such a favorite, but still he came into the essays frequently after the publication of Miss Tarbell's *History of the Standard Oil Company*. The change this bit of muckraking brought about in the oil magnate's life was presented in this way by Mr. Dooley:

> "Three years ago he seemed insured against punishment ayether here or hereafter. A happy man, a religious man. He had squared th' legislachures, th' coorts, th' pollyticians an' th' Baptist clargy. He saw th' dollars hoppin' out iv ivry lamp chimbley in th' wurruld an' hurryin' to'rd him. His heart was pure seein' that he had niver done wrong save in th' way iv business. . . . A good man! What cud harm him? An' so it seemed he might proceed to th' grave whin, lo an' behold, up in his path leaps a lady with a pen in hand an' off goes Jawn D. f'r th' tall timbers. . . . A year ago annybody wud take his money. Now if he wanted to give it even to Chancellor Day he'd have to meet him in a barn at midnight." [James R. Day was the chancellor of Syracuse University and a through-thick-and-thin defender of great wealth.]

In presenting Rockefeller's enormous fine, handed down by Judge Landis for violating the Interstate Commerce Act, Mr. Dooley assured Mr. Hennessy:

" He don't care f'r money in th' passionate way that you an' me do, Hinnissy. Th' likes iv us are as crazy about a dollar as a man is about his child whin he has on'y wan. Th' chances are we'll spoil it. But Jawn D., havin' a large an' growin' fam'ly iv dollars, takes on'y a kind iv gin'ral inthrest in thim. He's issued a statement sayin' that he's a custojeen iv money appinted be himsilf. He looks afther his own money an' th' money iv other people. He takes it an' puts it where it won't hurt thim an' they won't spoil it. He's a kind iv a society f'r th' previntion iv croolty to money. If he finds a man misusing his money he takes it away fr'm him an' adopts it. Ivry Saturdah night he lets th' man see it f'r a few hours. An' he says he's surprised to find that whin, with th' purest intintions in th' wurruld, he is found thryin' to coax our little money to his home where it'll find conjanial surroundings an' have other money to play with, th' people thry to lynch him an' th' polis arrest him f'r abduction."

Close to these essays in interest and quality was Dunne's presentation of Dooley's opinion on international peace, as represented by The Hague Conference. He had made sorrowful comment on the hopes for an international police force before:

" Be Hivins, Hinnissy, I looked forward to th' day whin, if a king, impror, or czar started a rough-house, th' blue bus wud come clangin' through th' sthreets an' they'd be hauled off to Holland f'r trile. . . . I thought th' coort wud have a kind iv a bridewell built, where they'd sind th' internaytional dhrunks an' disordhlies, an' where ye cud go anny day an' see Willum Hohenzollern cooperin' a bar'l, an' me frind Joe Chamberlain peggin' shoes. . . . But it hasn't come. . . . I want to see th' day whin just as Bill Hohenzollern an' Edward [of England] meets on th' corner an' prepares a raid on a laundhry a big polisman will step out iv a dure an' say: ' I want ye, Bill, an' ye might as well come along quiet.' But I suppose it wud be just th' same thing as it is now in rale life."

"How's that?" asked Mr. Hennessy.

"All th' biggest crooks wud get on th' polis foorce," said Mr. Dooley.

His comment on the second Hague Conference was healthful satire on its lack of real accomplishment. "Th' convintion thin discussed a risolution offered be th' Turkish dillygate abolishin' war altogether. This also carrid, on'y England, France, Rooshya, Germany, Italy, Austhree, Japan, an' th' United States votin' 'no.'" Joseph Choate, American delegate, was made to play a role that gave tone to the entire piece. Every few paragraphs Choate was made to inject an entirely valueless proposition, such as "Th' Hon'rable Joe Choate moved that in future wars horses shud be fed with hay wheriver possible. Carrid." Mr. Dooley continued:

"Th' entire South American dillygation said that no nation ought to go to war because another nation wanted to put a bill on th' slate. Th' English dillygate was much incensed. 'Why, gintlemen," says he, 'if ye deprived us iv th' right to collect debts be killin' th' debtor ye wud take away fr'm war its entire moral purpose. I must ask ye again to cease thinkin' on this subjick in a gross mateeryal way an' considher th' moral side alone,' he says. Th' conference was much moved be this pathetic speech, th' dillygate fr'm France wept softly into his hankerchef, an' th' dillygate fr'm Germany wint over an' forcibly took an openface goold watch fr'm th' dillygate fr'm Vinzwara."

Dunne had turned over the manuscript of a new collection of the Dooley essays to Charles Scribner's Sons in 1910, and the seventh book in the series, under the title *Mr. Dooley Says*, was soon on the market. In contrast to the fifty shorter essays in his first collection, this contained twenty-one longer pieces. The quality was high, and it contained what was perhaps the best political satire Dunne ever wrote. This was on the Payne-Aldrich tariff. Dunne's interest in tariff was of long standing, going back to his boyhood. He had once made careful preparation to write a Dooley essay on the tariff for *The Century*, but had not completed it. In various other articles he had commented on protection, and it was a frequent subject for his editorial discussion. His wide knowledge formed the necessary basis for a great satire. After making clear the promise of tariff reduction back of the bill, Mr. Dooley listed items on the free list, such as alazarin, apatite, hog bristles, works of art more than twenty years old, kelp, marshmallows, foreign newspapers, turtles, leeches, and yachts. Mr. Dooley pointed out that opium was also there.

"Th' tariff bill wudden't be complete without that there item. But it ought to read: 'Opyum f'r smokin' while readin' th' tariff bill.' Ye can take this sterlin' piece iv lithrachoor to a bunk with ye an' light a ball iv hop. Befure ye smoke up p'raps ye can't see where th' tariff has been rejooced. But afther ye've had a long dhraw it all becomes clear to ye. Ye'er worries about th' childhern's shoes disappear an' ye see ye'ersilf floatin' over a purple sea iv alazarin, in ye'er private yacht, lulled be th' London *Times*, surrounded be wurruks iv art more thin twenty years old, atin' marshmallows an' canary burrd seed, while th' turtles an' leeches frisk on th' binnacle."

After a devastating satire on senatorial tariff oratory and log-rolling, Dooley continues:

"An' so it goes, Hinnissy. Niver a sordid wurrud, mind ye, but ivrything done on th' fine old principle iv give an' take."

"Well," said Mr. Hennessy, repeating an old pro-tariff chestnut, "what diff'rence does it make? Th' foreigner pays th' tax, annyhow."

"He does," said Mr. Dooley, "if he ain't turned back at Castle Garden."

The book received little attention from the reviewers, although those who commented expressed the usual surprise that the quality held up as it did. Its sales were the smallest of all the Dooley books. Dunne and Scribner had tentatively planned to follow it with another volume in 1911, but gave it up because of the disappointing market.

Mr. Dooley had his usual campaign comment to offer on the exciting presidential contest of 1912. Although Dunne himself took a quiet part in promoting Theodore Roosevelt's campaign, first for the Republican nomination and later as a candidate of the Progressive Party, Mr. Dooley continued to reflect his customary "outside the battle" attitude in political campaigns. When Roosevelt was making excited oratory about the issues, Mr. Dooley observed:

"I had no idee it was so bad. I wint to bed last night thinkin' th' counthry was safe. . . . Whin I got up I had a feelin' that somethin' was burnin', th' same as I had th' mornin' iv th' big fire. But I cudden't find annything wrong till I opened up th' papers an', much to me relief, found it was not me pants but th' republic that was on fire. Yes, sir, th' republic is doomed to desthruction again."

The campaign of 1912 brought Norman Hapgood's editorship of *Collier's* to an end. He and Robert Collier quarreled over the editorial policy to be followed during the campaign. Basic to the disagreement was Collier's partisanship for Roosevelt and Hapgood's for Wilson. Although Dunne was not involved directly, he felt the quarrel between his two friends keenly, and his sympathies were with Collier when it was over. After a short time, Mark Sullivan, who had established *Collier's* notable Washington bureau, succeeded to the editorship in Hapgood's place. When Dunne left the associates on *The American* in 1913, he drifted gradually into the Collier organization for his last venture in journalism. At first he merely wrote a share of the editorials, but by the end of 1915, he induced Sullivan to give him a page of his own to be filled irregularly in addition to his share of the editorials. This page, called variously " Comment on Politics " and " Comment on Congress," was published intermittently during the following year and a half. It was carried anonymously and part of it may have come from other pens than Dunne's.

In his work for *Collier's*, Dunne's interests, outside of national politics, were concerned with the great war then raging in Europe. The war itself and the accompanying decline of all civilized standards weighed oppressively upon him. In spite of the strong anti-British trend in his thinking, the aggressive course of German foreign policy and her near-deification of militarism had always been an object of his hatred and a subject of his satire. The possibility of Germany's overcoming France and Great Britain seemed appalling. With this strong pro-Ally point of view, he became, as did others of similar mind, a strong advocate of preparedness, especially naval expansion. Collier and Sullivan were of similar opinion, and Dunne's writing for the magazine was frequently on this subject. In it he was strongly encouraged by Theodore Roosevelt, who was working for similar ends, although with greater emphasis upon American aid to the Allies. During 1916 Dunne spent a part of each week in Washington while Congress was in session, finding material for these articles, forming strong friendships with people there who felt the same way, especially A. P. Gardner, Congressman from Massachusetts, and Franklin D. Roosevelt, Assistant Secretary of the Navy. His most regular companion, however, was Francis P. Garvan, who was now in the Attorney General's office.

On one of his first trips to the Capital for *Collier's*, Dunne saw his old friend Brand Whitlock, just returned from war-torn Belgium, and a national hero for the courage and intelligence which he had displayed as minister to that unfortunate country. Of him, at this time, Dunne wrote one of his amusing sketches for the eye of a mutual friend:

I saw Brand Whitlock the other night. He looks much the same as ever and *is* quite the same amiable and simple soul, but with a little added touch of solemnity, which is also simple. He wears spats, if you can believe it, and a silk hat and broadens his a's, even those in "and," "man," and "fan." I hear he can have a first class ambassadorship – probably France – if he wants it and there is considerable talk of nominating him for vice president. I hope he gets anything he wishes for he is a wonderfully nice fellow and I liked him more than ever this time, in spite of, – no, more because of his boyish stateliness of demeanor, his graceful bow, and the exquisite flavoring of his talk with unusual French terms, "Alors!" "Eh bien" "Comment?" "Quelle dommage." Really it's a shame to make fun of him but I can't help doing it — a little. Don't think he was stiff. He wasn't. He was just as fine as anyone could be. But he had never been abroad before he went over as minister and landed just in time to see the last of Ypres and Louvain. You can't blame him for wearing the air of one who has looked into the terrible heart of things as they are and will never again hear the birds sing. It is most becoming to him, especially when accompanied by a certain gesture of the hand and the half whispered words: "Don't ask me, please." If I had it I would guarantee to start a harem with it.[1]

With the intrusion of the war and its psychology, Dunne gave up writing Mr. Dooley. The essays no longer paid him in the sense that the emotional satisfaction in their production was greater than the difficulty of driving himself to produce them. His depression over the war made it difficult for him to write either satire or humor. With all his intellectual resources, he did not feel sure enough of himself for the first, and he felt the tragedy of the day too deeply for the latter. No comment on Dunne's career written after 1920 is commoner than the expression of regret that Mr. Dooley was not vocal during the war period of 1915 to 1919, to keep officials from taking themselves too seriously and to give comic relief to the long-suffering public.

Some of Dunne's most vigorous writing for *Collier's* centered about the campaign of 1916. Collier and Dunne were hopeful that Theodore Roosevelt would be the candidate of a united Republican and Progres-

[1] To Robert Hamill, December 14, 1915. Hamill letters.

sive party, and as such would defeat Woodrow Wilson. When Charles E. Hughes was made the Republican nominee, *Collier's* placed its support behind his campaign. In line with its policy of presenting both sides of the case, it published articles by partisans of both candidates. Ray Stannard Baker and Ida Tarbell wrote those supporting Wilson, but Dunne wrote rebuttals of each of them for the editorial page. While the progressive-liberalism of *Collier's* was still apparent in its editorials, the war had become the dominating theme, and the preference for Hughes over Wilson was made almost entirely because of disagreement with Wilson's foreign and armament policies.

After the United States' entry into the war in April, 1917, Dunne was given charge of the publicity for the War Savings Stamp campaign in New York City, and edited a small publication called *The Pioneer Bulletin.* But most of his efforts went into *Collier's.* Robert Collier, in serious mental and physical condition, had permitted the weekly to become heavily involved in debt. As early as 1912, Payne Whitney had come to its rescue with financial support. After Mark Sullivan retired as editor in the fall of 1917, Collier's health broke down, and Dunne took charge of the magazine as its editor. In fact, Dunne, Payne Whitney, and Francis Garvan as a group took charge in an attempt to keep the magazine for Collier and to save it from falling into hands they did not wish to see control it. Whitney supplied the money to keep disaster away, Garvan the legal talent, and Dunne, during 1918 and 1919 at least, gave it general editorial management.

These were not the happiest years of Peter Dunne's

life. The war, with its intolerances on the part of an excited public, was heavily depressing. Soon after the entry of the United States, Dunne ran into his old cartoonist friend, Art Young, now under arrest for his cartoons in *The Masses*, which were critical of the government. They talked of the war, and Young thought Dunne seemed a bit sympathetic toward his pacifist-socialist point of view. But as they parted, Dunne gave him this advice: " Art, when the whole world goes crazy, you have to go crazy too." [2]

Dunne did enjoy the editorial management of *Collier's*. It revived some of his old dreams of editorial achievement. He busied himself in finding authors for the articles he wanted, and sought to stimulate them by courtly deference and judicious praise. When he added the inexperienced Gilbert Seldes to the staff after reading some sample editorials the young man had submitted, Dunne told him: " We haven't been satisfied with the quality of our editorial pages in the last few months and we will be very happy if you would join us in our effort to improve them." [3] He did very little writing himself, and the direction of policy for a great popular journal was not a wholly unsatisfactory prospect for a journalist who had lost the sharp edge of his writing ability.

Collier died on almost the very day the war ended. When the publisher's will was read, it was found that he had bequeathed the weekly, or his equity in it, to the three friends who had labored so hard to save it for him: Whitney, Garvan, and Dunne. Apparently

---

2 Art Young: *Art Young: His Life and Times*, p. 438.

3 Gilbert Seldes to author, April 2, 1941.

assuming that Mrs. Collier had sufficient wealth in her own name, the bequest can be understood only as an attempt to compensate the three men for their efforts in the magazine's behalf. But there were complications. It turned out that Mrs. Collier's resources were not as great as her husband had imagined. There was a distinct feeling of taking something from the widow which she needed, and the three decided to refuse the bequest and allow it to go to Mrs. Collier.

While the magazine was not a very profitable property, it had increased its circulation steadily over several years, and, about the time when Dunne became its editor, this passed the million mark. With less wasteful management than Robert Collier's, it seems that it could easily have been made into a well-paying property. Dunne continued the editorship for nearly a year after Collier's death, and then Mrs. Collier sold the magazine to the Crowell Publishing Co. Dunne was highly disappointed and chagrined at this turn of events, and his version of it was confided to Robert Hamill:

> I have meant to write you every day for a month, knowing you would want to know what has happened at *Collier's*. I am out of it. Apparently the widow was so amazed by the will that she forgot everything else and under the persuasion of a swindling lawyer named —— (Yale '93) and that pleasant Charlie Davis she practically gave the property away. She gets very little money, perhaps none, after the debts are paid, and ten per cent of stock in a new company of very doubtful present value. The head of the buying syndicate (which includes your friends Peabody, Houghteling & Co.) is Tom Lamont. Isn't it weird that the prop-

erty should go to the very man whose attempt to get hold of it in 1912 was the cause of the appeal to Payne Whitney? Collier was in a bad situation then, and the Astor Trust Co. which Lamont controls called his loan, expecting of course that he would be forced to throw the property into the hands of the Crowell Publishing Co. (a Lamont concern). Mrs. Collier knew all of this but her ladylike asperity was too great to be overcome by any consideration so [illegible] as might be suggested by the situation. On the whole, I am rather glad to be out of it. Feeling the way she did (she has never even written me since I renounced the legacy) and under the influence of a crook and a chump, nothing we could do in reorganizing the company would have satisfied her. As it is, by prompt and, in the end, none too [illegible] action the entire loan with interest was saved for Payne. In the final settlement I did not suffer and my anxiety about the future is removed for a while.

Of course, I am disappointed at the outcome. I had things going well at the time we first heard of Mrs. C. secret negotiations but I am not unhappy and Payne and Lewis Ledyard have acted with the utmost generosity. But to be destroyed by Charlie Davis! I am like the antique hero who died at the bite of a louse.[4]

Dunne was left without an occupation, although not entirely without income. His bitter feeling about losing control of *Collier's* gave him an outlook on life for a short time that was dark indeed. The only advice he received from friends was to revive Mr. Dooley. " Of course everybody is giving you one piece of advice — ' Dooley.' I met a venerable college professor who was crying for him just as much as the drummers in the smoking cars and the ladies' knitting circle. . . . You've twenty years before you of in-

[4] September 17, 1919. Hamill letters.

creasing wisdom and grace." Or, so wrote Frederick Palmer.[5]

Perhaps to test the popularity of the old philosopher in the post-war America, Dunne brought out a book of nineteen Dooley essays in the fall of 1919. Except for two articles, all those in the book had been written before 1915, and consequently none of them concerned recent public affairs. Nearly all of them celebrated favorite general subjects: St. Patrick's Day, oratory, the summer resort, heroes, criminal trials, old age, baseball, gambling, golf, and the practice of medicine. All of them were Dunne's authentic humor, shrewd, witty, and satirical. But none of them dealt with crucial public questions in any serious way. There was some satire of William Jennings Bryan, carried over from Dunne's antagonism to Bryan's pacifistic policies as Secretary of State. But that was all. The book attracted more public attention than the one of nine years before. Among the commentators, none seemed to find that Dunne had lost his power as a humorist, although many regretted the absence of comment on public affairs, and especially the lack of discussion on current trends.

Francis Hackett in *The New Republic* gave the book its most serious treatment, and he found it lacking in this very concentration upon " the patent trivialities and jocularities of the paper made American world. . . . He scores hard and often — on a newspaper target. Only occasionally does he disregard that target and pierce the heart of life." [6] This was an

---

[5] August 22, 1919. F. P. Dunne letters.
[6] XX (September 24, 1919), 234–36.

accurate judgment, but it could not have been written of any of the first six books. It represented not so much a change in Dunne, although that was there, as it did the result of his unproductiveness as a writer of satire over the past ten years.

Morris R. Werner, in an extended article on Dunne the year following the book's publication, was to point this out with a sharp warning: " The only reason why Finley Peter Dunne has not gone down hill in his humor is because he seems to take periodic rests from the strenuousness of making Mr. Dooley our national character. We hope that his creator is taking a good rest but a short one." [7]

While not completely disappointing, the reception of the book was far from the great enthusiasm of 1898 and 1902. There was no longer any possibility of popular songs to celebrate Mr. Dooley. The prospect of driving himself as would be necessary to turn out the kind of dialect essays that were expected of him was not attractive to Dunne in 1920. The dread of having to make the deadline was real, and it was easy to procrastinate and let it go. Dunne's own recollections of a year earlier give, in a humorous vein, what must have been an essentially true picture of his working habits at this time:

One bright morning in late May or early June I awoke with a consciousness that I had much important work to do. Accordingly I took a long time over breakfast, studied the morning papers with the greatest care and having exhausted all other devices for postponing labor, like playing with the

[7] " Mr. Dooley Alias Finley Peter Dunne," *The Bookman*, LI (August 1920), 677.

dog and winding the clock, settled down to work when suddenly it occurred to me that I had still a small balance left in the bank. It was not only small, it was puny, but large enough to shut the door on Inspiration. Every great artist knows that without inspiration he can't create; so letters and art are left to the working classes. When the Genius calls for Inspiration he finds she is howling at the door of a slave who has locked himself in and, cursing the fate that made him an artist rather than a bricklayer, settled down before a blank pad of paper to "make copy." Anyhow with the thought of my bank balance all Inspiration fled and there was nothing left for a sensible man to do but practise his mashie shots.[8]

---

[8] Recollections of Peter Dunne.

CHAPTER XV

## THE REVIVAL OF MR. DOOLEY

PETER DUNNE's retirement from editorial work in 1919 did not find him lacking in interesting things to do. During his twenty years in New York he had built up an enormous number of friendships, and, as one of the most popular of dinner or luncheon companions, he could always choose his own society.

A former Chicago acquaintance, Charles B. Macdonald, had organized a golf club that would sponsor the building of an ideal course, for which Macdonald had detailed plans. Dunne helped him frame a list of possible charter members, and soon the National Golf Links of America course at Southampton, Long Island, was under way. After it was completed, the Dunnes took a house at Southampton every summer. Another fraternal group was made up of men with whom Dunne had become intimate soon after he came to New York. It included Collier; both sons of W. C. Whitney, Harry Payne and Payne; the sportsman, Lewis C. Thompson; F. P. Garvan; John Fox, Jr.;

and a few others. These made up a small private club, called the Meeting House, which was Dunne's favorite as long as it existed. Most of the fourteen members were wealthy, but some of them, like Dunne and Fox, were not. Dunne's close relationship with this small group, between 1910 and 1927, meant a withdrawal from some of his other clubs, and a considerable lessening of the number of friendships which he had formerly maintained with a wide variety of people.

In the meantime, Dunne's domestic life had changed but little. The lively family in the Dunne house now included four children: Finley Peter, Jr., born in 1903; Philip, born in 1908; and the twins, Margaret and Leonard, born in 1910. Peter Dunne seemed only mildly interested in his children until they were grown, and the task of rearing them fell upon their mother. Perhaps his attitude is best illustrated by his reminiscence of the summer of 1918, when the lawn of the house he had rented — selected because the lawn was an excellent place to practise mashie shots — was converted into a war garden.

When I got out to the lawn there was scarcely enough of it left to provide room for one of those divots that have caused so many chairmen of green committees to shoot themselves. The lawn, although the hour was early, had all but disappeared, and in its place stood a jagged tract that with a little barbed wire and a few dead Germans, might have been a miniature reproduction of No Man's Land. In the near foreground stood a stately figure looking incomparably lovely, cool, and authoritative in a white muslin dress, gauntlet gloves, and a most becoming broad hat with a black velvet band and roses — such a hat, in short, as Eng-

MR. AND MRS. DUNNE (MARGARET ABBOTT)
*and their three sons, Philip, Leonard, and FPD Jr.*

lish farmers' wives wore for the spring planting in Robert Herrick's day.

It is needless to say that this apparition was the Food and General Administratrix, bless her, of the household. But who were these insane infants, their eyes ablaze, their faces streaked with grime or red from passion, who were hacking the green sward with hoe and spade and rake? They were none other than my four lovely children whose devotion to the good cause was beyond all reason. My considered opinion, proved by later developments, was that they had little interest in saving the army. They thought it reward enough for a soldier to be allowed to kill his fellow men without interference by the police. Why should these pampered darlings of fortune be stuffed with potatoes and spinach? No, their gentle souls were excited solely by the prospect of destroying something and my lawn was easy prey. I nourished a secret and traitorous hope that the potatoes would not grow. . . . When the time came for planting, the children were absent. They were busy destroying the Ford car.

As the children grew older, their father's attitude of amused tolerance toward them changed to one of active interest in their personalities and prospective careers. This was especially true of the two older boys, Finley and Philip, who were inclined to become professional writers. A strong fatherly pride in their work, both at Harvard and after they began to make careers for themselves, is evident in Dunne's correspondence during the twenties and thirties, whereas he had seldom mentioned them when they were younger. "The children are away at school," he wrote to Robert Hamill in the fall of 1925. "Fin is working on the Boston Globe. He writes better than he did and the editor tells me that he is the best young man he has had for a long time. But I dunno.

It's a rotten trade at best. Phil (at Harvard) goes strong but banged up his knee trying for the freshman team. I am rather glad of it for it was bound to happen soon or late. He is sad because the coach had told Fin he had the best chance for center rush. Maybe now he will learn something." [1]

Peter Dunne remained a Catholic Christian in sympathy and partisanship all his life. His friends sometimes remarked that his attitude toward his church was in one respect like that toward his family. He himself criticized both at times, but he permitted no one else to do so in his presence. After he left Chicago, he saw little of his relatives who were members of the Catholic clergy, but he once called on his distinguished cousin, Father Patrick W. Riordan, now Archbishop of San Francisco, who as a young priest had baptized Peter Dunne and his twin brother. "He is a creditable member of the family," he had written to his sister, Charlotte. "We need a few archbishops to keep up the average now that Bill has come in." [2]

In spite of Peter Dunne's sense of loyalty to the church, he was not a practising Catholic. He and Margaret Dunne, who, like her mother, was an Episcopalian, were married within the Catholic Church. He insisted that the children be baptized in accordance with Catholic rites and be made to observe fast days at home. But Peter himself stopped observing fast days and seldom went near a church after the death of his own father. He was later to tell one of his sons that he had never known an unworthy priest,

---

[1] Oct. 7, 1925, Hamill letters.

[2] Dec. 1, 1901, Charlotte Dunne letters.

but he added the advice: " the less you have to do with them the better." His intellectual convictions were not involved in this lack of conformity, for among his friends Dunne was often found defending the validity of religion against materialistic arguments.

The Dunnes continued to live in New York for most of the year, with the summers regularly spent at Southampton, and with frequently a winter trip to Palm Beach or Aiken, South Carolina. Being a member of the National, the Meeting House, and numerous other clubs meant that Dunne had acquired extraordinarily expensive habits. He enjoyed luxurious living as few persons did who could have its privileges, and, as he was never willing to practise personal economy, he did little to lessen its financial burdens. With four children to put through costly schools, and with his own wasteful habits, Dunne could not manage for very long without some remunerative employment. But for the present, he had sufficient resources and made no move toward either a new syndicate arrangement or an editorial connection.

In some ways the episode in Dunne's life which found him most completely out of his usual character was his connection with the candidacy of Warren G. Harding for the presidency in 1920. His sympathetic appreciation of the politician as a type was part of the cause, but behind it was also the subtle change in his political perceptions which had taken place during the ten years before 1920. He had been strongly opposed to Taft's administration and favorable toward Theodore Roosevelt in the campaign of 1912. His disagreement with Woodrow Wilson's policies had been intense during the period after 1914. These attachments and antagonisms continued, and tied Dunne in with Republican politics in a small way in 1916. Had Roosevelt lived, Dunne would have been supporting him for the presidency in 1920, but his death in 1918 did not leave the humorist a follower of either Leonard Wood or Hiram Johnson, as it did most of Roosevelt's friends.

Dunne had a lively friendship for Senator Harding, which dated back to his visits to Washington for *Collier's*. Later Dunne's memories of Harding were of this nature:

> I first met Harding in 1915 – I think it was – at a dinner of the Gridiron Club. President Wilson was guest of honor and made a memorable speech. . . . Harding also spoke. I don't remember what he talked about but he had a most commanding presence, – tall, broadshouldered and handsome, with the face and head of the ideal – not the actual – senator. The countenance betrayed a nature benignant, patient and humorous.
>
> I saw him frequently afterward and dined and played dollar limit poker at his house. He was a pleasant host. . . .

In 1920 Harry Daugherty was in charge of Harding's campaign for the Republican presidential nomination. In a conversation with Senator Davis Elkins, Dunne had expressed the idea that Harding had real presidential possibilities, considering the way the race was shaping up. Elkins passed on the remark to Daugherty, and when the latter came to New York to raise funds for Harding's campaign for delegates to the convention, he looked up Dunne and asked for help. Dunne agreed, and together they made up a list of possible contributors. Daugherty asked Dunne to try his hand at collecting. Dunne's own recollection continues:

In Daugherty's request I saw possibilities for myself as a Warwick. I could be a president maker like Whitney and Hanna. So I went to call on the gentleman at the head of the sucker list. He refused to give anything and did so with a speed and abruptness that left no doubt as to his feeling. He added this gratuitous information "Poor old Warren hasn't a Chinaman's chance." I told this to Daugherty that afternoon. "Then," he said, "can you get an interview with [Harry] Sinclair for me." I knew Sinco pretty well and I had no hesitation in asking for a meeting. We got together in an open room in plain sight and hearing of the clerks. Sinclair was cold and anxious to get away. But by this time I was a furious, a demonical advocate of Harding. I was determined that he'd get to Chicago and have headquarters there if I had to go out with a gun and stick up a bank. If I do say it, who shouldn't, I made such a speech as would have inflamed the iciest heart. It must have affected Sinclair deeply for after I had poured out my raptures over the good, the great, the generous and the possibly useful Harding, he turned wearily to Daugherty and said: "Oh, for God's sake, Harry, I'll lend you $7500. It's not a contribution. I'm for Wood. It's a loan. Harding hasn't a chance in the world."

The next day Sinclair called me up to say that Harry Whitney would lend Daugherty another $7500 to oblige Harding, whom he knew well and liked. Harry was partner of Sinclair in Sinclair Oil. So Daugherty had now $15,000 and he was grateful. He was so grateful that he asked for more. This convinced one anew that Mr. Daugherty was a regular Ohio statesman. But it also chilled my ardor. I no longer regarded myself as a Warwick. I was definitely down on the Ohio list as a sucker. . . . Yet it was with some pride that I read of Warren Harding's departure from Columbus, the opening of headquarters in the Sherman House in Chicago, the favorable personal impression made by my candidate.[3]

With this small but important task, Dunne's efforts ended, but his reward was to be in on the beginning of the Harding tragedy. Dunne was at Palm Beach a few weeks before the inauguration, when the President-elect and a party, consisting of Daugherty and a group of Republican senators, arrived. Dunne played golf with Harding, and saw himself afterwards on the motion-picture screen " clearly revealed not only as a man who couldn't play golf . . . but as one who couldn't even act and dress like a golfer." He sat next to Harding that night at a dinner which Daugherty gave. Harding was glum. " The sad austerity of Power had begun to envelop him like a garment." He told Dunne that he was going to appoint Daugherty Attorney General. That did not surprise Dunne; but it did surprise him that Daugherty had no better conception of his pending responsibilities than to go to one of the notorious gambling places of the resort city later in the evening!

When visiting Frank Garvan in Washington nearly a year later, Dunne was invited to lunch at the White House with the President and Daugherty. At the

[3] Recollections of Peter Dunne. This part of the manuscript which Dunne prepared was published in a bowdlerized form after Dunne's death in *The Saturday Evening Post* (September 12, 1936). Reasonably typical of the changes from the original to the *Post* version is this sentence in which the italicized words were eliminated. " It must have affected Sinclair deeply for *after I had poured out my raptures over the good, the great, the generous and the possibly useful Harding,* he turned wearily to Daugherty . . ." Many of the details of Dunne's relation to the campaign are borne out by letters from Daugherty to Dunne. F. P. Dunne letters.

Attorney General's office, Dunne met Daugherty's confidant, Jesse Smith, and, to his amazement, found him in the company of a notoriously corrupt New York lawyer. Dunne went to the luncheon, and it was the last time that he saw the President.

Two minor appointments were made which Dunne had suggested, and that ended Dunne's connection with the administration.[4] He never believed that either Harding or Daugherty was guilty of anything more than inattention to his duties. More important, perhaps, is the fact that Dunne appeared as a character witness for Harry F. Sinclair in 1928, when Sinclair was charged with conspiracy to commit fraud in connection with the naval oil leases. Dunne did this reluctantly, and only after the pleadings of Harry Payne Whitney had overcome his natural disinclination. Afterwards Sinclair wrote Dunne, expressing his appreciation and testifying to his belief that Dunne's testimony had resulted in the acquittal.[5]

In the meantime, Dunne had gone through periods of extremely bad health. A long illness was followed in 1923 by two operations that left him improved but hardly vigorous. Shortly before this, the need of income forced him to revive Mr. Dooley. It was done reluctantly, and begun by supplying the Bell Syndicate with a series of old Dooley articles, cut to conform to a definite space limit. These ran for nearly two years, and were followed in 1924 by a series of new essays on the pending presidential campaign,

---

[4] Harry M. Daugherty to Dunne, April 8, 1922 and May 23, 1923. F. P. Dunne letters.

[5] Sinclair to Dunne, April 27, 1928. F. P. Dunne letters.

which were distributed more widely and returned a much higher income. These began to appear in the spring, and Dunne kept them up with reasonable regularity until the campaign was nearly over. Then, as had been the case in many of his series after 1905, he began to miss issues, and one editor who had been publishing the articles wrote a parody entitled " Mr. Dooley on the Disappearance of Mr. Dunne," which some others published. There was some disagreement with the syndicate management, and the essays stopped entirely, the last to be published in newspapers.

Although the series had been well syndicated and was displayed prominently in such papers as the *New York World* and *Boston Globe*, it did not generate enough interest to encourage Dunne in his work. A little over a year after it ended, he was ready for another trial in the weekly magazine *Liberty*, then owned by the *Chicago Tribune* and managed by an old friend, Joseph M. Patterson. Patterson was looking for material to secure a wide circle of readers for his weekly, and it was natural that he should think of Mr. Dooley. He made Dunne an unusually remunerative offer for an article each week, and when Dunne accepted, Patterson secured E. W. Kemble to illustrate the series. Kemble had illustrated some of the Dooley articles several years before with much better success than most artists who had tried it. Dunne seemed to find these *Liberty* essays easier to do than he had expected. They were better on the whole than the 1924 series. Spurred on by congratulatory letters and comments from old friends, it was at first a great pleasure to be turning out the kind of copy that had made his great reputation. The series lasted without a break for six months, and then Dunne discontinued it. Perhaps he had his finances in passable shape again and, with that pressure removed, plus the passing of the stimulation of the first acclaim that greeted the revival, found it too difficult to continue. He knew well that he was not adding to his reputation, even though the new series was better than the one of two years before. Both series of dialect essays had been written after such a long vacation from Mr. Dooley that Dunne had considerable difficulty in getting his character back into his old intellectual form. The new articles showed also that Dunne's political partisanship of these years and the social isolation had taken a considerable toll on his knowledge of public affairs. Flashes of the old fire were there in every essay, but there was none that equaled the quality of the better old ones. The political satires were weak, and found Dunne defending in an indirect way some of his recent friends such as Daugherty. His association with the administration had destroyed his powers as a satirist. One piece in 1924 which dealt with a "Cousin Tim," who attended the Democratic National Convention in New York, was the best of the political comments, and enabled Dunne to make high-class humor out of the contrast between the popular conceptions of the life of such a delegate in New York and his actual experiences. However, the *Liberty* series proved that under the proper circumstances Dunne could write dialect essays good enough to approach his old standards, and do it with considerable regularity. Few of the new ones were more able than Dunne's review of *The Intimate Papers of Colonel House.* It fell short of the " Alone in Cubia " essay only as House failed to measure up to Theodore Roosevelt as a subject for satire. Fresher and more timely were his comments on prohibition:

" What's this Anti-Saloon League, annyhow? " Mr. Hennessy asked.

" Well," said Mr. Dooley, " it's a fine organ-ization. It's like th' Anti-Anti-Saloon League. It's wan way iv makin' a livin'." [6]

Mr. Dooley was here, of course, in keeping with the twenties, dispensing his " fluid extracts iv hell " in the humiliating atmosphere of a soft-drink parlor.

" Th' scepter has gone with th' crown. . . . To see me, what was wanst a free an' law-abidin' citizen that cud give th' back iv me hand an' th' sole iv me fut to th' very loot at th' station now keepin' wan eye on th' customer an' th' other on th' dure, to see ye lurkin' in like a tom-cat an' me sellin' ye hop that Thomas A. Edison wudden't handle with rubber gloves an' handin' it to ye as if I was passin' countherfit money, is grajally breakin' me heart. 'Tis thrue I have more coin thin I iver see before. But what is money, afther all? As Hogan says, where wealth accumylates man decays. What does it profit me, as th' good book says, if I gain th' whole wurruld be sellin' ye conthraband juice, if th' next I see iv ye a little dog is leadin' ye around at th' end iv a string. . . .

" An' there ye are, I've got to go on in th' on'y business I know. Th' saloon desthroyed th' home, but th' home has turned like a rattlesnake an' desthroyed th' saloon – th' home an' th' home brew. . . .

---

[6] *Liberty,* April 17, 1926.

"There ain't as much dhrunkenness as there was. I know that," said Mr. Hennessy.

"No," said Mr. Dooley, "but what there is is a much more finished product."[7]

After the quite satisfactory series of 1926, Dunne might have continued to write dialect essays intermittently as economic necessity forced his lethargic hand from time to time. But that spur to his genius was removed in 1927. Payne Whitney, the leading spirit of the Meeting House, and from Dunne's first days in New York the writer's admiring friend, died unexpectedly. When his will was read it was found that he had left legacies out of his fortune of nearly two hundred million dollars to three of the Meeting House group. These legacies amounted to a half million dollars each, and one of them went to Peter Dunne. Mutual friends thought this was left to Dunne in compensation for the loss of the Collier inheritance, which Dunne alone of the group could ill afford to return to the widow, but that seems to have been only one factor in Whitney's mind. In fact, he had tried to relieve some of his relatively impecunious friends in the Meeting House of their financial worries by a stock market operation a few years earlier, but it had turned out disastrously. The bequest was simply another generous gift out of a rich supply of friendship. Dunne's own comment was confided to Robert Hamill:

Wasn't it a nice thing for him to do, and so characteristic? I wish you had known each other. I always hoped I could bring about a meeting but something always interfered. You

[7] The *Boston Globe,* June 8, 1924.

were much alike. Like you he was reticent, even taciturn with others but quite loquacious with me. Like you again he was stubborn not to say pig headed, in his few political beliefs, which might be summed up in an equal hatred of Roosevelt and Wilson. He abhorred Wall Street, never went to Clubs, wouldn't entrust his affairs to bankers, and clung with unbelievable tenacity to any enterprise in which he had ventured, whether it was winning racquet & tennis championships, building up his companies, organizing his medical centre, or secretly bossing the Yale crew. He had rather a liking for rogues but loathed humbug and the extent of his generosity to people in distress will never be known. . . . What a queer feeling it gives a fellow to find himself in the 7th decade or was I there all last year? I never was good at mathematics.[8]

[8] July 16, 1927. Hamill letters.

CHAPTER XVI

## PETER DUNNE BECOMES MR. DOOLEY

PERHAPS no expression can more adequately explain what happened to Peter Dunne after the decline in the volume of his writing than the title of this chapter. The emotional pleasure which his writing had given him was replaced by the satisfactions that came from his associations and friendships, especially those which came from his role of witty and profound commentator to his circle of intimates. Of course this was older than Mr. Dooley himself, but its part in Dunne's life became larger as the dialect essays declined. In his clubs, among his circle of friends, Dunne became Mr. Dooley incarnate, who provided wisdom and humor on every occasion. Within each group to which he belonged was a small clique of friends who made up the foundation of the circle. In the National at Southampton, for instance, the group included the popular orator Francis Patrick Murphy and Judge Morgan J. O'Brien. These two were in some respects the most satisfactory companions of Dunne's later years, and they helped to make up for some of the emotional losses which came with the decline of his hold on the fame of popular authorship.

The Meeting House became a thing of the past after Payne Whitney's death, and Dunne found most of his companions in the Links Club when in New York City. He could regularly be found there, with such intimates as John Grier or F. P. Garvan or Wayne Johnson. He was still the terror of all poseurs and stuffed shirts that he had been in the days of the Whitechapel Club. Always his like for honest characters without pretense or fake overcame every other consideration, and his dislike for the frauds and pretenders increased. On an ordinary club evening, as the time wore on and the talk livened up, the poseurs, who knew from sad experience the dangers of Dunne's company, could be seen edging out of the circle and finding some secluded spot where they would not be apt to call up one of Dunne's comments. It is impossible to recapture the tone of his wit and his conversation; all that remains are treasured memories of certain observations which were striking because of their spontaneity. When comments were being made on a new full-length portrait of a proud club member, Dunne suggested that the picture was not a portrait at all but merely a symbolical figure representing "modesty." At another time at the Links Club, one of Dunne's friends, who was known for the regularity of his consumption of liquor, was entertaining a Prohibitionist relative, and, out of respect for his guest's sentiments, the dinner was proceeding in dry and dolorous state. Someone called Dunne's attention to the lack of animation on their friend's face. " Yes," he observed, " blood *is* thicker than alcohol." In the locker room at the National after a round of golf, one of the foursome passed some uncomplimentary remark about the manner in which Dunne's girth was increasing with age. Dunne agreed: " My fat is piling up under my belt, while yours goes under your hat." Once he entered one of his clubs just in time to help to his feet an elderly doorman who had tripped on the entry rug and sprawled on the floor. " You'll have to be more careful, old man," Dunne warned, " or you'll be mistaken for one of our members." When Frank Ward O'Malley brought T. A. Daly, well-known editor and author of Italian dialect poetry, around to meet Dunne, the talk turned to the tendency of prize-fighters of various non-Celtic nationalities to assume Irish names. " No," said O'Malley, of one Clancy, " he looked more like a Greek." " Same thing," said Dunne, " these foreigners come over here and get into the limelight under Irish names. Now here's this fellow [chucking his thumb at Daly] who writes Dago poetry. Honest, Daly, what's your right name?" [1]

The Harvest Home Dinner at the National Golf Links in 1925 made Dunne its guest of honor. The hilarious tone of irresponsible good fellowship that dominated the gathering was characteristic of this aspect of Dunne's life. The songs that were sung — one, at least, was taken from the old Whitechapel Club's repertoire — and the toasts that were drunk

---

[1] T. A. Daly: " I see be th' Pa-apers," *Saturday Review of Literature,* XIV (May 9, 1936), 4.

belong to the realm of masculine good fellowship. DeLancey Nicoll, New York lawyer, read a poetic tribute, which even more than the dinner, carried the color of much of Dunne's personal friendships and club life:

. . .

Whence did he come
This son of mirth
Did some good angel give him birth
Or is he earthy of the earth
Like every one?

I cannot tell — but this I say
With sparkling wit and humor kind and
Satire keen
He wields, I ween, the brightest blade
That ere was seen.

The nation roars
When out he pours
His wit upon the page
The old and young
With joy are wrung
While all the heathen rage.

. . .

His eye is blue
His heart is true
The things are few
In friendship's name
He would not do.
So drink a toast
To our brave host
And also to good Peter Dunne
Our man of fun

Who drinks a tun
Without a bun
The man beloved by everyone.[2]

Most important to Dunne, perhaps, during the twenties and thirties, was his friendship with F. P. Garvan. The Garvan family and the Dunnes were very intimate, and the Garvans named a son after Peter Dunne. Of all Dunne's letters during his later years, those to F. P. Garvan are the most interesting and revealing. Peter and Margaret Dunne spent the late winter and spring of 1928 and 1929 at Palm Beach, and Dunne enjoyed burlesquing its qualities to Garvan. "The stately houses, which are a representation of what Keokuk might think was Spanish architecture, are inlaid with chalcedony and the other stones which the Old Testament reserves for the furnishing of the Heavenly Kingdom. After the dances the footmen, in the uniform of Kubla Khan, go about with dusters of peacock's tails, sweeping up diamonds, pearls, emeralds and rubies. The great take their pleasure seriously and seldom smile except to show that their teeeth are filled with real gold."[3] "When you go home you ought to consult Miller about spending your winters here. It would be fine if you would build a couple of houses on the sea and rent one to me. Thus you would realize your ambition to become an Irish landlord for an Irish tenant. We might even have an eviction for, of course, true to my race tradition, I would be behind in my payments and the

[2] Quoted in Joseph S. Auerbach: *The Bar of Other Days* (New York, 1940), pp. 348–51.
[3] March 8, 1928. Garvan letters.

neighbors would see you in white top hat and boots, ordering your bailiffs to do their hateful work, while the children huddled around Margaret; and I, after hurling a Gaelic curse at you, drove the pigs down to the Breakers, our only refuge from wind and rain at $50 a day per room. In the meantime, of course, Mabel would be sitting in her coach-and-four fanning herself and toying with her spaniel. Think it over." [4]

But it was not all burlesque, as the two Irishmen had more serious interests. To Garvan's praise of Garet Garrett's recent book, Dunne replied: " I have been reading ' The American Omen ' and I can't say I join in your enthusiasm over so slight an essay. . . . Now, if you want to read a good book get Winston Churchill's ' Aftermath ' — the fifth volume of his ' World Crisis,' which to my way of thinking, is the best history book written in our generation. I might go further and say that it is the best book I have ever read for it is almost the first to be written from the inside by a man of authority and genius." [5]

Although Dunne's contacts with new people were much more restricted than they had been thirty years before, he maintained his old interest in personalities, especially in young people. And he could overcome the handicap of much greater age and be the life of a party of younger people with little effort. Franklin P. Adams went to Bermuda with him in 1933, and Adams noted that while to the crowd of youngsters there Dunne " was a nice elderly gentle-

[4] March 13, 1928. Garvan letters.

[5] March 18, 1929. Garvan letters.

man who had done something in a literary way, back along about the Battle of Shiloh," they were "full of respect for his erudition and bowled over by his charm."[6] His experience in hospitals during his periods of illness invariably resulted in a new group of admiring friends — striking testimony to Dunne's personal qualities. His unwillingness to become old was due to his refusal to become saddened at the thought of old age. He could be deeply moved for short periods, but was never sorrowful for very long. When Michael Monahan wrote to him in a rather lugubrious tone, Dunne replied: "But why so melancholy? Alas, the fleeting years and lost youth! But what of it?"[7] And another time: "I wish you would not be so melancholy in everything you write about me. It was the Sweet Singer of Michigan who was accused of 'hitching her pegasus to a hearse.' You are not quite as bad as that but you are sombre. I would like to see you piping down the valley wild rather than playing 'Farewell Summer' on your reed. As a matter of fact, you and I were a good deal more melancholy a quarter of a century ago than we are today."[8]

In 1933, forty years after the World's Columbian Exposition, about which Colonel McNeery had commented so fully, another World's Fair was held in Chicago, and an anniversary meeting of the "Press Veterans of '93" was planned. Many friends of Dunne's were to be there, but Dunne could not be, as

[6] F. P. Dunne: *Mr. Dooley at His Best* (New York, 1938), p. xv.

[7] No date. Monahan letters.

[8] July 6, 1928. Monahan letters.

he had been ill for several weeks. To Herbert L. Jones, once of the *Journal* staff, he wrote: " I am still a wreck, and when I suggested going to Chicago my doctor told me flatly that he wouldn't be responsible for my safety if I attempted the journey. I should like nothing better than meeting my old friends and joining in the festivities, but it simply can't be done. Besides, if Ade and I were to wander into the Paleontological exhibit under the impression that it was the 1933 substitute for the Midway the curator would never let us out." [9]

His old habit of doing small favors for innumerable people stood him in good stead in these later years, for he had friends everywhere of highly varied ages. Some of them he had helped to their first jobs, others to find a publisher or to secure a tryout as an actor or musician. He never lost his interest in the drama of the daily news, and, after being a partisan of Alfred E. Smith's in 1928 and in the pre-convention campaign of 1932, he became an admiring supporter of Franklin D. Roosevelt, delighting in the sure hand with which the new President guided public affairs during his first years in office, and especially the astute way in which he overcame his opposition. He took considerable malicious delight in baiting some of his friends at the Links Club on the subject of the President's successes.

He seemed to enjoy giving advice. To a younger friend who had opportunities to go into politics he revealed some of his own reflections upon a career:

[9] June 30, 1933. Jones letters.

Perhaps I shouldn't give you advice. But one of the privileges of advanced age is to offer counsel whether it is wanted or not. . . . But will you get as much fun out of it, and will Gladys and the kids, as if you stuck to the law? My own opinion is that you ought to go out for it. In my time I have talked with many public men and without exception they have maintained that Big Politics (which includes and consolidates all kinds) is incomparably the most satisfactory of human pursuits. The control and leadership of men. That is the thing to exercise the mind to the very end. It seems to be a preservative of health and life, too. Statesmen live a long time, unfortunately, in some cases, for their country. In this respect, it is almost as antiseptic as avarice. Of course you ought to have money enough.[10]

Dunne's taste in reading did not change in his later years. He had already added Boswell's *Life of Samuel Johnson* and Burton's *Anatomy of Melancholy* to Montaigne to make a trio of favorites that never lost its savor for him. His wide-ranging search had made him familiar with rarities of literature little known outside of the ranks of scholars, such as John Wilson's *Noctes Ambrosianæ*. His taste was definitely Victorian, but he did enjoy and praise Ring Lardner's short stories when Lardner began to display his bent for realistic and sardonic sketches of American life. Perhaps Dunne saw in these a development close to a type of dialect essay of his own that he had frequently written in the nineties. Or, what is more probable, he found them like the early sketches of George Ade, for unlike Mr. Dooley's tragedies, which were a mirror that reflected through the pathetic

[10] To Wayne Johnson, February 19, 1934. Johnson letters.

things that were a vision of what they ought to be, Lardner's short stories and Ade's *Artie* and *Doc' Horne* were purely amoral in their conceptions. At any rate, Dunne remarked that Lardner had a great advantage over him in that the younger man had taken the more nearly average American for his mouthpiece, while Dooley represented the small minority of Irish descent which was rapidly losing its distinct character. Some of Ernest Hemingway's stories also won his praise, although he qualified it by observing that the author's use of profanity was a confession of weakness or laziness, as a capable writer ought to be able to gain his effects without resorting to such usage. Perhaps his most positive distaste was for the loud bellowing of H. L. Mencken, and he could rarely be induced to read one of his reviews or essays. Once he told of reading some recent critic who favored a modern writer over Sir Walter Scott. "I forgot who it was he preferred. It may have been Harold Bell Wright, or it may have been H. L. Mencken. . . . Now I maintain that if a man is suffering from this sort of malady, if he really does prefer so-and-so to the Wizard of the North, he shouldn't talk about it. It is a disease."[11]

Dunne's calm philosophy had not only been expounded in his Dooley essays, but it was an actual part of his own life. Thirty years earlier he had written:

"Life, Hinnissy, is like a Pullman dinin'-car: a fine bill iv fare but nawthin' to eat. Ye go in fresh an' hungry, tuck ye'er napkin in ye'er collar, an' square away at th' list iv gro-

---

[11] Recollections of Peter Dunne.

ceries that th' black man hands ye. What'll ye have first? Ye think ye'd like to be famous, an' ye ordher a dish iv fame an' bid th' waither make it good an' hot. He's gone an age, an' whin he comes back ye'er appytite is departed. Ye taste th' ordher, an' says ye: 'Why, it's cold an' full iv broken glass.' 'That's th' way we always sarve Fame on this car,' says th' coon. 'Don't ye think ye'd like money f'r th' second coorse? Misther Rockyfellar over there has had forty-two helpin's,' says he. 'It don't seem to agree with him,' says ye, 'but ye may bring me some,' ye say. Away he goes, an' stays till ye're bald an' ye'er teeth fall out an' ye set dhrummin' on th' table an' lookin' out at th' scenery. By-an'-by he comes back with ye'er ordher, but jus' as he's goin' to hand it to ye Rockyfellar grabs th' plate. 'What kind iv a car is this?' says ye. 'Don't I get annything to eat? Can't ye give me a little happiness?' 'I wudden't ricommend th' happiness,' says th' waither. 'It's canned, an' it kilt th' las' man that thried it.' 'Well, gracious,' says ye. 'I've got to have something. Give me a little good health, an' I'll thry to make a meal out iv that.' 'Sorry, sir,' says th' black man, 'but we're all out iv good health. Besides,' he says, takin' ye gently be th' arm, 'we're comin' into th' deepo an' ye'll have to get out,' he says."

And once when Mr. Hennessy had asked Mr. Dooley how long he wanted to live, Mr. Dooley, who had no quarrels with human existence, had answered: "Well, I wudden't want to have me life prolonged till I become a nuisance. I'd like to live as long as life is bearable to me an' as long afther that as I am bearable to life, an' thin I'd like a few years to think it over."

The Whitney bequest had placed Dunne beyond immediate financial necessities, and, although he lost a large share of it in the market crash of 1929, he never again was forced to work for a living. His two elder sons, Finley and Philip, had found work in scenario writing for the motion pictures, and, after spending parts of two winters with them in Los Angeles, Mrs. Dunne moved the rest of the family there. Peter Dunne preferred to stay in New York most of the time, and went to California only for a part of each winter. The new experience there interested him, as did all aspects of life. He wrote to Wayne Johnson about Hollywood:

> Most of the wickedness is in the newspapers. Free advertising takes the place of the delights of passion and the object of these cavaliers is not so much to enjoy the fruits of conquest as to get their names in the journals. They really work like coal miners under savage and bewildered capitalists from Seventh Avenue. But the directors – the fellows who do the actual work – are for the most part intelligent and companionable men, and on the whole the " industry " seems much better than I expected, from every point of view.[12]

Dunne had developed a persistent throat ailment in 1934, and was under treatment for it regularly thereafter. While in Los Angeles in 1935, a specialist told him that his difficulty was a cancer and recommended that he return to New York for treatment by specialists there. He left for New York immediately, but, characteristically, failed to inform his family of the reason. In New York he was given a long series of X-ray treatments and showed definite improvement. He was able to return to Los Angeles twice during the year for short visits, but he spent most of his time in New York under his doctor's care. " My treatment goes on tediously," he wrote to

[12] No date. Johnson letters.

Michael Straus. "The radiation is painless but the preliminaries are annoying. I am getting 204,000 volts a day. The doctor thinks I am doing well, progressively. At any rate I am not at the moment conscious of any lesion when I swallow. The cancer doesn't bother as much as the cost. I thought the Hebrew healers in California were high but these N. Y. experts have almost persuaded me to be a Zionist." [13]

The illness brought with it a certain loss of freedom and companionship that stimulated reflection upon his own career. In 1931 he had agreed to write a volume of reminiscences. Later at the urging of his son Philip, who was doing strikingly successful work for the motion pictures, he began to write. Not quite willing to admit that he still sought self-expression, he addressed his recollections to his son, as a sort of personal letter which Philip could publish or not as he chose. He wrote rapidly and well while in California, and when he returned to New York he had nearly forty thousand words completed. While confined to his rooms at Delmonico's, when undergoing his treatments, he tried to resume his writing, but with the greater pleasure of talking with his friends every day, the effort was more than he could bring himself to put forth. Wayne Johnson thought to urge him on by taking him the *Memoirs of U. S. Grant*, with the story of the brave general who had written against time while a cancer was gnawing at his throat. But Dunne merely reread Grant and talked Grant's career and his place in history every time Johnson came to see him. Even when Johnson sent a stenographer over

[13] January 14, 1936. Straus letters.

to encourage Dunne to dictate, it was useless, for Dunne found it easier than ever to believe that dictating was the enemy of good writing, and he spent the time visiting pleasantly with the girl.

Early in 1936, Dunne's cancer was pronounced completely checked, if not cured. Dunne felt much better, and wrote to Straus, promising to stop off in Chicago on his way back to Los Angeles. But on April 24, he had a hemorrhage at or near the site of the old growth, and died within a very short time.

His funeral was at St. Patrick's Cathedral in New York City, and his body was placed in the Garvan mausoleum in Woodlawn Cemetery. The Chicago City Council designated May 29 as "Scribes' Day" as a tribute to all in the field of letters who had contributed to the world's well being, but specifically to honor Finley Peter Dunne. On that day a memorial mass was celebrated at St. Bridget's Church on Archer Avenue; a delegation of students from St. Patrick's School laid a wreath at the site of the old Dunne home on West Adams Street; and the Old Time Printers Association placed a wreath on the West Division High School building. The press hailed Dunne's passing as the loss of our greatest humorist since Mark Twain, and many newspapers reprinted extensive selections from Mr. Dooley's wisdom and humor.

## JOURNALISM OR LITERATURE?

DUNNE's remarkable success as a writer of popular humor frequently raised the question among critics of the permanence of Mr. Dooley as literature. Almost invariably these commentators answered with predictions of lasting achievement. The exceptions were those who anticipated that Dunne would sometime do as striking work in pure English, for it was hard for them to conceive of such a non-literary language as Mr. Dooley spoke becoming permanent literature. The nature of Dunne's influence is somewhat easier to assess in 1941, although the question of the permanence of his dialect essays is still to be solved by time.

The most useful key to Dunne's success, and, conversely, the strongest feature of his writings, was his deep understanding of human nature. There was nothing superficial or merely smart about his knowledge of people and the springs of their action. His understanding went far beyond the cynical materialism of most exponents of realism or naturalism, and while including much that was valid in their analysis, he kept his picture in clear focus by leaving in it the emotional and idealistic elements that his own experience and faith had taught him made up part of man's life.

Peter Dunne knew human nature because he was honest about himself. In one of the most self-revealing essays which Dunne ever wrote, Mr. Dooley explained what was Dunne's own secret of his powers of character analysis:

> "I can tell be th' cut of a man's coat or his whiskers, be th' way he walks, be his attichood at th' bar, be a light wurrud spoke in jest or a heavy wurrud in anger, be a glance at th' side of his face as he passes a lookin'-glass, what kind iv a man he is. Wan thing I'll always bet on — he ain't much diff'rent fr'm anny other man. If I want to get a line on what he'd do in case iv a fire, I ask mesilf what I wud do in case iv a fire. I, mesilf, am ivry man. Barrin' iddycation an' th' business we're in, th' King iv England . . . an' Martin Dooley is all out iv th' same peck measure. If I know mesilf, I know thim all. King, Czar . . . they're all me with betther or worse clothes. . . . All men are ME. Th' little tape line that I use f'r mesilf is long enough an' acc'rate enough to measure anny man in th' wurruld, an' if it happens that I'm ladlin' out red impeeryalism at tin cints th' glass instead iv breakin' stone at Joliet or frinds in Wall Sthreet it's because I started th' way I did."[1]

Few things are more difficult to evaluate than the influence of a writer upon the life of his own generation. One qualification must always be kept in mind in attempting to evaluate Dunne's. Undoubtedly there were many levels of appreciation of Mr. Dooley.

[1] *Collier's Weekly*, December 6, 1902.

The lowest of these was the reader who found merely something comic in the fact that the saloon-keeper spoke in a quaint language, a dialect associated with unskilled laborers and household servants, and it was therefore an invitation for smiles to find it in print. How many of these were among Dunne's readers, one can only guess, but one fears there were many. Were it not a matter beyond dispute that he was also read and enjoyed by the best minds in every important field of endeavor, one might be inclined to scale down his influence unreasonably. Even the most bloodless intellectuals such as Henry Adams and Henry James were constant readers of Mr. Dooley, and that is clear proof not only of his varied appeal but also of the penetrating nature of his observations.

These levels of appreciation exist for many writers, although one searches in vain for another with Dunne's widespread appeal. Will Rogers had it at a later date, but only in his stage and radio appearances, as his written product never secured anything like the widespread demand which Mr. Dooley had from 1898 to 1905, and read today, Rogers' comments are far more clearly dated than Dunne's on the events of twenty years earlier.

In his function of censor, this very width of appeal, even leaving out the lower orders of enjoyment, made Dunne the most influential of the editorial writers of his day. Like all social satirists, his influence was discounted by the very human tendency for everyone to read such corrective literature for the enjoyment he gets from the pillory in which he finds an opponent or the manner in which a disliked argument is eviscerated, and this pleasure is not spoiled by equally trenchant blows upon himself and his concepts, because these strokes can be partly ignored or more quickly forgotten. Perhaps the mind should work differently, but it does not, and Dunne himself recognized this tendency as one of the weaknesses of popular satire. But it was far from universal, because of the good temper and humor in which Dunne usually dressed his most destructive blows. A remark that made one laugh, because he recognized the fundamental truth of the idea, was not likely to be forgotten, even if it contradicted a firmly held opinion. At least the holder would have to modify his belief to the extent of justifying his smile to his own conscience. And when one smiles at one of his own political opinions, he is well along the way to re-examine his stock of ideas with some hope of making a more rational framework. This was what was meant when an anonymous reviewer of the second Dooley book wrote ruefully: "If the American people continue to laugh with Dooley they will be Mugwumps before they know it."[2] They were, for Mr. Dooley was a strong factor in reducing the narrow partisanship that had been intensified by the sectional struggle of the sixties and its political consequences.

It is unnecessary, at this point, to list formally all of the traits in American life which Dunne tried to modify or destroy, but one should mention the two major ones. First and most persistently, he was against all demagoguery, whether vicious in intent or from well-meaning but self-deceived humbugs. A people

[2] *Life*, November 2, 1899.

deceived was the worst of all societies, and Dunne used every good opportunity to make clear such deceptions. He persistently labored against permitting the pocketbook interests of individuals or groups to parade as altruism, patriotism, or religion. A great share of his satire is directed at exposing such shams, and making clear to all who would read the underlying reality of personal interest. It was natural of people to use such excuses for their own selfishness. "If ye'd turn on th' gas in th' darkest heart, ye'd find it had a good raison f'r th' worst things it done, a good varchous raison, like needin' th' money, or punishin' th' wicked, or teachin' people a lesson to be more careful, or protectin' th' liberties iv mankind, or needin' th' money." But that was far from saying that the public should accept such testimony. The demagoguery of politician and reformer, of Wall Street operator and educational leader, of newspaper editor and labor leader — none escaped his pillory.

Next only to this, Dunne's greatest object of attack was the group of concepts underlying the definite American feeling of national and racial superiority that was basic to the more dangerous trends in popular thought, from imperialism in 1898 to the Ku-Klux Klan in 1924. Dunne's Irish Catholic background was helpful here in freeing him from some common nativistic emotions, and he struck at these anti-democratic and un-Christian concepts of superiority with a fury that can be explained only by the sudden strength they assumed during and after the Spanish-American War. It was not so much the Anglo-Saxon allegiance tea-talk, for that was a private feud, but it was the whole basic imperialistic policy as upheld by Lodge and Roosevelt, and more unblushingly maintained by Mahan and Beveridge. When the latter would talk about shedding blood for "our imperial destiny," strikingly like a Hitler or Mussolini of forty years later, it is not surprising that a democrat who understood people and their weakness for such intoxicants would try to laugh him and his kind out of countenance. And Dunne had notable successes in this field, as has been shown. "We're a great people," said Mr. Hennessy, earnestly. "We are," said Mr. Dooley. "We are that. An' th' best iv it is, we know we are." These same claims of superiority were attacked as vigorously when they appeared as the claims for class privilege by Mr. Baer or Mr. Worldly Wiseman. Intolerance of all kinds stemmed directly from the fiction of superiority of class, creed, or race. Dunne recognized it among all sorts of people, finding it in its most vicious forms in supposedly select circles. To him it seemed the most explosive and cruel element in American society, and he struck at it with his strongest weapons at every opportunity.

It should be recalled also that Dunne's satire on aspects of our national life was not only influential because of its effect upon the mind of the reading public, but it was also potent directly upon the leaders in all walks of life. Between 1898 and 1910 at least, presidents, Cabinet members, and congressmen read Mr. Dooley, and absorbed as much as their own characters and their fears of public reaction made necessary. Nor did it stop there. Prominent leaders in all walks of life read Mr. Dooley with some trepidation, fearing to find themselves being discussed in the Archey Road barroom. Theodore Roosevelt's assiduous cultivation of Dunne was probably not alone due to his appreciation of wisdom and humor. Certainly there could be few more unpleasant happenings to the high and mighty than to be made to strut before the world morally and mentally undressed as only Mr. Dooley could perform that revealing task. Not the least of Mr. Dooley's threat was that his exposure of hollowness and sham was so good-natured that one dare not risk resentment. Certainly one of the greatest pleasures of living, when Dunne was at his best, was the confidence one might have that the powerful of the world would be held immediately accountable for meanness and folly. Fortunate is an age and a nation so blessed!

Nearly as important a function in American life as being its satirist was Dunne's role as its humorist and wit. Conceiving of democracy as a form of society in which the conflicts of interests are compromised by peaceful means, Dunne's function here was one of lubricating the cog-wheels of peaceful adjustment. Compromise is made easier by laughter, especially when one can be made to laugh at himself. And after one has laughed at himself, it is not so easy to be led into the belief that an issue which concerns part of his personal income is a cause for which governments should be overthrown and mankind slaughtered. Mark Sullivan, who has made extremely intelligent use of Mr. Dooley in his history of the period, describes the influence of Dunne's humor in this manner: "Most useful of all, Mr. Dooley supplied the softening solvent of humor to the American atmosphere in times of acute controversy. Just when we were getting worked up into factional passion, with everybody searching the cellar of his vocabulary for verbal lumps of coal, Mr. Dooley would come out in the Sunday papers with a picture of the situation that made every reader laugh at it, and at himself."[3] Charles A. Beard, who would emphasize Dunne's role as a critic more, likewise agrees that the Dooley essays "relaxed the tension of the 'moral overstrain'" of public controversy.[4]

These two functions — the satirist and the humorist — frequently came into conflict in practice. As a satirist Dunne had to have Mr. Dooley possessed of a point of view and excoriate the other side. He might also satirize some of the arguments which his own side used, but with all his good humor there could be no real doubt as to where his heavy blows were falling. In every case of effective satire which Dunne wrote, this is clear. Imperialism, militarism, smug corruption in government and business, pretentious nonsense in education or religion, the protective tariff, fake reformers, self-deified aristocrats, and dishonest journalists — all of these he could and did satirize in his masterly fashion. And although each essay contained some other humorous elements, none of them was directed at easing the conflicts within society. They were aimed at influencing action. For real achievement in his second role, Mr. Dooley had to

[3] *Our Times*, I (New York, 1926), 206.

[4] *The Rise of American Civilization*, II (New York, 1927), 440.

take a position above or beside the battle, as he did in each political campaign; and while he could satirize the methods of all parties without limit, he could not become partisan to the immediate struggle itself. To do so immediately rendered his writing useless for lessening the friction of the struggle, but those who wanted him firing on the enemy from their side of the battlefront — and who did not? — naturally resented these lapses from satire. But forty years after the struggles one begins to suspect that the other function was just as significant to Dunne's readers and to American life of his day. As has been seen, the humorist function tended to encompass more and more of Dunne's writing as time went on, and after 1910 there is little of the satire in Mr. Dooley that had made him a modern scourge of princes. Most of what remains is directed against harmless popular pastimes. Perhaps, as some thought, this was a natural result of moving in the society of some of these very princes; perhaps it was a mellowness which came with greater age and a growing disinclination to throw bricks where they would do the most good in the old Archey Road manner. Or perhaps it was merely a greater personal pleasure from the humorous type of comment. At any rate the change was there.

A less obvious but very important influence on the America which read his essays was the political philosophy which Dunne expounded. While never explicit in a well-rounded form, and while it underwent slight modification in time, still a study of either his Dooley pieces or his non-dialect writing reveals a consistent theory, which underlay all that he wrote. He had no sharply visioned blueprint of a better day or an ideal society; in fact, his concept of human nature made any such clearly outlined society impossible. For this reason he was not a socialist — at least after 1893; nor did he become a defender of capitalism. Anarchists were sewer gas, like the life-insurance company officials of 1905. In his view of human nature, the system of organizing economic and political society was not of primary importance. The motives of people, the standards of value by which great numbers approved or disapproved of action, these were the important things.

Under any of the different social structures which Americans of the day visualized as desirable, Dunne saw little difference. Most of them, pending improvement in individuals, would operate essentially as the present one did. Those in positions of prestige and influence would try to hold their privileges by devices that would not require the constant effort that they should display for a well-functioning society. Other groups and individuals who believed their merits justified greater rewards in prestige would try to displace those already in power, by means which might vary from mild to substantial reforms. None but the few hopeless and desperate favored revolution. Whether one group or another of these outsiders succeeded in its efforts at any particular time was not important; what was important was that the avenues of peaceful displacement be kept open and free to all. Then those in power would not sit too securely in their seats; they would not be able to hide behind legal or emotional bulwarks; but instead would have to maintain a reasonable degree of efficiency and decency in order to hold what they had originally won. The great reform that would improve society was the elimination of the pretenses that made easy the exploitation of people by those who added little of social value to the group. If the pretenders, poseurs, and demagogues could be deflated, if arguments of interests were forced into the open as such, if Wall Street were recognized for what it was and not as some sacred institution to be worshiped as its beneficiaries desired, then an American democracy would be able to make life somewhat better. This would force or enable government more adequately to hedge about the " trough of trade " in order to protect the weak bargainers and prevent the hogs from monopolizing it to their personal advantage.

Beyond this, reform and progress were to Dunne as they were to priest and teacher, primarily an individual matter. Only as the individual was improved, as his understanding of society was sharpened, as his love of decency was deepened, as his sympathy for the distressed was quickened, as his consciousness of duty to his fellowman was made more acute, would society make real improvements.

Dunne was on the constant alert to keep progress from being defined in materialistic terms. He recognized the tendency to do that as one of the highly questionable trends in American thinking.

" I've been up to th' top iv th' very highest buildin' in town, Hinnissy, an' I wasn't anny nearer Hivin thin if I was in th' sthreet. Th' stars was as far away as iver. An' down beneath is a lot iv us runnin' an' lapin' an' jumpin' about, pushin' each other over, haulin' little strhips iv ir'n to pile up in little buildin's that are called sky-scrapers but not be th' sky; wurrukin' night an' day to make a masheen that'll carry us fr'm wan jack-rabbit colony to another an' yellin', 'Progress! ' Progress, oho! I can see th' stars winkin' at each other an' sayin': 'Ain't they funny! Don't they think they're playin' hell! '

"No, sir, masheens ain't done much f'r man. I can't get up anny kind iv fam'ly inthrest f'r a steam dredge or a hydhraulic hist. I want to see sky-scrapin' men. But I won't. We're about th' same hight as we always was, th' same hight an' build, composed iv th' same inflammable an' perishyable materryal, an' exthra hazardous risk, unimproved an' li'ble to collapse. We do make progress but it's th' same kind Julyus Caesar made an' ivry wan has made befure or since an' in this age iv masheenery we're still burrid be hand."

Unlike some writers who have a realistic view of the springs of action in most people, Dunne was not pessimistic or defeatist about it. Because most people insisted on being selfish most of the time, ignorant, jealous, covetous, and cruel, he did not despair of humanity and seek to pillory it as something unworthy of living in the world. He recognized human nature, with all its weakness, as a fact of life, and in accepting it, found that it was still worth while. He did not, like so many reformers, begin by setting up standards of conduct, and then reading out of decent society all who did not conform. In his essay on the muckrakers in 1905, Mr. Dooley told of a boarding-house run by a lady named Doherty.

"She was a good woman, but her idee iv life was a combination iv pneumony an' love. She was niver still. Th' sight iv a spot on th' wall where a gintleman boorder had laid his head afther dinner would give her nervous prostration. She was always polishin', scrubbin', sweepin', airin'. She had a plumber in to look at th' dhrains twice a week. Fifty-two times a year there was a rivolution in th' house that wud've made the Czar iv Rooshya want to go home to rest. An' yet th' house was niver really clean. It looked as if it was to us. It was so clean that I always was ashamed to go into it onless I'd shaved. But Mrs. Doherty said no; it was like a pig-pen. 'I don't know what to do,' says she. 'I'm worn out, an' it seems impossible to keep this house clean. What is th' throuble with it? ' says she. 'Madam,' says me frind Gallagher, 'wud ye have me tell ye? ' he says. 'I wud,' says she. 'Well,' says he, 'th' throuble with this house is that it is occypied entirely be human bein's,' he says. 'If 'twas a vacant house,' he says, 'it cud aisily be kept clean,' he says."

As Dunne accepted human nature as part of his environment, he never suffered from the frustration of defeat that comes to the short-sighted; as he did not expect Utopia, he was not shocked that it did not follow his preachments. "A man that'd expict to thrain lobsters to fly in a year is called a loonytic; but a man that thinks men can be turned into angels be an iliction is called a rayformer an' remains at large."

That the Dooley essays are journalism of the finest type few will dispute; that they are literature in the more permanent sense may not be so clear. Were the American-Irish brogue of Mr. Dooley still a living and growing language there might be no doubt about it, but Mr. Dooley's language has become at least obsolescent, and that puts the future of the Dooley essay in serious question.

As for the quality of the dialect itself, one can get argument without end. Mr. Dooley's more partisan admirers insisted that it was Roscommon Irish that was " phonographically correct "; while the few who did not like Dooley anyway denied that it was soundly constructed Irish dialect. The truth is, Dunne never claimed it was true Roscommon dialect. He had written that in Archey Road " you can hear all the various accents of Ireland, from the awkward brogue of the ' far-downer ' to the mild and aisy Elizabethan English of the southern Irishman, and all the exquisite variations to be heard between Armagh and Bantry Bay, with the difference that would naturally arise from substituting cinders and sulphuretted hydrogen for soft misty air and peat smoke." Dunne took pains to make clear that the saloon-keeper had been in America for many years. Consequently, Mr. Dooley spoke an Irish brogue and used an Irish idiom which was modified by many years' residence in Chicago. Dunne was no philologist, at the time he created Mr. Dooley, but he had a good ear, and Mr. Dooley's language is unquestionably the best representation of Irish-American methods of speaking that has been written. " One can hardly elsewhere, unless from the mouth of Kipling's Mulvaney, hear so mellow and lilting a Hibernian voice as this," wrote H. W. Boynton in 1904.[5] But too much should not be claimed for it. Dunne was not always consistent in his written representations of Mr. Dooley's speech. Besides having to contend with a variety of typesetters, he had to keep the spelling simple in order to be readable. Consequently, Mr. Dooley's chief interest is written as polytics, pollyticks, pollytics, and, at times, correctly

[5] *Journalism and Literature and Other Essays* (Boston and New York, 1904), p. 101.

as politics. Court is sometimes that and sometimes coort; world is both wur-ruld and wurrld. It is unlikely that different pronunciations are intended by such variations. Moreover, the idiom used is an excellent Irish-American combination which came naturally to Archer Avenue.[6]

More important is the fact that had Dunne depended upon dialect for his effects, his writing would probably be unknown even though the dialect were perfect. There were several attempts to duplicate his success with other Irish-dialect articles, and all of them failed miserably.[7] The significant thing is that Dunne's essays lose nothing today when rewritten into ordinary English words and the current American idiom. This cannot be said of the host of minor humorists of the past whose principal literary trick has been ingenious misspellings or manufactured dialect.

Dunne's humor was more American than Irish. There are Irish peculiarities in it, and typical Irish twists to expressions or thoughts, but the American characteristics clearly dominate. Now and then there is an Irish whimsy or a tragedy. He dearly loved an ingenious misquotation: "Shakespeare says, Be thrue to ye'ersilf an' ye will not thin be false to ivry man." He could not resist the temptation to analyze popular sayings. When Mr. Hennessy asked hopefully if he did not think drink was a necessary evil, Mr. Dooley

---

[6] P. W. Joyce, *English as We Speak It in Ireland* (London, 1910). Chapter VII shows many Dooley-like spellings, but unfortunately Joyce makes few distinctions between Roscommon English and the speech of other parts of Ireland.

[7] The two most important of these in Chicago journalism were "On the City Hall Corner," in the *Times-Herald*, and "Pat's Soliloquies," by William Bullock in the *Evening Post*.

answered: " Well, if it's an evil to man, it's not necessary, and if it's necessary it's an evil." Still, his tall tales, his lists of incongruous names, his caricatures, and his burlesques — all of these are peculiarly American. Perhaps Dunne's attraction to the tragic and somber is an Irish characteristic, but it is American also, and Dunne's selection among American writers shows his preference for those with similar outlook. " Emerson and Clemens, our greatest writers each within his own orbit. Emerson and Clemens, Hawthorne, Poe, Whitman, Abraham Lincoln " — that was Dunne's mature judgment.[8]

Mr. Dooley was as clearly of the tradition of the cracker-box philosopher of American literature as was Hosea Biglow, Abe Martin, or Will Rogers. In Mr. Dooley, the philosopher left the crossroads store for the city saloon, although that poor-man's club was in a village-like area of one-story business buildings, shanties, cabbage patches, and goat pastures. While Dunne had qualities of mind that are similar to Mark Twain's, his medium was entirely different, for Twain wrote novels, short stories, and travel books, while Dunne wrote short essays. It is through the line of Simon Suggs, Major Jack Downing, Hosea Biglow, Petroleum V. Nasby, Bill Arp, Artemus Ward, and Josh Billings that Mr. Dooley takes his place in the history of American humor.[9] From the dated char-

---

8 Recollections of Peter Dunne.

9 Jennette Tandy: *Crackerbox Philosophers in American Humor and Satire* (New York, 1925), pp. 158–63; Constance Rourke, *American Humor: A Study of the National Character* (New York, 1931), p. 288; Walter Blair: *Native American Humor, 1800–1900* (New York, 1937), pp. 105–21.

acter of this type of writing, it is clear that only the highest kind of achievement can insure survival as living literature.

Perhaps Dunne's finest characteristic, aside from the constantly flashing wit, was his ability to improvise situations and dialogue. Morgan and Harriman's contest in Wall Street over the Northern Pacific Railroad becomes a fight between two toughs in the Archey Road saloon; life is a dining-car, where each orders what he wants and takes what the waiter brings; a naval attack on a coast is two Irishmen with bricks, one of them on roller skates; McKinley in diplomacy is the proud villager in front of the tin-horn gambler at the rural fair. The ability to improvise conversation is one of Dunne's most striking literary qualities, and, consequently, whether it is Mr. Dooley quoting conversations between himself and Father Kelly or between Roosevelt and General Miles, or conversation between the Poet and the Worldly Wiseman in the "Interpreter's House," Dunne shows not only a good ear for language but a truly marvelous imaginative ability to think other men's thoughts. It is part of the same wisdom regarding human nature that his intimate friends always treasured so highly.

There is a tendency in comment on Dunne by Chicagoans and by some regionalists to regret his moving to New York in 1900, and to explain the decline of his productivity after 1910 to his distance from his original inspiration. This is largely a superficial judgment, and it is not unreasonable to suppose that the things that brought about a lessening of his productivity would have operated in nearly the same degree in both places. There is one partial exception; the pathetic and tragic pieces, which Dunne wrote between 1894 and 1897, were ended by national syndication. Why, is not clear. The only recurrence of these splendid elements in Dunne's writings after that date was in pure English, as in the essay on the *Titanic* disaster or in the reminiscent essay on capital punishment, "The Majesty of the Law," of the same period.[10]

Dunne's failure to continue writing this type of literature, which was not humor and not always satire, is a real cause for regret, for he was clearly a great master of it. One cannot read "Shaughnessy" or "The Wanderers" today without regretting deeply that the vein of pathetic tragedy with the dramatic overtones each possessed was not continued. It is possible that if Dunne had remained in Chicago, his wide acquaintance among all classes of people would have meant regular revivals of his inspiration for such essays. Against this belief is the fact that he had written very few of these during the last years he was in Chicago. The lack of such inspiration was probably more a result of his increasing ability to live better, and an unconscious attempt to avoid the painful experiences which came from direct contact with tragic circumstance. Once when he was leaving the office of *The American Magazine*, Dunne met the social worker, Robert Hunter, and Lincoln Steffens. Dunne asked where they were going for lunch, and Hunter replied that they could not take the time to eat until later, as he was showing Steffens some of New York's unemployed. "Then why don't you both come to Del-

[10] *The American Magazine*, February 1914.

monico's with me? " asked Dunne. The point here is not the humor of Dunne's remark, but the contrast in experience. Dunne had already seen enough tragedy to satisfy him, and he never went out of his way to look for more. But in avoiding it, he had also removed himself from one source of inspiration for a type of great literature which he could write. It is possible that had he maintained this contact, it would have given him an enriched product whose composition would have been easier in later years because of the greater number of avenues of expression it would have opened to his imagination.

But when one has expressed the common regret that Dunne did not write more, it is but fair to recall that no other American humorist, who used the form of the short essay as distinguished from more space-filling types of humor such as novels, and certainly none of the cracker-box philosopher type, produced more copy for current journals which was worthy of republication in book form. In all, Dunne wrote over seven hundred dialect essays of which about one-third were republished in his eight books. There was enough high-class material left to have made at least four more volumes had Dunne been a person of greater energy, or had he been slightly less careful and critical of his own work. Considering the concentrated character of his writing, it is hardly fair to accuse him of not being sufficiently productive.

The question of permanence can be answered only by time, but certain of its elements can be pointed out. Comment on current affairs is always quickly dated, and as one cannot read Hosea Biglow today without heavy annotations or a deep knowledge of the politics of the forties and sixties, so one cannot read many of the Dooley essays without similar aids. But even here there will be elements of permanence as long as history of the period of 1890 to 1910 has an interest to readers; for no writer can treat either the general history of the United States after 1890 or the special history of aspects of its life without resorting helpfully to Dunne's penetrating characterizations. "He niver done annythin' wrong save in th' way iv business," is a comment on Rockefeller that ought to last. "I'd like to tell me frind Tiddy that they'se a sthrenuse life an' a sthrenuseless life," is as good as a chapter on Roosevelt. "Ivry time he gives a libry he gives himsilf away in a speech," carries a flavor of Carnegie that biographers usually miss. A discussion of American imperialism of 1900 is incomplete without this concept: "To most people a savage nation is wan that doesn't wear uncomfortable clothes." "A Morman" defined Mr. Dooley, "is a man that has th' bad taste an' th' relligion to do what a good many other men are restrained fr'm doin' be conscientious scruples an' th' police." And this liquor-dealer's definition of the promoter of the turn of the century is at least suggestive: "A Titan iv Finance is a man that's got more money thin he can carry without bein' disordherly." "I do not care who makes th' laws iv a nation if I can get out an injunction," carries an entire chapter of the struggle of organized labor for recognition. Quite adequate for a longer period is this philological judgment: "Whin we Americans are through with th' English language, it will look as if it'd been run over be a musical comedy."

The most dated element in the Dooley stories turns out to be the dialect. Readers born after 1910 are not apt to be familiar with Irish immigrant ways of speaking English, and reading Mr. Dooley's spellings not only fails to tickle their risibilities, but until some familiarity is secured it provides some positive handicaps to grasping the meanings. This promises to become progressively worse as that speech becomes less and less familiar. Dunne himself recognized it, and once told Charles Scribner that if the Dooley essays were to live they would have to be rewritten in ordinary English. In reviewing a recent anthology, *Mr. Dooley at His Best*, John Chamberlain makes a similar observation. "If you try quoting Mr. Dooley's brogue to the average listener [1938] you will be rewarded with a look of intense pain. But if you translate Mr. Dooley into ordinary English nearly everything precipitates out as pure wisdom." [11]

When these dated elements in Dunne's writing are specified, there remain many elements that look toward the continuance of Mr. Dooley as living literature. The greatest of these is the character, Mr. Dooley, brought out almost entirely by his own conversation.[12] Surely he is one of the most real persons in American literature. "Few of our friends are more

---

[11] *The New Republic*, vol. 97 (November 23, 1938), 77.

[12] Stephen Leacock holds that "Mr. Dooley belongs to the humor of character, a far higher thing than the mere fun of words or incongruity of situation." *The Greatest Pages of American Humor* (New York, 1936), p. 173.

alive than this mythical bar-tender,"[13] observed an English critic. One of the most distinguished of American historians was once asked whom, among all the characters in American history, would he prefer to interview, were he given that supernatural power. He answered with scholarly hesitation, mentioning Franklin first, then Jefferson, and finally, as the privileges of the proposal dawned upon him, he declared that he would pick Mr. Dooley as the third. When one contrasts the well-rounded way in which Mr. Dooley is realized, with the fragmentary manner in which Lowell sketches Hosea Biglow, Dunne's high achievement is clearly revealed.

Next to this is the aptness and wisdom of Mr. Dooley's characterizations, not of dated things but those which are timeless. Such things will tend to be treasured permanently, just as his expression " the Supreme Court follows the election returns " will live as long as that institution is a matter of political discussion. Certainly none of the cracker-box philosophers, old or recent, is quoted today with anything like the regularity of Mr. Dooley — quoted, be it noted, usually without dialect. " D'ye think republics are ongrateful? " asked Mr. Hennessy. " I do," said Mr. Dooley. " That's why they continued to be republics." " Among men, Hinnissy, wet eye manes a dhry heart." " A fanatic is a man that does what he thinks th' Lord wud do if He knew th' facts iv th' case." " Miracles are laughed at be a nation that reads thirty millyon newspapers a day an' supports Wall Sthreet." " Onaisy, as Hogan says, is th' head that wears a

[13] *The Spectator*, vol. 90 (February 14, 1903), 259.

crown. They'se other heads that 're onaisy too; but ye don't hear iv thim." "Me experyence with goold minin' is it's always in th' nex' county." "Th' further ye get away fr'm anny peeryod th' better ye can write about it. Ye aren't subject to interruptions be people that were there." "The past always looks betther thin it was. It's only pleasant because it isn't here." "Many a man that cudden't direct ye to th' dhrug store on th' corner whin he was thirty will get a respectful hearin' whin age has further impaired his mind." "Annyhow, th' truth is a tough boss in lithrachoor. He don't even pay board wages, an' if ye go to wurruk f'r him ye want to have a job on th' side." "Wise is he who says: 'I on'y know yisterday. I must look out to-morrah.'" "All ye've got to do is to believe what ye hear, an' if ye do that enough, afther a while ye'll hear what ye believe."

As Dunne's non-dialect writing is still buried in non-literary periodicals, it has never been subjected to critical evaluation. But Howells characterized the pure English preface to *Mr. Dooley In Peace and In War* as a graphic piece of analysis, as "brilliant . . . as I have ever seen."[14] Dunne's associates on *The American Magazine* have never changed the tone of high praise which they have always directed toward "In the Interpreter's House." These and the equally distinguished "From the Bleachers" essays await republication in book form before anything definite can be predicted as to their chances of survival. While they lack some of the earthiness of Mr. Dooley as well

[14] "Certain of the Chicago School of Fiction," *North American Review*, vol. 176 (May 1903), 744.

as his humor, they escape the handicap of dialect.

Regardless of the fate of these, one cannot help but believe that those dialect essays which deal with timeless subjects will never cease to find some admiring readers. Thomas L. Masson quotes Mr. Dooley on "Avarice and Generosity," and compares it favorably with "The Avaricious Man" by the minor Greek philosopher, Theophrastus.[15] It would be a rash commentator who would try to prove that Peter Dunne's essay will not be as timely two thousand years from now as Theophrastus' is today. Whether it will or not depends upon the world itself. If it continues to accept the values which Dunne cherished — personal integrity, plain speaking, catholic tolerance, compassion for the weak, good humor, and salty wit — if it continues to treasure these, then Peter Dunne will surely continue to be read.

---

[15] *Our American Humorists*, Revised Edition (New York, 1931), pp. 113–18.

# INDEX